TREATMENT RESISTANCE *and* PATIENT AUTHORITY

A Norton Professional Book

Treatment Resistance
and Patient Authority

The Austen Riggs Reader

Eric M. Plakun, Editor

W. W. Norton & Company
New York • London

Please note that clinical material has been disguised and names changed when they are used.

Chapter 9 is a revised version of a chapter that first appeared in *The Inner World and the Outer World* (1997), copyright Yale University Press, and used with their permission.

For information about special discounts for bulk purchases, please contact W. W. Norton Special Sales at specialsales@wwnorton.com or 800-233-4830

Manufacturing by R.R. Donnelley, Bloomsburg
Production manager: Leeann Graham

Library of Congress Cataloging-in-Publication Data

Treatment resistance and patient authority : the Austen Riggs reader / Eric M. Plakun, editor. — 1st ed.
    p. ; cm.
"A Norton professional book."
Includes bibliographical references and index.
ISBN 978-0-393-70661-1 (hardcover)
  1. Psychotherapy. 2. Psychotherapist and patient. 3. Austen Riggs Center.
I. Plakun, Eric M., 1947–
[DNLM: 1. Austen Riggs Center. 2. Psychotherapy—methods. 3. Mental
Disorders—therapy. 4. Patient Participation. 5. Physician-Patient Relations.
6. Psychotherapeutic Processes. 7. Treatment Failure. WM 420]
RC480.5.T754 2011
616.89'14—dc22   2010052143

ISBN: 978-0-393-70661-1

W. W. Norton & Company, Inc., 500 Fifth Avenue, New York, N.Y. 10110
  www.wwnorton.com
W. W. Norton & Company Ltd., Castle House, 75/76 Wells Street, London W1T 3QT

1 2 3 4 5 6 7 8 9 0

For Ed Shapiro, retiring as Riggs Medical Director in July 2011, whose passion, integrity, wisdom, and leadership helped develop our own as we built an institution together.

CONTENTS

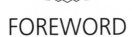

FOREWORD

Otto F. Kernberg, MD

The present volume represents a major breakthrough in the treatment of so-called "treatment-resistant" patients, a significant and growing group of patients that does not respond to our standard psychopharmacological or psychotherapeutic procedures. This population includes patients with major depressive disorders; some chronic, nonresponding patients with schizophrenia or other psychotic spectrum disorders; and, particularly, treatment-resistant severe personality disorders. Among the latter, patients with severe borderline and narcissistic personality disorders, who also present with chronic suicidal behavior, eating disorders, drug abuse and addiction, and antisocial behavior, constitute an unusually complex diagnostic group with various kinds of symptomatic comorbidity superimposed and centered on an underlying severe personality disorder.

This book reports on the experience of the Austen Riggs Center, which provides a fully voluntary and unrestrictive hospital-based continuum of care, with programs ranging from inpatient to residential to day treatment to outpatient care. Riggs treats previously treatment-resistant patients within a specially developed therapeutic community setting offering intensive individual psychodynamic psychotherapy, psychopharmacological treatment, the psychodynamic analysis and utilization of the therapeutic milieu, exploration and utilization of patients' family dynamics, as well as a subtle study of the interaction between patient and institutional dynamics. All of this is integrated in a specific treatment approach that has proven highly successful in many cases previously considered resistant or impossible to treat.

The treatment approach developed at Austen Riggs reflects an original and sophisticated extension of earlier findings within psychoanalytic hospital settings—that is, an integration of contemporary understanding of family and group dynamics in the analysis of patients' multiple transference dispositions. These dynamics are played out in a structured social setting that, in turn, reacts with its own dynamics to the activation of the unconscious conflicts of patients in that environment. The Austen Riggs Center has defied the serious difficulties that have impinged on psychiatric hospital treatment in this country in the last 20 years. It has avoided the excessive orientation toward restrictive, locked settings; the focus on a unimodal psychopharmacological approach that tends to ignore the interaction between medication, the patient's total personality structure, and the patient–therapist relationship; and the widespread social ambiance in which financial pressures tend to corrupt treatment. The Riggs staff has developed an original, specific, highly focused approach that complements evidenced-based treatment approaches that focus on clearly defined diagnostic syndromes, which, by design, exclude the patient population with multiple comorbidities under consideration here.

In a series of mutually complementary chapters that build on one another, this book describes the basic theoretical approach that combines a strong focus on the patient's authority and responsibility to participate actively in decisions regarding his or her own treatment plan, with systematic analysis of all relationships in which the patient engages within the therapeutic community, and methods for analyzing transgenerational and infantile traumata affecting the patient's early development and his or her unconscious adaptation to the family structure. The authors carefully explore the influence of patients' temperamental dispositions as well as the unconscious dynamics of the family, the influence of the patients' personality structure and their unconscious agendas on their reaction to psychopharmacological treatment, the consideration of patients' authority and that of the social milieu that they are negotiating with, and, very centrally, the development of the unconscious dynamics of transference and countertransference that impact all these other factors in the treatment situation. Within such a complex frame of reference, patients' maladaptive behavior patterns may be decoded to reveal the unconscious messages expressed by them, acting out and enactment may be transformed into affective-cognitive communication, and patients can acquire tools for more adaptive and functional ways of establishing their authority and autonomy and re-establishing gratifying relations with significant others. This approach clearly transcends the ordinary dyadic relationship of psychodynamic psychotherapy, permitting an optimal integration of transference and countertransference analysis while understanding and managing the role of medication and facilitating the development of new ways for dealing with these patients' frequent crises and life threatening behaviors, particularly chronic suicidal tendencies.

In contrast to the reduction of the therapeutic programs offered by psychiatric hospitals under the impact of financial restrictions and managed care, Riggs has been able to continue and transcend the tradition of the psychodynamic hospital with the incorporation of new knowledge regarding groups and organizations and the interrelationship between psychopharmacological, psychodynamic, cognitive behavioral and supportive approaches. This represents, I believe, a new psychiatry that, hopefully, will again integrate body and mind, neurobiological, psychodynamic and social dynamic knowledge and approaches.

I am pleased if, as Dr. Plakun states in the Introduction, my own comments and suggestion while visiting Riggs some years ago helped initiate the process that led to this volume. The reader will find in this text an overall definition and explanation of these concepts and approaches to treatment resistance, well illustrated by abundant clinical material that reflects the problems that are a major source of challenge and frustration in clinical practice with this patient population. Further, the authors have extracted from each chapter a set of concise principles that will help focus clinical thinking about work with complex patients.

I warmly recommend this volume to all psychiatrists, it is an indispensable reading for psychodynamic psychotherapists and should help a wide range of clinicians better work with treatment resistant patients, whether in relatively isolated outpatient settings or other inpatient, partial hospital or residential settings. There is much for clinicians and the field to gain from what Riggs has been learning on our behalf about work with treatment resistant patients.

TREATMENT RESISTANCE *and* PATIENT AUTHORITY

INTRODUCTION

Eric M. Plakun, MD

This book began as a result of two unrelated conversations. In the first, during a visit to Riggs Otto Kernberg wondered why we at Riggs had not yet developed a coherent voice within the field, articulating our distinctive way of working and what we were learning. The response of Riggs staff, under the leadership of medical director/CEO Edward Shapiro, MD, was to begin to publish more about our work, speaking as individuals with multiple voices in a range of journals rather than with a recognizable and distinct (or even formally negotiated) voice of the institution. The second conversation occurred several years later with Douglas Ingram, then editor of the *Journal of the Academy of Psychoanalysis and Dynamic Psychiatry*, who was familiar with the work emerging from Riggs. He asked if there was interest in publishing more about what we were learning. After speaking to Shapiro and other colleagues at Riggs and negotiating the articulation of a theme about "a" (not necessarily "the only") way we work with so-called treatment-resistant patients who have failed to benefit from less intensive treatment, I accepted the offer to edit such a series and set out to select material for six papers. As the papers began to emerge and interest in them and in Riggs's work grew, I realized we had more to say, and negotiated with Ingram a total series of 12 papers (see references to the series below). Once the series of papers was completed, Norton Professional Books expressed interest in publishing this material as a volume discussing what we are learning about a psychodynamic approach to working with treatment-resistant patients. I am grateful to Guilford Press for authorizing republication of the original 12 papers in revised form (see citations below), but this volume also expands beyond the original material. Editing the series and the book has proven rewarding if sometimes daunting, but I am pleased that it is a step in the direction of shaping a voice of Riggs within the field.

Riggs serves as a psychodynamic beacon in a biologically focused clinical world, showing the value of our way of working through empirical research, catching the attention of clinical audiences, and, despite its small size, repeatedly being recognized as one of America's best psychiatric hospitals by *US News & World Report*.

The Riggs treatment program emphasizes careful attention to meaning as a central task of treatment, emphasizes human relationships with treaters and peers that continue over time, and, through the medium of a completely open and voluntary therapeutic milieu—with no use of seclusion, restriction, or restraint—does so with a commitment to approach patients as having authority over and responsibility for taking charge of their own lives. This book is not meant to present or prescribe *one* right way to approach treatment-refractory patients, nor is it intended to offer a blueprint for "how we do it at Riggs," nor to convey every aspect of the point of view from which clinical care is offered at Riggs. However, based on what is presented in what follows and on the reality that Riggs has not only survived, but thrived, with a median 6-month length of treatment and a waiting list for admission for the last decade, despite expanding the census from 50 to 75 patients, we may have a way of working that could help other clinicians improve their own therapeutic work with treatment-resistant patients in outpatient and other settings.

Riggs is an unusual institution that treats a small number of treatment-refractory patients who have access to enough financial resources of their own or from third parties to support a mobilization of intensive and extensive treatment resources that include individual, group, family, and milieu treatments. Few will work in an institution like Riggs or have our clinical resources. Some might argue that such intensive work cannot be relevant to a field for which a principal focus is how to provide the greatest good to the greatest number. Others, like Kernberg and Ingram, recognize that the way of working at Riggs, developed over nearly a century, has served as a clinical laboratory for the study and treatment of the most difficult patients as individuals and within a social context. What makes Riggs and this volume relevant to the field is the way that what we are learning can be applied by practitioners from a range of mental health disciplines in outpatient, inpatient, partial hospital, residential, and other settings, and potentially help our colleagues work more effectively with the disturbingly large number of patients who fail the usual treatments.

In an effort to facilitate the application of what we are learning to other settings and to those with limited familiarity with psychodynamic theory, the chapters are written in accessible language. Throughout the book, in reporting what we are learning about working with treatment-refractory disorders, we endeavor to define core principles that are applicable to other treatment settings in which clinicians are struggling to work with similarly disturbed patients. Text boxes dispersed throughout or at the end of chapters highlight these principles.

I want to thank the authors for their contributions and for enduring my editorial hand, Otto Kernberg for challenging us to speak about what we believe as well as for offering his Foreword to the volume, and Doug Ingram, Guilford Press, and Norton Professional Books for giving us this window on the world. This volume is dedicated, though, to Edward Shapiro, whose 20 years of inspired and inspiring leadership challenged us in innumerable, helpful ways to discover and articulate our voice within the field.

REFERENCES

Listed chronologically

Plakun, E.M. (2006). A view from Riggs: Treatment resistance and patient authority—I. A psychodynamic perspective. *Journal of the American Academy of Psychoanalysis and Dynamic Psychiatry, 34*(2), 349–366.

Plakun, E.M. (2006). A view from Riggs: Treatment resistance and patient authority—introductions to papers II and III. *Journal of the American Academy of Psychoanalysis and Dynamic Psychiatry, 34*(3), 441–443; *34*(4) 579–580.

Fromm, M.G. (2006). A view from Riggs: Treatment resistance and patient authority—II. Transmission of trauma. *Journal of the American Academy of Psychoanalysis and Dynamic Psychiatry, 34*(3), 445–459.

Mintz, D., & Belnap, B.A. (2006). A view from Riggs: Treatment resistance and patient authority—III. What is psychodynamic psychopharmacology? *Journal of the American Academy of Psychoanalysis and Dynamic Psychiatry, 34*(4), 581–602.

Plakun, E.M. (2007). A view from Riggs: Treatment resistance and patient authority—introductions to papers IV, V, and VI. *Journal of the Amer-*

ican Academy of Psychoanalysis and Dynamic Psychiatry, 35(2), 219–220; 35(3), 373–374; 35(4), 605–606.

Muller, J.P. (2007). A view from Riggs: Treatment resistance and patient authority—IV. Why the pair needs the third. *Journal of the American Academy of Psychoanalysis and Dynamic Psychiatry*, 35(2), 221–241.

Elmendorf, D.M., & Parish, M. (2007). A view from Riggs: Treatment resistance and patient authority—V. Silencing the messenger: The social dynamics of treatment resistance. *Journal of the American Academy of Psychoanalysis and Dynamic Psychiatry*, 35(3), 375–392.

Schwartz, A. (2007). A view from Riggs: Treatment resistance and patient authority—VI. Working with family resistance to treatment. *Journal of the American Academy of Psychoanalysis and Dynamic Psychiatry*, 35(4), 607–625.

Plakun, E.M. (2008). A view from Riggs: Treatment and Patient Authority—introductions to papers VII and VIII. *Journal of the American Academy of Psychoanalysis and Dynamic Psychiatry*, 36(2), 351–352; 36(3), 543–545.

Krikorian, S.E., & Fowler, J.C. (2008). A view from Riggs: Treatment resistance and patient authority—VII. A team approach to treatment resistance. *Journal of the American Academy of Psychoanalysis and Dynamic Psychiatry*, 36(2), 353–373.

Charles, M. (2008). A view from Riggs: Treatment Resistance and Patient authority—VIII. System pressures, ethics, and autonomy. *Journal of American Academy of Psychoanalysis and Dynamic Psychiatry*, 36(3), 547–560.

Plakun, E.M. (2009). A view from Riggs: Treatment resistance and patient authority—introduction to paper IX. *Journal of the American Academy of Psychoanalysis and Dynamic Psychiatry*, 36(4), 737–738.

Tillman, J.G. (2009). A view from Riggs: Treatment resistance and patient authority—IX. Integrative psychodynamic treatment of psychotic disorders. *Journal of the American Academy of Psychoanalysis and Dynamic Psychiatry*, 36(4), 739–762.

Kayatekin, M.S., & Plakun, E.M. (2009). A view from Riggs: Treatment resistance and patient authority—X. From acting out to enactment in treatment resistant disorders. *Journal of the American Academy of Psychoanalysis and Dynamic Psychiatry*, 37(2), 365–381.

Plakun, E.M. (2009). A view from Riggs: Treatment resistance and patient authority—XI. ABIS: An alliance based intervention for suicide.

Journal of the American Academy of Psychoanalysis and Dynamic Psychiatry, 37(3), 539–560.

Shapiro, E.R. (2009). A view from Riggs: Treatment resistance and patient authority—XII. Examined living: A psychodynamic treatment system. *Journal of the American Academy of Psychoanalysis and Dynamic Psychiatry, 37*(4), 683–698.

Plakun, E.M. (2009). A view from Riggs: Treatment resistance and patient authority—series epilogue. *Journal of the American Academy of Psychoanalysis and Dynamic Psychiatry, 37*(4), 699–700.

Chapter 1
Treatment Resistance

J. Christopher Fowler, PhD, Eric M. Plakun, MD, and Edward R. Shapiro, MD

Despite scientific advances in treating the mentally ill through biological and psychosocial treatments, clinicians, patients, and families struggle with the limitations of medications, psychotherapies, and inpatient approaches. Clinicians and researchers are searching for answers as to why some individuals get worse or see little response to biological or psychotherapeutic interventions.

Broadly defined, the term *treatment resistance* signifies a less than 50% improvement in target symptoms and failure to return to baseline functioning despite adequate dose and duration of a treatment known to be effective (Greden, 2001). In some cases, failure to respond may be related to the patient's poor adherence to an otherwise efficacious and previously agreed-to treatment regimen. In other cases the "resistance" may be thought of as reflecting the limitations of our current treatments.

The Austen Riggs Center has focused its clinical and research mission on the treatment and study of treatment-resistant psychiatric disorders. Close to 100 years of intensive engagement with patients have helped focus our comprehensive psychodynamic approach on the meaning of symptoms, the importance of relationships, and the centrality of patient authority in bringing about lasting change in symptoms, relationships, and occupational functioning. Because our patients require integrated treatment in order to make gains, we have refined our multimodal approach, defined a set of core psychodynamic principles for individual psychotherapy, and created a therapeutic milieu program to support social and inter-personal learning.

Looking over hundreds of case histories, we find a prototypic trajectory for Austen Riggs patients. Most began experiencing psychological difficulties relatively early in adolescence, yet first-line treatment strategies, comprised of multiple medication trials, including augmentation strategies, failed to bring about improvement in functioning. Various psychotherapy modalities (including psychodynamic, behavioral, cognitive–behavioral, and dialectical behavioral therapies) were added to medication regimens to produce modest improvements, but profound disturbances in social, relational, and vocational functioning persisted. Deteriorating courses and increasing self-destructive behavior frequently resulted in one or more acute and/or longer-term hospitalizations, but few future Riggs patients were able to sustain short-term gains following discharge, and most were generally unable to function in work or social roles without massive external support.

We came to understand that these patients' deteriorating courses—sometimes decades long—reflected the complexity and severity of their illnesses as well as the limitations of modern psychiatry to adequately address their illnesses. These patients appeared to be located within a spectrum of treatment resistance, within which we could discern a set of markers that distinguished them from others and that contributed to their limited response to standard treatment approaches.

THE SPECTRUM OF TREATMENT RESISTANCE

Although randomized controlled trials and high-quality efficacy studies have demonstrated improvement and recovery in many individuals with a range of psychiatric conditions, there is increasing recognition that failure to respond is frequent, ranging from 15 to 50% depending on the disorder (Berlim & Turecki, 2007; Lieberman et al., 2005; Perlis et al., 2006; Thase & Rush, 1997; Thase et al., 2007; Thase, Friedman, & Howland, 2001). Thus, treatment-resistant disorders represent a significant proportion of all psychiatric outcomes—and this is true whether we examine patients with single disorders or with more complex, comorbid disorders. There are few systematic approaches to the problem of treatment resistance. The American Psychiatric Association addresses the problem of treatment resistance in only two of its past practice guidelines: those for schizophrenia and for major depressive disorder (American Psychiatric Association, 2000, 2004).

But with emerging research on the scope of treatment resistance in the past few years, the psychiatric community is developing approaches to improve outcomes. For example, the American Psychiatric Association's Practice Guideline Watch for major depressive disorders (Fochtmann & Gelenberg, 2005) suggests strategies for treating patients who are unresponsive to first-line agents. These include increasing dosages of antidepressants, switching medications, augmenting primary agents with other classes of medications, adding psychosocial treatments such as psychotherapy, and using electroconvulsive therapy. Algorithms for treatment-resistant depression are under investigation, yet no consistently effective approach has emerged (Stimpson, Agrawal, & Lewis, 2002). Sequential treatment approaches are gaining ground, yet definitive evidence for "best practices" for treatment-resistant depression is still unavailable. When we consider that major depressive disorders are the most widely researched psychiatric disorder, it becomes clear that our understanding of the scope and breadth of treatment resistance is in its infancy.

Single-Disorder Treatment Resistance

Results from outcome studies suggest that patients suffering from even one psychiatric disorder often experience limited benefit, drop out of treatment, or experience recurrence of illness after a period of improved functioning. For example, in schizophrenia 10–30% of patients fail to respond to treatment, and another 30% respond only partially (American Psychiatric Association, 2004, p. 24). Nearly 75% of patients with schizophrenia in the Clinical Antipsychotic Trials in Intervention Effectiveness (CATIE) study discontinued their medication regimen before 18 months of treatment (Lieberman et al., 2005). For patients with mood disorders, between 15 and 50% appear as treatment-resistant cases (Thase et al., 2001), and only a minority of patients with major depressive disorder recover fully with medications alone (Rush & Trivedi, 1995). The Sequenced Treatment Alternatives to Relieve Depression (STAR*D) study demonstrated that substantial numbers of patients with major depressive disorder fail to respond adequately either to the initial treatment or to various switch or augmentation strategies, including augmentation with short-term cognitive–behavioral therapy (Thase et al., 2007). In bipolar disorder, the Systematic Treatment Enhancement Program for Bipolar Disorder (STEP-BD) study reported that only 58% of subjects achieved recovery from the index mood episode, and half of these experienced a recurrence of a mood episode within 2 years (Perlis et al., 2006).

Comorbidity and Treatment Resistance

Evidence is mounting that the presence of comorbid Axis I and II disorders substantially increases the risk of poor outcome, even when patients and clinicians are adherent to otherwise demonstrably efficacious treatments. Various studies report an association between comorbidity (especially anxiety, substance use, and personality disorders) and treatment-resistant depression (Fagiolini & Kupfer, 2003; Kornstein & Schnieder, 2001; Souery, Lipp, Massat, & Mendlewicz, 2001). In general psychiatric practice, comorbid disorders are often missed or considered irrelevant, leading to suboptimal treatment (Grote & Frank, 2003). A recent meta-analysis explored the impact of comorbid personality disorders on the treatment of major depression, revealing that the risk for poor outcome is doubled when patients have a comorbid personality disorder compared to those depressed subjects without a personality disorder (Newton-Howe, Tyrer, & Johnson, 2006). In a reanalysis of the STAR*D data, researchers (Wisniewski et al., 2009) found that despite similar medication dosing, those patients without comorbidity tolerated medication better, had higher rates of treatment response (51.6% vs. 39.1%), and better rates of remission from depressive symptoms (34.4% vs. 24.7%) than patients with comorbidity. Of great concern is the fact that 78% of all STAR*D participants exhibited comorbid disorders or other traits, such as suicidal ideation, that are exclusion criteria for most treatment trials. These findings strongly suggest that these trials do not recruit clinically representative samples of depressed individuals.

Many clinicians would agree that the patients they see in their offices are more like the 78% with higher comorbidity and poorer outcomes. This impression is supported by the National Comorbidity Survey Replication (Kessler et al., 2003), which found that individuals with single psychiatric disorders represent a minority of patients seeking treatment.

Severity of Illness and Functional Impairment

Although comorbidity is a significant risk factor for developing treatment-resistant psychiatric illness, there is clear evidence that severity of symptoms and degree of impairment in social and occupational functioning also impact response to treatment (Fawcett, 2008; Lehman, Alexopoulos, Goldman, Jeste, & Üstün, 2002; Skodol & Bender, 2009). Secondary analyses of several large-scale studies shed light on characteristics associated with poor outcomes. In a reanalysis of the National Institute of Mental

Health (NIMH) Treatment of Depression Collaborative Research Program (Sotsky, Glass, Shea, & Pilkonis, 1991) seven patient characteristics predicted outcome across all treatments: pretreatment depression severity, social dysfunction, cognitive dysfunction, low expectation of improvement, endogenous depression, double depression (i.e., the presence of major depressive disorder and dysthymia), and duration of current episode. In a 2-year follow-up of subjects with borderline personality disorder in the Collaborative Longitudinal Personality Disorders (CLPS) study, Gunderson and colleagues (2006) had similar findings. Pretreatment characteristics such as more severe psychopathology (as manifested by higher number of borderline personality disorder criteria, greater functional impairment, and greater interpersonal relationship instability) as well as a history of childhood trauma predicted differential outcome at the 2-year follow-up. Taken together, these findings indicate that treatment resistance may be a function of severity, chronicity, degree of associated cognitive impairment, social impairment, low expectation of improvement, as well as comorbidity.

This and other evidence suggests that patients with treatment-resistant disorders present a high social and financial burden in terms of lowered quality of life, lost income, lost lives through suicide, and markedly increased treatment costs. Crown and colleagues (2002) report that treatment-refractory patients with unipolar or bipolar depression were at least twice as likely to require medical or psychiatric hospitalization as a more treatment-responsive comparison group of depressed patients. They also report that the hospitalized treatment-refractory group had 6 times the mean total medical costs and 19 times the total depression-related costs of the comparison group.

Clinicians who treat hospitalized patients with personality disorders confirm these findings, suggesting the massive burden of treatment resistance (Munich & Allen, 2003; Plakun, 1994, 2003; Shapiro & Plakun, 2008). For example, a recent study of 219 hospitalized inpatients at the Austen Riggs Center (Perry et al., 2009) reveals high rates of comorbidity, symptom severity, and functional impairment. Study subjects had an average of six Axis I and II disorders: 80% had treatment-refractory mood disorders, 50% substance use disorders, 26% eating disorders, and 15% psychotic spectrum disorders. More than 80% of patients in the Riggs sample met criteria for one or more personality disorders, most commonly borderline personality disorder. Their psychiatric histories were replete with failed treatments: 79% had undergone previous psychiatric hospitalizations, 74% had experienced regression (i.e., psychological and functional deterioration) during previous psychiatric treatments, and virtually all had had multiple outpatient psychotherapies combined with psychotropic medication trials without clear improvement. Two-thirds of these patients had histories suggesting significant early adverse experiences of abuse, trauma, neglect, loss, or deprivation, and approximately 30% met criteria for posttraumatic stress disorder. Half (49%) had made at least one serious suicide attempt, 88% had histories of nonsuicidal self-injury, and 76% reported frequent suicidal ideation.

High rates of comorbidity, multiple failed treatments, sustained social and interpersonal impairment, and self-destructive behaviors in our patient population have contributed to the development and refinement of an integrated approach to treatment at the Austen Riggs Center, out of which comes a set of principles that may be applicable to clinicians working with these patients across a range of settings.

CAN A PSYCHODYNAMIC APPROACH HELP TREATMENT-RESISTANT PATIENTS BECOME TREATMENT RESPONDERS?

In recognition that many patients fail to benefit from initial treatment, algorithms have been developed in psychiatry to maximize therapeutic response. These algorithms generally structure a rational sequence of trials of biological treatments, with appropriate augmentation strategies and an emphasis on maximizing patient compliance with medication, given the evidence that poor compliance is a significant factor in treatment resistance (Boudes, 1998; Cramer & Rosenheck, 1998). Nevertheless, clinicians know that these patients frequently struggle with far more than a failure to respond to prescribed medications. The intractable severity of these patients' symptoms leads to serious impairment in relationship and role functioning, while repeated treatment failures, coupled with disappointment in authority figures, leads such patients to mistrust those charged with caring for them, including medical and psychiatric professionals (Shapiro & Plakun, 2008). Power struggles and ruptures in social and therapeutic relationships are common (Munich & Allen, 2003), as are patients' difficulties adhering to prescribed medication regimens due to extreme sensitivity to side effects and limited treatment response (Mintz, 2002).

These patients often express intense and unbearable emotions through such self-destructive behaviors as substance use, recurrent self-injury, and/

or suicidal behavior. Given the intensity of their distress, the often chaotic and stormy nature of relationships, and the significant risk for serious injury, optimal treatment requires an intensive, multimodal approach (including, but not limited to, medications) in order to help these patients take charge of their lives and shift from a trajectory of treatment resistance toward becoming treatment responders. Considering the broad range of phenomena that contribute to treatment resistance and its burdens, we must look beyond the scope of biological treatments for these patients. A psychodynamic systems approach is one way of integrating such a multimodal treatment program.

Our emphasis on the value of a multimodal psychodynamic treatment approach is in contrast with the last two decades' emphasis on biological treatments and tendency toward biological reductionism in psychiatry. Practice guidelines, for example, emphasize biological treatments for nearly all disorders. In part this emphasis reflects psychiatry's preference for "evidence-based" treatments found efficacious in randomized controlled trials, while eschewing the clinical consensus of experts. Randomized trials are most easily designed and conducted with biological and short-term psychotherapeutic treatments for one disorder at a time—the reality of the high incidence of comorbidity notwithstanding (Westen & Morrison, 2001).

Other medical specialties do not necessarily share psychiatry's reluctance to rely on expert consensus in selecting recommendations for practice guidelines. A review of the cardiovascular practice guidelines of the American College of Cardiology and the American Heart Association showed that only 11% of 2,711 treatment recommendations in the practice guidelines were supported by the highest level of evidence involving multiple replicated randomized controlled trials or meta-analyses (Tricoci, Allen, Kramer, Califf, & Smith, 2009). Almost half of the cardiology recommendations (48%) were based on expert consensus. Perhaps the wide acceptance of expert consensus in cardiology will help us rethink the kind of recommendations included in psychiatry practice guidelines.

The biological focus of general psychiatry has also been associated with a substantial decrease in the provision of psychotherapy by psychiatrists (Mojtabai & Olfson, 2008) and a concomitant decrease in teaching psychotherapy skills to residents (Plakun, 2006). However, there is growing reason to be concerned that we may have overestimated the efficacy of medications while underestimating the efficacy of psychotherapy. A review of published and unpublished studies of antidepressants concluded that the efficacy of antidepressants has been overestimated by about a third through publication bias or other neglect of negative studies (Turner, Matthews, Linardatos, Tell, & Rosenthal, 2008), while Kirsch (Kirsch, et al., 2008) reports that perhaps 75% of the effects ascribed to antidepressant medications appears to be due to the placebo effect.

Meanwhile, there is growing evidence that psychotherapy is an effective treatment for more complex cases. For example, Nemeroff et al. (2003) studied 681 patients with chronic major depressive disorders, many of whom had histories of early adverse life experiences. They found that a form of cognitive–behavioral therapy (CBT) called "cognitive behavioral analysis system of psychotherapy" was superior to nefazadone for those chronically depressed and treatment-resistant patients who also had abuse histories. Nemeroff notes (p. 14293), "Our findings suggest that psychotherapy may be an essential element in the treatment of patients with chronic forms of major depression and a history of childhood trauma." A series of well-designed studies has demonstrated that psychotherapy is an effective treatment for patients with borderline personality disorder (Bateman & Fonagy, 2008, Clarkin, Levy, Lenzenweger & Kernberg, 2007; Doering et al., 2010; Levy et al., 2006; Linehan et al., 2006). There is also evidence that psychotherapy is associated with brain changes and that imaging studies can distinguish therapy responders from nonresponders (Schwartz, Stoessel, Baxter, Martin, & Phelps, 1996).

Furthermore, a high-quality meta-analysis of 23 studies of long-term psychodynamic treatments (Leichsenring & Rabung, 2008) revealed that complex and often treatment-resistant patients receiving at least 50 sessions of long-term psychodynamic psychotherapy showed better outcomes in terms of overall effectiveness, target problems, and personality functioning than did patients who experienced short-term forms of psychotherapy. In addition, after long-term psychodynamic psychotherapy, patients with complex mental disorders were better off than 96% of the patients in the comparison groups, suggesting that it is an effective treatment for complex mental disorders. Addressing the overall efficacy of psychodynamic psychotherapy compared to other therapies and medications, Shedler (2010) suggests that the effect sizes of psychodynamic therapy are equivalent to other forms of treatment, and that patients receiving long-term psychodynamic psychotherapy maintain their treatment gains and continue to improve after therapy ends, unlike the outcomes of patients who undergo other forms of therapy.

RESEARCH RESULTS FROM THE
AUSTEN RIGGS CENTER

Several naturalistic studies of symptomatic and functional outcomes focus on patients at the Austen Riggs Center. Plakun, Burkhardt, and Muller (1985) reported that between 60 and 80% of 237 patients had good outcomes, depending on diagnosis, with patients with borderline personality disorder appearing as impaired at admission as those with schizophrenia, but with substantially better long-term outcome. Among patients with borderline personality disorder who were free of significant comorbidity, self-destructive behavior that emerged in the course of treatment, but that was associated with engagement of the behavior in the treatment and repair of the therapeutic relationship, was associated with better outcome (Plakun, 1991).

Blatt and Ford (1994) examined treatment outcomes in 90 seriously disturbed Riggs patients, noting change across an average of 15 months of intensive psychodynamic treatment. These investigators found marked improvement in domains of interpersonal relating, motivation for treatment, and greater emotional expressiveness. Patients demonstrated more modest improvement in degree of thought disorder, greater capacity to engage in adaptive fantasy, and improvement in their representations of self and others. The authors then assessed how treatment affected functioning based on two global character styles: the anaclitic and introjective. For patients primarily concerned with maintaining need-gratifying relationships (anaclitic type), changes were noted in quality of object representations, improved social competence, and motivation for treatment. For patients with introjective (more constricted) character organizations, the greatest change occurred in decreased thought disorder, with a corresponding improvement in clinician assessment of psychotic symptoms and affect modulation.

A similar study, (Fowler et al., 2004) examined treatment outcomes of 77 inpatients suffering from complex, comorbid treatment-resistant disorders during an average of 16 months of intensive residential treatment at Austen Riggs. Overall, patients were significantly improved on measures of symptom severity, quality of relationship functioning, and ability to function in work roles as well as on measures of personality functioning, including degree of thought disorder, quality of representations, and capacity to understand social relationships in more complex and nuanced ways. Rates of improvement were promising: 69% had at least modest improvement in symptom severity, 61% improved in quality of inter-personal relating, and 57% improved in capacity to function in work roles.

In the latest study of patients at Riggs with past suicide attempts, 75% had recovered from suicide as an issue in their lives after an average of 7 years, and 50% had completely recovered from experiencing suicidal ide-ation within 8 years (Perry et al., 2009). As is typical, for these patients, whose median length of stay at Riggs was 6 months, one focus of their Riggs treatment was helping them function more successfully than previ-ously in outpatient treatment.

Based on this data from Riggs and elsewhere, we argue in this volume that there is a subset of patients with treatment-resistant disorders for whom a psychodynamic approach, including individual psychodynamic psychotherapy and a range of psychodynamically integrated psychiatric treatments, is the best way to engage and grapple with the character issues that contribute to treatment resistance.

> There is a subset of patients with treatment-resistant disorders for whom a psychodynamic approach, including individual psychody-namic psychotherapy and a range of psychodynamically integrated psychiatric treatments, is the best way to engage and grapple with the character issues that contribute to treatment resistance.

SPECIFIC THERAPEUTIC TASKS

A major task of psychodynamic work with these patients is translating the (usually unconscious) meanings communicated through symptoms and behavior into words. Patients reveal to us in their character, in their de-fenses, in the evolving transference, and in their symptoms, the impact of adverse experiences on their development. The task of the clinical staff is to help them translate these nonverbal communications into words. When patients can shift from enacting their messages in behavior and learn to speak meaning in words, they are better able to acknowledge, bear, and put into perspective painful life experiences in ways that allow them to take charge of themselves and often to emerge from treatment resistance. When viewed this way, treatment resistance becomes not only a clinical reality but also a powerful metaphor for aspects of the patient's life history and character structure that can best be engaged on the level of human relationships.

> Treatment resistance is not only a clinical reality but also a powerful metaphor for aspects of the patient's life history and character structure that can best be engaged on the level of human relationships.

Helping a treatment-resistant patient transform into a treatment responder who can take charge of his or her life requires an approach that includes several features generally absent from current psychiatric practice, including (1) an emphasis on the therapeutic value of human relationships; (2) careful attention to deciphering the encoded psychological meaning embedded within a patient's symptoms and character structure, particularly meaning related to treatment resistance; and (3) recognition that treatment resistance often includes a response to the loss of the patient's authority, as he or she becomes a passive recipient expected to "comply" with a doctor's orders. Resistance to treatment may be the only way left for a patient to exercise authority if he or she has lived a life of abuse, loss, deprivation, and neglect. Treatments work best when patient authority is restored within human relationships that include efforts to discover and translate hidden meaning and that do not shrink from facing a patient's rage toward those in authority on whom he or she must nevertheless depend.

> Treatment-resistant patients are most likely to respond to treatments that include:
>
> - Emphasis on the therapeutic value of human relationships
> - Attention to deciphering the encoded psychological meaning embedded within a patients' symptoms and character structure
> - Recognition that treatment resistance may come from loss of patients' authority.

PSYCHODYNAMIC PRINCIPLES IN TREATMENT-REFRACTORY DISORDERS

One of the first efforts to extract what we were doing in work with treatment-resistant patients at Riggs came in response to detailed follow-up revealing that many of our previously treatment-resistant patients, especially those with treatment-refractory mood disorders comorbid with personality disorders, were showing significant evidence of improvement. We focused our attention on particular elements in the treatment approach that might be associated with good outcome and determined that 10 psychodynamic treatment principles stood out (Plakun, 2003).

Psychodynamic principles for treating patients with treatment-resistant disorders:

- Attend to diagnostic comorbidity.
- Carefully negotiate and use the therapeutic alliance.
- Listen beneath the symptoms for recurring themes in the patient's life story.
- Integrate medication and therapy.
- Attend to and use transference and countertransference.
- Find and put into words the unavailable affects.
- Detect and use enactments.
- Use interpretation.
- Implement a treatment plan that integrates treatment by all providers.
- Use psychotherapy consultation.

Attention to diagnostic comorbidity, particularly to Axis II disorders and to the role trauma, neglect, loss, and deprivation may be playing in the patient's treatment- resistant presentation, facilitates access to behavioral communication. In a treatment system such as the one in place at Riggs, this means developing specialized approaches to particular disorders that complement the psychodynamic psychotherapy, including treatment of substance use disorders and skills training for patients with borderline personality disorder or other disorders for which learning skills to contain intense affects may be valuable.

Negotiating the terms of the *therapeutic alliance* is a way to engage difficult issues such as suicide. Taking seriously the patient's effort to resume development can help clinicians from a range of disciplines join the patient's efforts rather than take over for him or her (see Chapters 8 and 11).

Listening beneath the symptoms for recurring themes in the patient's life story goes beyond diagnostic criteria and symptoms. These "therapeutic stories," as Volkan (2010) calls them, are often metaphorical communications about the nature of a patient's core struggles. This way of listening follows the patient's emotions and requires learning to listen with a psychodynamic ear. The themes revealed in a patient's narrative often offer clues about how treatment resistance may "make sense" for a patient.

Integrating medication and therapy is valuable for many of these patients, for whom the use of medication has particular meanings that must be grasped in order to engage them, whether or not the therapist is the prescriber (see Chapter 3).

Transference and countertransference are the principal means through which a patient's dynamic struggles come to life in the consulting room, often in ways that bring themes from therapeutic stories to life in the transference and countertransference.

Treatment-resistant patients of the sort we are describing often communicate important information through behavior rather than words, with behavior expressing feelings that patients cannot bear. Therefore, one of the tasks of clinicians is to help patients *find and put into words previously unavailable affects*. These important but unavailable affects may include grief, rage, envy, shame, and their discovery contributes to making sense of treatment resistance. Another task is to *attend to enactments* and use them to deepen the work (see Chapter 2).

Interpretation is a central vehicle for change in psychodynamic therapy because it is a way to show that actions, even impulsive ones, have an underlying and discoverable logic that can be broken down into graspable parts that make sense of the apparently irrational. Interpretation can also show patients how they are caught in a repetition of memories that are out of their awareness and thus out of their control. Discovering a language for these painful experiences allows patients to begin to bear the feelings and put their past in perspective. In a treatment system, interpretation is used in individual therapy and in group work.

Implementing a treatment plan that integrates treatment by all providers is a crucial way to protect the treatment from fragmenting through dispersed transferences and splitting. Such a plan should be guided by a dynamic formulation that all members of the treatment team participate in creating (see Chapter 13).

Psychotherapy consultation is always useful when therapists become lost in the work or caught in enactments. Consultation offers an outside perspective that can help a pair caught up in impasses or other struggles related to transference–countertransference enactments.

These principles are illustrated throughout this volume. Patients find different pathways to symptomatic and functional improvement in our setting. The treatment center, with its various formal therapeutic modalities, the social learning foci of the therapeutic community program, and the opportunities to experiment with work and student roles provide an enriching environment for each patient to discover his or her unique path.

REFERENCES

American Psychiatric Association. (2000). Practice guideline for the treatment of major depressive disorders in adults, second edition. *Journal of the American Psychiatric Association, 157,* April supplement.

American Psychiatric Association. (2004). Practice guideline for the treatment of patients with schizophrenia, second edition. *Journal of the American Psychiatric Association, 161,* February supplement.

Bateman, A., & Fonagy, P. (2008). 8-year follow-up of patients treated for borderline personality disorder: Mentalization-based treatment versus treatment as usual. *American Journal of Psychiatry, 165*(5), 631–638.

Berlim, M.T., & Turecki, G. (2007). Definition, assessment, and staging of treatment-resistant refractory major depression: A review of current concepts and methods. *Canadian Journal of Psychiatry, 52,* 46–54.

Blatt, S. J., & Ford, R. (1994). *Therapeutic change: An object relations perspective.* New York: Plenum Press.

Boudes, P. (1998). Drug compliance in therapeutic trials: A review. *Controlled Clinical Trials, 19,* 257–268.

Clarkin, J. F., Levy, K. N., Lenzenweger, M. F., & Kernberg, O. F. (2007). Evaluating three treatments for borderline personality disorder: A multi-wave study. *American Journal of Psychiatry, 164,* 922–928.

Cramer, J.A., & Rosenheck, R. (1998). Compliance with medication regimens for mental and physical disorders. *Psychiatric Services, 49,* 196–201.

Crown, W.H., Finkelstein, S., Berndt, E.R., Ling, D., Poret, A.W., Rush, A.J., et al. (2002). The impact of treatment-resistant depression on health care utilization and costs. *Journal of Clinical Psychiatry, 63,* 963–971.

Doering, S., Hörz, S., Rentrop, M., Fischer-Kern, M., Schuster, P., Benecke, C., et al. (2010). Transference-focused psychotherapy v. treatment by community psychotherapists for borderline personality disorder: Randomised controlled trial. *British Journal of Psychiatry, 196,* 389–395.

Fagiolini, A., & Kupfer, D.J. (2003). Is treatment-resistant depression a unique subtype of depression?. *Biological Psychiatry, 53,* 640–648.

Fawcett, J. (2008). The role of comorbidity in severity and outcome. *Psychiatric Annals, 38*, 702–702.

Fochtmann, L.J., & Gelenberg, A.J. (2005). Guideline watch: Practice guideline for the treatment of patients with major depressive disorder, second edition. *Focus, 3*, 34–42.

Fonagy, P., & Bateman, A.W. (2007). Mentalizing and borderline personality disorder. *Journal of Mental Health, 16*, 83–101.

Fowler, J.C., Ackerman, A., Blagys, M., Speanburg, S., & Bailey, A., & Conklin, A.C. (2004). Personality and symptom change in treatment-refractory inpatients: Evaluation of the phase model of change using Rorschach, TAT and DSM Axis V. *Journal of Personality Assessment, 83*, 306–322.

Greden, J.F. (2001). The burden of disease for treatment-resistant depression. *Journal of Clinical Psychiatry, 62*(Suppl. 16), 26–31.

Grote, N.K., & Frank, E. (2003). Difficult-to-treat depression: The role of contexts and comorbidities. *Biological Psychiatry, 53*(8), 660–670.

Gunderson, J., Daversa, M., Grilo, C., McGlashan, T.H., Zanarini, M.C., Shea, M.T., et al. (2006). Predictors of 2-year outcome for patients with borderline personality disorder. *American Journal of Psychiatry, 163*(5), 822–826.

Kessler, R.C., Berglund, P., Demler, O., Jin, R., Koretz, D., Merikangas, K.R., et al. (2003). The epidemiology of major depressive disorder: Results from the National Comorbidity Survey Replication (NCS-R). *Journal of the American Medical Association, 289*, 3095–3105.

Kirsch, I., Deacon, B.J., Huedo-Medina, T.B., Scoboria, A., Moore, T.J., & Johnson, B.T. (2008). Initial severity and antidepressant benefits: A meta-analysis of data submitted to the Food and Drug Administration. *Public Library of Science: Medicine, 5*(2), e45. doi:10.1371/journal.pmed.0050045, February.

Kornstein, S.G., & Schneider, R.K. (2001). Clinical features of treatment-resistant depression. *Clinical Psychiatry, 62*(Suppl. 16), 18–25.

Lehman, A., Alexopoulos, G., Goldman, H., Jeste, D., & Üstün, B. (2002). Mental disorders and disability: Time to reevaluate the relationship? In D.J. Kupfer, M. B. First, D.A. Regier (Eds.) *A research agenda for DSM-V,* (201–218). Washington, DC: American Psychiatric Association.

Leichsenring, F., & Rabung S. (2008). Effectiveness of long-term psychodynamic psychotherapy: A meta-analysis. *Journal of the American Medical Association, 300*(13), 1551–1565.

Levy, K. N., Meehan, K. B., Kelly, K. M., Reynoso, J. S., Weber, M., Clarkin, J. F., et al. (2006). Change in attachment patterns and reflective function in a randomized controlled trial of transference-focused psychotherapy for borderline personality disorder. *Journal of Consulting and Clinical Psychology, 74*, 1027–1040.

Lieberman, J.A., Stroup, T.S., McEvoy, J.P., Swartz, M.S., Rosenheck, R.A., Perkins, D.O., et al. (2005). Effectiveness of antipsychotic drugs in patients with chronic schizophrenia. *New England Journal of Medicine, 35*, 1209–1223.

Linehan, M., Comtois, K., Murray, A., Brown, M., Gallop, R., Heard, H., et al. (2006). Two-year randomized controlled trial and follow-up of dialectical behavior therapy versus therapy by experts for suicidal behaviors and borderline personality disorder. *Archives of General Psychiatry, 63*(7), 757–766.

Milrod, B., Leon, A.C., Busch, F., Rudden, M., Schwalberg, M., Clarkin, J., Aronson, A., Singer, M., Turchin, W., Klass, E.T., Graf, E., Teres, J.J., Shear, M.K. A randomized controlled trial of psychoanalytic psychotherapy for panic disorder. American Journal of Psychiatry, 2007; 164:265-272.

Mintz, D. (2002). Meaning and medication in the care of treatment-resistant patients. *American Journal of Psychotherapy, 56*(3), 322–337.

Mojtabai, R., & Olfson, M. (2008). National trends in psychotherapy by office-based psychiatrists. *Archives of General Psychiatry, 65*(8), 962–970.

Munich, R.L., & Allen, J.G. (2003). Psychiatric and sociotherapeutic perspectives on the difficult-to-treat patient. *Psychiatry: Interpersonal and Biological Processes, 66*, 346–357.

Nemeroff, C.B., Heim, C.M., Thase, M.E., Klein, D.N., Rush, A.J., Schatzberg, A.F., et al. (2003). Differential response to psychotherapy versus pharmacotherapy in patients with chronic forms of major depression and childhood trauma. *Proceedings of the National Academy of Sciences, 100*, 14293–14296.

Newton-Howes, G., Tyrer, P., & Johnson, T. (2006). Personality disorder and the outcome of depression: Meta-analysis of published studies. *British Journal of Psychiatry, 188*, 13–20.

Perlis, R.H., Ostacher, M.J., Patel, J.K., Marangell, L.B., Zhang, H., Wisniewski, S.R., et al. (2006). Predictors of recurrence in bipolar disorder: Primary outcomes from the Systematic Treatment Enhancement Program for Bipolar Disorder (STEP-BD). *American Journal of Psychiatry, 163*, 217–224.

Perry, J.C., Fowler, J.C., Bailey, A., Clemence, A.J., Plakun, E.M., Zheutlin, B., et al. (2009). Improvement and recovery from suicidal and self-destructive phenomena in treatment-refractory disorders. *Journal of Nervous and Mental Disease, 197*(1), 28–34.

Plakun, E.M. (1991). Prediction of outcome in borderline personality disorder. *Journal of Personality Disorders, 5*, 93–101.

Plakun, E.M. (1994). Principles in the psychotherapy of self-destructive borderline patients. *Journal of Psychotherapy Practice Research, 3*, 138–148.

Plakun, E.M. (2001). Making the alliance and taking the transference in work with suicidal borderline patients. Journal of Psychotherapy Practice and Research, 10, 269-276.

Plakun, E.M. (2003). Treatment refractory mood disorders: A psychodynamic perspective. *Journal of Psychiatric Practice, 9*, 209–218.

Plakun, E.M. (2006). Finding psychodynamic psychiatry's lost generation. *Journal of the American Academy of Psychoanalysis and Dynamic Psychiatry, 34*(1), 135–150.

Plakun, E.M., Burkhardt, P.E., & Muller, J.P. (1985). 14-year follow-up of borderline and schizotypal personality disorders. *Comprehensive Psychiatry, 26*, 448–455.

Rush, A.J., & Trivedi, M.H. (1995). Treating depression to remission. *Psychiatric Annals, 25*, 704–709.

Schwartz, J.M., Stoessel, P.W., Baxter, L.R., Martin, K.M., & Phelps, M.E. (1996). Systematic changes in cerebral glucose metabolic rate after successful behavior modification treatment of obsessive–compulsive disorder. *Archives of General Psychiatry, 53*, 109–113.

Shapiro, E.R., & Plakun, E.M. (2008). Residential psychotherapeutic treatment: An intensive psychodynamic approach for patients with treatment-resistant disorders. In S. Sharfstein (Ed.), *Textbook of hospital psychiatry* (pp. 285–297). Washington, DC: American Psychiatric Association.

Shedler, J. (2010). The efficacy of psychodynamic therapy. *American Psychologist, 65(2)*, 98–109.

Skodol, A.E., & Bender, D.S. (2009). The future of personality disorders in DSM-V. *American Journal of Psychiatry, 166*, 388–391.

Sotsky, S., Glass, D., Shea, M., & Pilkonis, P. (1991). Patient predictors of response to psychotherapy and pharmacotherapy: Findings in the NIMH Treatment of Depression Collaborative Research Program. *American Journal of Psychiatry, 148*(8), 997–1008.

Souery, D., Lipp, O., Massat, I., & Mendlewicz, J. (2001). The characterization and definition of treatment-resistant mood disorders. In J.D. Amsterdam, M. Hornig, & A.A. Nierenberg (Eds.), *Treatment-resistant mood disorders* (pp. 3–29). New York: Cambridge University Press.

Stimpson, N., Agrawal, N., & Lewis, G. (2002). Randomised controlled trials investigating pharmacological and psychological interventions for treatment-refractory depression: Systematic review. *British Journal of Psychiatry, 181,* 284–294.

Thase, M.E. (2006). Predictors of recurrence in bipolar disorder: primary outcomes from the Systematic Treatment Enhancement Program for Bipolar Disorder (STEP-BD). *American Journal of Psychiatry, 163,* 217–224.

Thase, M.E., Friedman, E.S., Biggs, M.M., Wisniewski, S.R., Trivedi, M.H., Luther, J.F., et al. (2007). Cognitive therapy versus medication in augmentation and switch strategies as second-step treatments: A STAR*D report. *American Journal of Psychiatry, 164,* 739–752.

Thase, M.E., Friedman, E.S., & Howland, R.H. (2001). Management of treatment-resistant depression: Psychotherapeutic perspectives. *Journal of Clinical Psychiatry, 62*(Suppl.), 18–24.

Thase, M.E., & Rush, A.J. (1997). When at first you don't succeed: Sequential strategies for antidepressant nonresponders. *Journal of Clinical Psychiatry, 58*(Suppl. 13), 23–29.

Tricoci, P., Allen, J.M., Kramer, J.M., Califf, R.M., & Smith, S.C., Jr. (2009). Scientific evidence underlying the ACC/AHA clinical practice guidelines. *Journal of the American Medical Association, 25,* 831–841.

Turner, E.H., Matthews, A.M., Linardatos, E., Tell, R.A., & Rosenthal, R. (2008). Selective publication of antidepressant trials and its influence on apparent efficacy. *New England Journal of Medicine, 358*(3), 252–260.

Volkan, V.D. (2010). *Psychoanalytic technique expanded: A textbook on psychoanalytic treatment.* London & Istanbul: OA Press.

Westen, D., & Morrison, K. (2001). A multidimensional meta-analysis of treatments for depression, panic, generalized anxiety disorder: An empirical examination of the status of empirically supported treatments. *Journal of Consulting and Clinical Psychology, 69,* 875–899.

Wisniewski, S.R., Rush, A.J., Nierenberg, A.A., Gaynes, B.N., Warden, D., Luther, J.F., et al. (2009). Can phase III trial results of antidepressant medications be generalized to clinical practice?: A STAR*D report. *American Journal of Psychiatry, 166,* 599–607.

Chapter 2

From Acting Out to Enactment in Treatment-Resistant Disorders

M. Sagman Kayatekin, MD, and Eric M. Plakun, MD

Action defenses are a conspicuous part of the phenomenon of treatment resistance. These defenses, often referred to as "acting out," pose serious challenges in treatment that lead to stalemates by creating an endless series of crises that derail therapeutic work and evoke desperation in patients, families, and treaters alike. Worse still, these actions may end treatment and sometimes lead to the death of patients by suicide. Therapists are faced with the dilemma of how to formulate and approach these phenomena in a way that does not simply label them, but that also engages patients in a way that can deepen and enhance the effectiveness of therapy.

> With treatment-resistant patients look beyond the notion of acting out toward the notion of enactment.

With difficult-to-treat patients it is often useful to look beyond the notion of acting out toward the notion of enactment. The former is a one-person formulation, locating the action in the patient, whereas the latter is a two-person formulation that locates the action in both parties in the therapeutic endeavor. Beyond the therapy dyad, though, enactments also occur between patients and other staff, between patients and patients, and between staff, whenever one person's character issues engage those of another or the issues in a group, as will be made clear in later chapters. Recognizing the limitations of the notion of acting out and reconceptualizing acting out as an enactment we unwittingly join is one of the major technical approaches that makes it possible to work with treatment-resistant patients.

FROM ACTING OUT TO ENACTMENT

The conceptual progression from acting out to enactment has been part of the evolution of our field. In 1945 Fenichel illustrated the "one-person" formulation when he noted:

> Neurotic acting out is an acting which unconsciously relieves inner tension and brings a partial discharge to warded off impulses. . . . The present situation, somehow associatively connected with the repressed content, is used as an occasion for the discharge of repressed energies; the cathexis is displaced from the repressed memories to the present "derivative," and this displacement makes the discharge possible. (p. 197)

In contrast to this intrapsychic formulation centered on concepts of drive, energy, and repression, some contemporary theoreticians were developing different ideas. Johnson and Szurek (1952),who were working with patients prone to acting out, observed parallels between superego lacunae in the parent and the patient. They hypothesized that parents "may find vicarious gratification of their own poorly-integrated forbidden impulses in the acting out of the child, through their unconscious permissiveness or inconsistency toward the child in these spheres of behavior" (p. 323), and asserted that the child was vicariously gratifying parents' "poorly integrated, forbidden impulses" (p. 342).

Bird (1957) agreed with this observation, stating that acting out is "a direct action response to stimulation by another person" that is motivated to "please or to influence another person, or perhaps to do both" (p. 630). He emphasized that this was an unconscious phenomenon using mainly behavioral channels of communication.

Contributions from International Psycho-Analytic Congress of 1968 sessions devoted to the topic of acting out crystallized these disagreements. On one pole, Anna Freud (1968) suggested that in acting out, "excessive quantitative cathexis of the revived strivings is responsible for the *irruptions* from analysis which land the patient in repetitive *reality actions* of a psychopathic nature" (p. 170). On the other hand, Grinberg (1968, p. 171) asserted: "Acting out, to my mind, can be regarded as a process that always calls for two participants."

Analysts working with patients with psychotic disorders were aware of the importance of the therapist as a central and ubiquitous "other" in analytic work. Margaret Little (1951) made references to the paranoid or phobic stance toward countertransference feelings that may impede the work: "I have shown above that unconscious (and uninterpreted) countertransference may be responsible for the prolonging [or] premature ending of analysis" (p. 38). In 1973 Searles proposed the notion of "therapeutic symbiosis," which required an understanding "of the extent to which the patient is himself devoted to functioning as a therapist in relationship to his officially designated analyst, as well as in his relationships with other persons in his life" (p. 248). In another foreshadowing of the notion of enactment, Boyer (1979) discussed his treatment of a woman with whom he became sleepy in sessions. His sleepiness led to a chain of associations and to an analysis of his own dream, which led to awareness of the way his countertransference to the patient engaged conflicted issues from his own past. Boyer realized that his sleepiness involved "expressing my anger by withdrawal and refusal to recognize her. . . . Such knowledge permitted me to regain my objectivity" (p. 361).

Writing from Riggs, Cooperman (1983) offered an innovative formulation: "Although the basic unit of biological functioning is the individual, the basic unit of psychological functioning seems always to be a twosome. That is, such behavior is always in relation to another person" (p. 22).

While therapists working with patients with psychotic disorders were elaborating on the vicissitudes of countertransference and paving the way toward the concept of enactment, within mainstream British psychoanalysis there was an early inclination toward the evolution of a two-person psychology. The Kleinians were instrumental in the development of two-person theories with their concepts of projection, introjection, and projective identification (Grotstein, 1994, 1995). Winnicott's (1947) observation that "there is no such thing as a baby" (p. 137) was a reference to the mother–baby twosome as an initially inseparable unit. Sandler (1976), from the Anna Freud School, foreshadowed the concept of enactment when he suggested that the analyst

> will, unless he becomes aware of it, tend to comply with the
> role demanded of him, to integrate it into his mode of re-

sponding and relating to the patient. Normally, of course, he can catch this counter-response in himself, particularly if it appears to be in the direction of being inappropriate. However, he may only become aware of it through observing his own behavior, responses and attitudes, *after these have been carried over into action.* (p. 47, italics in original)

Mainstream American psychoanalysis, dominated by one-person ego psychology for decades, gradually incorporated the two-person approaches that came from work with patients with psychotic disorders and from the theories of the British school. In 1972 Bird, writing about analysts developing transferences and transference neuroses to their patients, suggested that the transference of the analyst was often the central obstacle in therapeutic stalemates. He asserted that "stalemate in the analysis, an implacable resistance, an unchanging negative therapeutic reaction—anything of this kind should be suspected of consisting of a silent, secret, but actual destructive act engaged in by *both* patient and analyst" (p. 294, italics in original).

Over time the field has seen a clear shift toward two-person formulations and toward recognition of the concept of enactment. Reporting on the work of a panel of the American Psychoanalytic Association, Johan (1992, p. 841) defined enactment as a pattern of nonverbal interactional behavior between the two parties in a therapeutic situation. However, fully grasping the notion of enactment may require unpacking of this condensed definition. The link between enactment and projective identification is central (Plakun, 1999; Shapiro & Carr, 1991). Shapiro and Carr note eight components of projective identification (p. 24), including noticing that the analyst has "an attribute that corresponds" to that disavowed and projected by the patient, that the therapist is involved in "an unconscious collusion" with the process that sustains the projection, and that there is a "complementarity of projections—both participants project" aspects of their own life history into the other.

Plakun (1999) further elaborated the components of enactment as follows:

One might think of enactment as a multistep process in which, first, there is the usual "reenactment" in the transference relationship of part of the patient's conflicted or traumatic past. . . . However, in an enactment, the patient's associated unconscious self experience is next disavowed and projected into the therapist. . . . Enactment begins to become a unique concept, though, when the therapist then participates unwittingly by projecting back into the patient reciprocal and complementary unconscious conflicted countertransference material from the therapist's own life history. The therapist unwittingly colludes with the patient in a process of mutual and complementary projective identification organized around significant past events from the lives of both participants. Within such an enactment, the therapist is as much a participant as the patient. (p. 286)

> In an enactment the "therapist unwittingly colludes with the patient in a process of mutual and complementary projective identification organized around significant past events from the lives of both participants" (Plakun, 1999, p. 286).

Although some (e.g., Chused, 1997) view enactments as undesirable, others (Renik, 1993) have argued that they are inevitable and useful. For example, Renik suggests that "it is helpful to see countertransference enactment as the ever-present raw material of productive analytic technique" (p. 153). Based on our experience at Riggs, we agree with those who see enactments as inevitable therapeutic phenomena, particularly in work with "enactment-prone" patients with primitive (e.g., action) defenses (Plakun, 1998). *Enactment* is an integrative concept with connections to the central issues we emphasize in this volume: the importance of relationships, the elucidation of meaning, and recognition of patients' authority when working with patients who have treatment-refractory disorders. The following further elaborates the notion of the inevitability and utility of enactment (Plakun, 2007):

The situation is a bit like that in skiing. In the complex interpersonal terrain of therapy, enactments seem as inevitable a part of the work as sliding downhill is on skis. In both situations one is pulled inexorably in a certain direction, either by the unfolding of the transference–countertransference relationship or by gravity. This is neither good nor bad, but part of the experience. A good skier learns the skill of finding and using his or her edges on the slippery slope, allowing control of the fall downhill. Similarly, a good therapist learns there will be enactments. The trick is to find the edge on this slippery slope that allows him or her to stay poised in a position of technical neutrality and abstinence as best one can. (p. 106)

Whether or not enactments are inevitable is, in many ways, a less compelling issue than learning to know when they occur, how to unravel what is going on in an enactment, and what to do with what has been learned. In an earlier publication (Plakun, 2007) steps in the detection, analysis, and utilization of enactments were explored. Detection is an essential step; without the ability or willingness to detect enactments the therapist is in danger of acting out the countertransference in an ongoing, undisciplined manner, even to the extent of serious boundary transgression (Plakun, 1999). Detection of enactments is facilitated by cultivating self-knowledge and awareness of one's thoughts, perceptions, bodily responses, and gut sense that something may be different from the usual. Supervision and personal analysis are key to this kind of self-knowledge.

> Learn to detect, analyze, and utilize enactments to deepen therapeutic work with treatment-resistant patients. Supervision and/or peer consultation are often essential steps in facilitating this process.

Analysis of enactments—that is, unraveling their meaning—is best carried out in a state of forbearance. This means *stopping* any acting out in the countertransference rather than simply continuing it or reporting it to the patient. This part of the analysis of an enactment is performed in a way that observes the therapeutic dyad as if from the outside—that is, from a transdyadic perspective of the "Third" (see Chapter 6). Sometimes the therapist is able to complete the analysis of an enactment alone, but often it is necessary to seek supervision or consult with colleagues to concretize the perspective from this third vantage point.

Utilization of what has been learned in the analysis occurs in a range of ways. Utilization may take the form of an interpretation, an apology if the enactment has led to inadvertent injury of the patient with a sadistic remark or condescending tone, a new way of looking at things, recovery of an abstinent and technically neutral stance, a fuller elaboration of the formulation of the patient's dynamics, and/or emergence from a therapeutic impasse.

ACTING OUT AND ENACTMENT AT RIGGS

At Riggs, action patterns that have been part of a patient's treatment resistance inevitably emerge in the individual therapy and larger patient community. These actions may manifest themselves in a wide range of behaviors, from coming late to, or missing, sessions, to more overt self-destructive behaviors such as cutting, burning, restricting food, and threatening or even attempting suicide. Although they may have no explicit conscious meanings for the patient, these actions are understood and often interpreted as potential behavioral communications and will likely generate a complicated array of responses within staff and the patient community. In the environment of Riggs there is an opportunity to slow down these actions, "rewind" and examine them from different angles, including their unconscious meaning, their transference implications within therapy, the interpersonal implications within the therapeutic community, and their historical genesis within the family. Much that we have been learning about this complicated phenomenon at Riggs is directly applicable in outpatient and other settings, as will be apparent in the case examples that follow.

> The concept of enactment helps us see that what may seem to be a countertherapeutic action initiated by a patient is generally co-created by therapist and patient.

Our experience at Riggs repeatedly reminds us that what may seem to be a countertherapeutic action initiated by a patient is generally co-created by therapist and patient. In other words, what might be understood as acting out in one-person terms is usually an enactment that, in two-person terms, involves the therapist as a main actor. The following case material, constructed from composites of several cases, illustrates this point. The first case example illustrates a potential enactment that is contained by the therapist's awareness of countertransference. The second illustrates an enactment that unfolds in the therapy.

The Case of G: An Enactment Forestalled

G was a man in his late 30s. Following graduation from college he began displaying serious difficulties, failing at graduate school and unable to hold a job. He would start a job enthusiastically, excel for a while, and then collapse into depression that was refractory to outpatient psychotherapy and medications for his bipolar II disorder. G would disappear from work, isolate himself in his home in a deeply depressed state, and stay in bed, often asleep, for days at a time. All through his life he had vacillated between two self-presentations. Whenever he was seen as a competent person who was able to take care of himself, G would collapse into depressed states that would evoke deep worries in his family members, who would intrude into his life to rescue him. The parents vacillated between infantilizing him—giving advice on every decision he needed to make and rescuing him in the face of adversity—or insisting that he was an independent, capable person who ought to be able to pull himself up by his bootstraps. G felt confused and ambivalent in his life and in relation to his family. He felt invaded and intruded upon, but he also derived conscious pleasure from his family's caretaking and rescuing of him when he regressed.

G began four-times-weekly therapy with a female therapist at Riggs who was an eldest child who'd had significant caretaking responsibilities for her younger siblings while growing up because her mother was ill and her father was largely absent. In the course of supervision and in her personal analysis, G's therapist had learned about the powerful pull toward rescuing and caretaking others that had been part of her choice of a career in psychiatry. She often struggled to contain therapeutic zeal with her patients while remaining in a technically neutral, but compassionate and empathic, stance.

The first several months of the treatment were uneventful. G developed an idealizing transference toward the therapist as he explored his personal development. At the same time he began to function as an elected leader in the patient government. Around the sixth month, during a routine family session, his parents asked G about the progress he was making. They were interested in learning whether their financial support of the treatment was proving to be a good investment. G was surprised, angry, and frustrated with this inquiry, and deferred the question to his therapist, hoping she would help him out. The therapist was aware of strong wishes to offer a response that would protect the patient and the treatment, but she recalled that a similar discussion had occurred a month or so earlier. She contained her impulse, instead suggesting to G that he might have a point of view about what his parents were asking. In fact, G did offer a summary of what he thought he was learning in treatment.

In the next individual therapy session G became angry with the therapist for the first time. He blamed her for not standing up for him and for making him do the work. He felt lonely, abandoned, and betrayed. The therapist acknowledged that G was feeling hurt and abandoned, but noted that G seemed to omit that he had handled the question competently himself.

Soon G began missing most sessions; he stayed in bed, and, of course, resigned from his position in the patient government. This behavior evoked concern in the therapist and the treatment team. Now G was raising questions in their minds about how well he was using the treatment. There were team discussions about whether G was regressing and whether there was a need for an administrative intervention or a family meeting to report his absences from sessions. When G finally did come to a session the therapist was curious about why G had missed sessions. G told his therapist that he was avoiding some sessions because he felt overwhelmed. He asked the therapist whether he should attend or skip sessions when he felt overwhelmed. The therapist recognized a strong wish to suggest that he come to the sessions, but, aware of G's parents' tendency to give such advice and of her own characterological inclination to rescue and take care of him, recognized and contained her countertransference impulse. Instead of making a suggestion about G's decision to come to or skip sessions, she suggested that perhaps G might attend to what was going on in his mind during the moment of decision.

The next week G missed the first session, but came to the next and reported the following to his therapist:

> "As you suggested, I paid attention to what was going on in
> my mind when I was struggling with the decision about com-
> ing. I recognized that if you told me I had to come, that
> would have made me mad and I would have opposed the
> idea. Since you gave no specific recommendations, I was con-
> flicted. On the one hand I was thinking that I should go. But
> this thought made me angry and I opposed it. This in turn,
> made me feel good. Then I recognized I didn't want to go—

that was what I wanted. The first sessions of the week are always too overwhelming for me so I needed an extra day off. When I made this decision, though, I felt guilty about it."

In subsequent sessions G and his therapist were able to elaborate the way G's life pattern of alternation between competence and collapse were being played out in his treatment at Riggs, as well as to note how G's "regression" seemed related to "aggression"—that is, to anger at his therapist for not taking care of him adequately. G's regression from competent functioning and from active participation in his treatment had a quality of revenge for failing him, and invited treating him as incapable, as lacking both personal agency and the full authority to make his own decisions. He had found and recreated in his treatment the very issues with which he was grappling in his life. Over time G took ownership of his role in initiating and evoking the very behaviors from his family that he found so intrusive and infantilizing, and was able to return to his therapy sessions and to competent functioning as a member of the patient community in a way that was sustained through discharge several months later.

The family therapy session was a critical moment in which G, in a familiar role, was unwittingly pulling the therapist into the position of doing something for him that he was perfectly capable of executing himself. The therapist's detection, analysis, and containment of her countertransference rescue fantasies, while remaining in a technically neutral stance, allowed the patient to practice his newly developing skills, while evoking negative transference anger in relation to the therapist for not rescuing him. It was a moment of separation and differentiation out of which the patient emerged with a sense of accomplishment and pride in exercising his budding sense authority.

In the later issue involving missed sessions, G illustrates the process of internalization. What could have unfolded into a familiar action pattern if the therapist had made a suggestion, instead turned into an internal conflict with which G could grapple. G's therapist's early detection and analysis of countertransference feelings and impulses led to their containment and minimized the evolution of an enactment that would simply repeat the problem G had with his family in the transference and treatment, without either G or his therapist seeing what was happening or how the problem was being co-created.

Early detection, analysis, and utilization of a potential enactment by a self-aware and self-reflective therapist who forbears acting on countertransference impulses is a laudable goal, but it is not always achieved. The following is an example of such a situation.

The Case of W: An Enactment

W was in her 30s when she came to Riggs. The only child of a divorced musician couple, she had an extended history of a profound schizoid adaptation and social phobia. As a child she was frequently abandoned, physically and emotionally, while her parents rehearsed and performed in their demanding musical careers. During adolescence she was uninterested in developing friendships, attending social functions, or inviting friends to her home. She was deeply attached to her maternal grandparents and would spend most of her time with them. In her teens she dated a boy she eventually married. It became the one stable relationship in her life.

In contrast to the emptiness of her interpersonal life, W excelled academically, feeling this aspect of her life compensated for what she lacked in her interpersonal world. After college she applied for graduate studies but dropped these plans, married her boyfriend, who worked in a blue-collar job, and became a homemaker and mother when she discovered she was pregnant. W was deeply but guiltily resentful about her life. In her late 20s, not long after the death of both maternal grandparents, she became symptomatic, developing significant depression, restricting food and losing large amounts of weight, often smashing her hands with a mallet and burning herself. She made several suicide attempts, was repeatedly hospitalized, and her marriage deteriorated. Several attempts at outpatient psychotherapy, including dialectical behavior therapy (DBT), and numerous medication trials failed, leading to referral to Riggs.

At Riggs W consciously tried to emerge from her schizoid cocoon. She gradually became more outspoken in various groups and tried to deepen and expand conversations with peers outside of groups. This was a wearing task. After periods of such attempts to reach out to people, W would isolate herself in her room, read books, listen to music, or paint to recuperate. While she struggled in the Riggs therapeutic community for several months, she filled the therapy hours with explorations of her lonely childhood and sense of abandonment by her parents.

The therapist was a man known for his relatively quiet and patient personality. The therapist's own parents had been distracted during his youth by the needs of his chronically ill younger brother. The therapist had been an inhibited adolescent who was seen as mature rather than shy.

Unlike other adolescents, whose rebelliousness caused all sorts of trouble, the therapist was never a concern for his family. This history created a conflicted self-image for the therapist. Although he longed to be less inhibited and felt shame about his reticence, he was also proud of the image of himself as mature—as were his parents, who took pride in their mature, healthy son who was such a good boy.

As the therapist listened to W's themes of loneliness and abandonment, he felt interested, but he was also left with an impression that he was an inanimate object in the room or at best a silent spectator of W's lonely explorations. In his work with W, the therapist had a clear therapeutic formulation and strategy that he shared with the treatment team. He saw himself as allowing the patient to expand and unfold into the therapeutic space. He was using interpretations sparsely to try to help W settle in and become accustomed to the presence of another person within the small physical space of the office, but he was aware of having difficulty feeling genuinely "with" W. Despite the therapist's experience of being a spectator, there was also evidence that the patient was revisiting important aspects of her past and sharing the narrative of her life.

After several months W began flirting with male patients and then engaged in brief sexual liaisons with a few of them. This behavior caused a stir in the patient community and in the treatment team since it was not consistent with behavioral expectations. Despite sharing some concern about these actions, the therapist also saw them as comparable to the developmental struggles of a teenager and as potentially useful for W. However, as often happens in splitting, what felt like developmentally appropriate mischief to the therapist felt like an intolerable flouting of rules to the larger community. W was referred by another patient to the patient group that examines and contextualizes, ideally in a nonpunitive way, worrisome behaviors carried out by members of the patient community (see Chapter 11). In the meeting with her peers she was angrily confronted about her promiscuous behavior.

This was a turning point for W, who felt that her efforts to emerge from her schizoid cocoon had failed—that her efforts were seen as nothing but a performance, like the musical performances her parents would put on before audiences. She was confused, deeply hurt, humiliated, and angry. W severed her ties with the patient community and withdrew to her schizoid self. She had fantasies of hammering her hands or burning herself with cigarettes, but managed to contain these with the help of interpretive work about her humiliation and rage. Working on her paintings in the activities department and coming to therapy became the only spaces she attended regularly.

As she withdrew, W spoke of hopelessness, despair, and wishes to commit suicide. She became deeply resentful about her therapist's inability to help her emerge from the schizoid shell, demeaning the therapist's mind and technique, mocking his clothing, and threatening to destroy his office. At one point she attempted to smoke in his office, eliciting a strong sense of resentment, futility, and anger in the therapist. Nevertheless the therapist felt he was helping by keeping his composure and continuing to be present as a listening, empathic other in the sessions. From the therapist's theoretical perspective, it felt like the work was unfolding, with a negative transference emerging as he held to a technically neutral stance.

Several months passed with this intense, contagious sense of hopelessness and attacks on herself, the therapist, and others. During the therapist's 2-week vacation, W overdosed on over-the-counter pills. She was immediately transferred to an emergency department and spent 2 weeks in an intensive care unit being monitored for liver failure. The therapist, who was becoming increasingly hopeless about the work, had been relieved by his vacation and the break from the work, but was shocked to hear of her suicide attempt when he returned. For several weeks the patient and the treatment became the main topic of discussion in team meetings and larger clinical staff meetings. The therapist felt like he, his patient, and their work were under scrutiny and shamefully exposed. Colleagues confronted the therapist about his lack of affect and sense of numbness in his presentations of the work with W. They questioned his technique. Was he "addressing the aggression," was W "medicated enough"? W's actions evoked a strong response in the therapist compounded by responses from the patient community. The therapist felt enraged, exhausted, humiliated, and defeated. Even though she was now hospitalized elsewhere on a locked unit, W seemed to be invading all aspects of his life, even disturbing his sleep.

Once stabilized, W was readmitted to Riggs to review what had happened and reach a decision about whether the work would continue. In addition to exploration of what led to the suicide attempt, the therapist also renegotiated with W the terms of a viable treatment (see Chapter 8). He made it clear to the patient that there was one very definite requirement if they were to continue working together: The patient had to be open with him in therapy or with nursing staff about any wishes to die, instead of acting on them, so that they could determine if W's treatment could continue, and they could explore the meaning of suicide together. W agreed to this condition, reporting that she was fearful of losing her treatment at Riggs and understood the implications of secrecy around suicidal wishes and plans. She gradually became aware of the link between the therapist's vacation abandonment of her and her suicide attempt. From this perspective her attempt looked like acting out.

After W's suicide attempt, the therapist's colleagues were instrumental in helping him become aware of his own role in the process that had unfolded with her. They offered a sometimes difficult-to-experience but helpful perspective from the "Third" to the therapist, who sometimes experienced shame about what he had not seen. This consultation helped him emerge from his position as lost in the dyad during a regressed enactment. The therapist became more aware of unforeseen implications of his version of a "technically neutral stance." In this instance he had been defensively avoiding the multiple negative feelings that W had evoked in him. Realizing this, he became more aware of and comfortable with interpreting such motives as brutal, enraging, sadistic aspects of W. In response she felt, somewhat to the therapist's surprise, confirmed, acknowledged, and seen. Along with her negative transference, W also showed more caring and tender sides of herself to the therapist.

Gradually, with consultation from colleagues and with self-analysis, the therapist was able to recognize how his countertransference led to his own role in the enactment. W developed transferences that were congruent with conflicted, narcissistic aspects of the therapist's self-representation. The content of these transferences provided fault lines for the development of complementary countertransferences in the therapist, as described by Racker (1968). The subsequent mutual and complementary regression organized around these fault lines became an enactment.

As the therapist consulted with colleagues about his work with W, he realized several components of his role in the enactment. When W engaged in sexual relationships, the therapist realized he had silently colluded with her breaking of the Riggs behavioral expectation for abstinence from sexual relationships with fellow patients because of the way her behavior resonated with his own unfulfilled and inhibited adolescent sexual longings.

In addition, an aspect of the therapist's conflicted, grandiose self-image was engaged in the work with W. Both he and W shared the experience of neglect by their respective parents. As W complained about this experience from her own childhood, it hooked the therapist in his childhood and adolescent response of patiently enduring parental neglect in the service of being complimented as mature. What he experienced as being a mature and patient therapist, albeit without much emotional connection to W, she experienced as evidence of his neglect. Whereas the therapist found in W someone to be patient with, at a distance, waiting for the reward of being seen in a flattering way, W found in her therapist her neglectful, distant, and professionally preoccupied parents. The therapist came to realize that the "acting out" of W's overdose was actually an enraged rejection of the absent parent she found in him, and that his "patience" concealed his own emotional retreat from her, with previously unconscious wishes from him to be rid of her—wishes with which she unwittingly ultimately complied in her overdose.

As is so often the case in work with previously treatment-refractory patients, what appeared from one perspective to be W's "acting out" was, in fact, an enactment involving both therapist and patient. W, through her relentless, sadistic attacks on the therapist, had recreated a situation from her past, turning the therapist into the kind of "numb," passive, and absent listeners her parents had been. This time, though, it was the analyst who was a co-actor and "enactor" of this old theme. Detection of the enactment coupled with self-analysis on the part of the therapist, with help from colleagues, allowed the work to deepen. Once conscious of his role in the enactment, the therapist was able to contain and metabolize his countertransference and return to a technically neutral analytic stance within which he could be emotionally more available to W and no longer numb. This kind of detection, analysis, and utilization of an enactment is facilitated by working in a treatment environment with colleagues to turn to for consultation, but can usually be replicated in other treatment settings. Supervision, including peer supervision groups, and consultation at difficult moments in treatment allow even relatively isolated solo outpatient therapists to create something comparable.

It is also worth noting that W helped the therapist become aware of grandiosely held, conflicted aspects of his self-image. W's attacks on this image were clearly destructive—as she was being dangerously destructive with herself. On the other hand, they led to a moment of increased self-awareness for the therapist, thus offering a chance for reparation, reworking, and recreation of a less conflicted self-image. This is an example of the treatment-resistant patient unwittingly becoming therapist to his or her therapist in the transference as part of moving toward a healthier adaptation (Chasseguet-Smirgel, 1984; Riviere, 1936; Searles, 1973).

CONCLUSION

Among the preconditions for an optimal therapeutic handling of enactments are a good-enough therapeutic relationship (as embodied in the therapeutic alliance), careful attention to the elucidation of meaning as a mutually agreed-upon task of the therapy, and acceptance of the fallible humanity and legitimate authority of both participants. With these in place, the therapist's role is to carefully monitor the evolving transference and countertransference in the service of early detection of enactments. Countertransference feelings, impressions, and fantasies are invaluable sources of data. It is imperative for the therapist to "hear" and to achieve understanding in words of the actions of both the patient and him- or herself.

If the therapist can detect and make sense of countertransference feelings and the impulse to act, he or she has a chance to contain them, as illustrated in the case of G. However, since these feelings and impulses are often preconscious or unconscious phenomena, their recognition may only be possible retroactively or with the perspective of an outside "Third," as in the case of W. Once an enactment is detected, the therapist's task is to analyze it in a state of forbearance and then to determine how to utilize and bring it to the work.

The moment of enactment often brings therapeutic work to a crucial fork in the road. Down one direction lies stalemate or impasse, whereas down the other lies an opportunity to deepen understanding of the patient's struggles, strengthen the alliance, and advance the therapeutic work. While deepening a therapist's self-knowledge is another result, this sometimes painful if rewarding learning for therapists is not a negotiated goal of treatment—but rather part of the learning that unfolds with experience.

REFERENCES

Bird, B. (1957). A specific peculiarity of acting out. *Journal of American Psychoanalytic Association, 5*, 630–647.

Bird, B. (1972). Notes on transference: Universal phenomenon and hardest part of analysis. *Journal of American Psychoanalytic Association, 20*, 267–301.

Boyer, L. B. (1979). Countertransference with severely regressed patients. In L. Epstein & A.H. Feiner (Eds.), *Countertransference* (pp. 347–374). New York: Jason Aronson.

Chasseguet-Smirgel, J. (1984). Thoughts on the concept of reparation and the hierarchy of creative acts. *International Review of Psycho-Analysis, 11*, 399–406.

Chused, J. (1997). Discussion of "Observing-participation, mutual enactment, and the new classical models," by Hirsch I. *Contemporary Psychoanalysis, 33*, 263–277.

Cooperman M. (1983). Some observations regarding psychoanalytic psychotherapy in a hospital setting. *The Psychiatric Hospital, 14*(1), 21–28.

Fenichel, O. (1945). Neurotic acting out. *Psychoanalytic Review, 32*, 197–206.

Freud, A. (1968). Acting out. *International Journal of Psychoanalysis, 49*, 165–170.

Grinberg, L. (1968). On acting out and its role in the psychoanalytic process. International Journal of Psycho-Analysis, *49*, 171–178.

Grotstein, J.S. (1994). Projective identification reappraised: Part I. Projective identification, introjective identification, the transference/countertransference neurosis/psychosis, and their consummate expression in the crucifixion, the *Pietà*, and "therapeutic exorcism." *Contemporary Psychoanalysis, 30*, 708–746.

Grotstein, J.S. (1995). Projective identification reappraised—projective identification, introjective identification, the transference/countertransference neurosis/psychosis, and their consummate expression in the crucifixion, the *Pietà*, and "therapeutic exorcism," Part II: The countertransference complex. *Contemporary Psychoanalysis, 31*, 479.

Johan, M. (1992). Report of the panel on enactments in psychoanalysis. *Journal of the American Psychoanalytic Association, 40*, 827–841.

Johnson, A.M., & Szurek, S.A. (1952). The genesis of antisocial acting out in children and adults. *Psychoanalytic Quarterly, 21*, 323–343.

Little, M. (1951). Counter-transference and the patient's response to it. *International Journal of Psycho-Analysis, 32*, 32–40.

Plakun, E.M. (1998). Enactment and the treatment of abuse survivors, *Harvard Review of Psychiatry, 5*, 318–325.

Plakun, E. M. (1999). Sexual misconduct and enactment. *Journal of Psychotherapy Practice and Research, 8*, 284–291.

Plakun E.M. (2007). Perspectives on embodiment: From symptom to enactment and from enactment to sexual misconduct. In J. P. Muller & J. G. Tillman (Eds.), *The embodied subject: Minding the body in psychoanalysis* (pp. 103–116). Lanham, MD: Rowman & Littlefield.

Racker, H. (1968). *Transference and countertransference*. London: Hogarth Press and the Institute of Psycho-Analysis.

Renik, O. (1993). Countertransference enactment and the psychoanalytic process. In M. J. Horowitz, O. F. Kernberg, & E. M. Weinshel (Eds.), *Psychic structure and psychic change: Essays in honor of Robert S. Wallerstein* (pp. 135–138). Madison, CT: International Universities Press.

Riviere, J. (1936). A contribution to the analysis of the negative therapeutic reaction. *International Journal of Psycho-Analysis, 17*, 304–320.

Sandler, J. (1976). Countertransference and role-responsiveness. *International Review of Psycho-Analysis, 3*, 43-47.

Searles, H.F. (1973). Concerning therapeutic symbiosis. *Annual of Psychoanalysis, 1*, 247–262.

Shapiro, E. R., & Carr A. W. (1991). *Lost in familiar places* (pp. 23–26). New Haven, CT: Yale University Press.

Winnicott, D.W. (1947). Further thoughts on babies as persons. In D.W. Winnicott (Ed.) (1964), *The child, the family and the outside world* (pp. 85–92). New York: Basic Books.

Chapter 3
What Is Psychodynamic Psychopharmacology?

An Approach to Pharmacological
Treatment Resistance

David Mintz, MD, and Barri A. Belnap, MD

A review of *Medline* citations concerning treatment-resistant psychiatric conditions shows a disconcerting trend. Whereas the number of annual citations for all articles increased by 25% over the past two decades, articles citing psychiatric treatment resistance have increased by over 800%, doubling approximately every 5 years (Mintz, 2010). With significant advances in neurobiology and psychopharmacology, we have become increasingly aware of limitations in the standard treatment approaches to most psychiatric illnesses (Mintz, 2002). We propose that one cause of treatment resistance to biological treatments is an approach that neglects the importance of meaning in the patient's symptoms and in treatment.

> Psychodynamic psychopharmacology attends to the meanings that patients and others attach to medications and symptoms

"Psychodynamic psychopharmacology" is a discipline that explicitly acknowledges and addresses the central role of meaning and interpersonal factors in psychopharmacological treatment. From our point of view psychodynamic psychopharmacology is not in conflict with a traditional objective-descriptive approach to psychopharmacology. Rather, the dynamic and biological frames of reference actually complement each other and lead to fuller understanding of the patient as well as to enhanced treatment effectiveness.

A conventional symptom- or diagnosis-based treatment approach considers the ways that patients are similar. This kind of approach brings with it an established evidence base and is a foundation of rational psychopharmacological practice, offering critical guidance about what to prescribe to enhance the likelihood of a positive outcome. In a complementary fashion, psychodynamic psychopharmacology considers what is unique to the individual patient. This approach can become especially important for treatment-resistant patients, who do not respond to treatment as expected. For these patients it is useful to understand what makes them different. Part of the "evidence base" for the psychodynamic approach derives from the patient's unique life history, repeating patterns in the patient's life, current developmental needs, and the patient's subjectivity. Rather than telling the psychopharmacologist *what* to prescribe, the psychodynamic approach to psychopharmacology informs prescribers *how* to prescribe to enhance treatment outcomes.

MEANING EFFECTS IN PSYCHOPHARMACOLOGY

Widely accepted psychiatric treatment algorithms are concerned primarily with proper medication choice, adequacy of dose and treatment duration, and correct diagnosis. Treatment resistance is sometimes explained by noting the presence of a personality disorder, since comorbid personality disorders have been found to contribute to treatment resistance (Thase, 1996; see also Chapter 1). It is not clear, however, how or why "personality disorders" make antidepressants or other psychotropics ineffective. Algorithms do not generally consider that the problem may relate to nonbiological factors, such as the meaning of the patient's symptom or the patient's relationship to medications, nor do they consider that treatment resistance may emerge in the context of personality disorders when people with disordered object relations have corresponding disturbances in relation to their medications. The meanings that medications have for patients can have a profound impact on medication effectiveness.

An emerging body of evidence comparing biological and symbolic effects of medication points to the importance of meaning in pharmacology. A series of meta-analyses (Khan, Warner, & Brown, 2000; Kirsch, Moore,

Scoboria, & Nicholls, 2002; Kirsch & Sapirstein, 1998) of Food and Drug Administration (FDA) databases (which include unpublished negative study results) shows that, though antidepressant medications are effective, the placebo effect accounts for between 76 and 81% of treatment effectiveness. Placebos produce real, clinically significant and objectively measurable improvements in a wide range of medical conditions (Brody, 1977; Moerman & Jonas, 2002), including psychiatric conditions.

The patient's "readiness to change" is a central factor in pharmacological treatment response. Beitman, Beck, Deuser, Carter, Davidson, and Maddock (1994) found in a placebo-controlled trial that, among patients treated for anxiety, those who were highly motivated to change and received a benzodiazepine had the most robust response. However, patients who were highly motivated to change and received a placebo had a greater reduction in anxiety than patients receiving the active drug, but who were less ready to change. Readiness to change (Prochaska & DiClemente, 1983) was found to be the single most powerful determinant of treatment effectiveness, even more potent than drug condition (i.e., active vs. placebo).

Similarly, the doctor–patient alliance seems to be more important for pharmacological treatment outcome than medication. A large, multi-center National Institute of Mental Health (NIMH) supported study (Krupnick, Sotsky, Simmens, Moyer, Elkin, et al., 1996) found that in pharmacological treatment, patients had the greatest reduction in symptoms when a strong alliance was paired with active drug. However, patients receiving a placebo who had a good alliance with their doctor had a greater reduction in symptoms than patients with a poor therapeutic alliance who received an active drug. Taken together, these studies support a basic premise of psychodynamic psychopharmacology, suggesting that symbolic aspects of medications are at least as potent as the "biologically active" ingredients and should not be neglected in the care of treatment-resistant patients.

WHAT MAKES A PATIENT TREATMENT RESISTANT?

There are as many different kinds of treatment resistance as there are treatment-resistant patients. Nevertheless, it may still be useful to consider resistance to treatment to fall into broad psychopharmacological categories. Writers on the subject have suggested dynamic approaches to pharmacological treatment resistance based on character structure (Forrest, 2004; Marcus, 1990). For the purposes of this chapter, however, we divide treatment-resistant patients into two broad categories—those who are treatment resistant *to* medications and those who are treatment resistant *from* medications—and look within categories to consider dynamics that interfere with pharmacological effectiveness.

Treatment Resistance to *Medications*

Patients who are resistant to medications have conscious or unconscious factors that interfere with the desired effect of the medications. Often, resistance in this category takes the form of nonadherence to treatment, but it also includes the group of patients that develops adverse psychological and/or physical responses to medications that are experienced as new or worsening symptoms and/or side effects to medication. This is in contrast with patients who are resistant *from* medications. These patients are eager to receive the medication or some benefit that they ascribe to it. Here the pills may relieve symptoms but do not contribute to an improvement in the patient's quality of life.

It is not difficult to understand why a patient with manic euphoria might resist getting better, but what of a depressed patient who is nonadherent to prescribed medications? If this patient is not simply lazy or irresponsible, what sense does this behavior make? The fundamental psychoanalytic notion of unconscious motivation suggests that patients are often ambivalent about relinquishing their symptoms, albeit generally unconsciously. This concept helps us understand why such patients may not be ready to change. Although patients' symptoms may create painful difficulties for them, at the same time those symptoms may solve other problems. An adolescent who is worried about whether or not he can live up to his parents' expectations and who feels that the only way to be loved and recognized by them is try to be who *they* think he is, is in the type of dilemma that "illness" temporarily cures. While he remains sick, there is a moratorium on the need to satisfy his parents' expectations. He and his family may make an implicit deal not to judge him as a "failure" until the illness has passed. Even when there is a serious biologically determined illness, patients may be able to derive some benefit from their symptoms, at least at some point in the illness. Other patients may find that, paradoxically, they are far more potent when ill than they ever were when they were well. When illness partially ameliorates deep feelings of powerlessness, patients are understandably ambivalent about relinquishing their symptoms.

> Remember that symptoms are not only problems—they are also so-
> lutions.

Patients may be reluctant to relinquish symptoms when those symptoms are needed to communicate something important that cannot be
said to, or heard by, important others in the patient's life—for example,
expressing a desperate longing for care that the patient cannot consciously bear to acknowledge. When patients find ways to put these encoded
communications into words, they may become able to let treatments, including pharmacological treatments, work.

Successful pharmacological treatment may be unconsciously resisted
because it undercuts important intrapsychic defenses. For example,
consider Mrs. A, who sought help at her family's urging for treatment-
refractory schizophrenia. She had previously been able to organize herself
enough to competently raise a child with support from her parents. After
her son's death from cancer, she could only tolerate antipsychotics that
were ineffective. Invariably, when considering a switch to potentially more
effective medications, she became frightened of becoming depressed and
killing herself. Her preoccupation with the hallucinated voice of her dead
child and delusional conviction that she could bring back the dead revealed the powerful logic behind her treatment resistance. If she became
nonpsychotic, then her child was forever lost; she feared that the grief of
this loss would kill her. She unconsciously resisted effective treatment
because improved reality testing could interfere with restitutive psychotic
efforts (Havens, 1968; Nevins, 1977), with the potential to precipitate a
grief reaction that could overwhelm her already limited capacities and
risk suicidal depression.

Patients who have disordered object relations are likely to bring these
problems into the pharmacotherapeutic relationship, and these problems
interfere with a straightforward pharmacological response. Though the
ingestion of a pill may activate positive object representations, such as the
oral gratification of the nursing situation, in some patients with predominantly positive object representations, ingestion of a pill can also activate
profoundly negative object representations, including toxic experiences of
rejection, of sexual intrusion, or other forms of physical or psychological
control by another.

If prescribers do not recognize that patients, despite presenting to their doctors in a manifestly trusting request for help, are often deeply suspicious of that help, they may be ill prepared to help patients who form disguised negative transferences. When such patients are healthy enough to mobilize a straightforward resistance, they cannot submit trustfully to the doctor's medication because it is experienced as harmful. These patients are often recognizable by recurrent struggles for control that occur around medications. They will question our motives, express fears of loss of control, show particular interest in the side effects of the medications (i.e., our capacity to harm them), or negotiate in excruciating detail the timing and dosages of the pills, raising questions for the prescriber of whether to insist on rational use of medications or tolerate the patient's irrational efforts at control for some time-limited therapeutic purpose.

In situations where the prescriber asserts control, the patient may attempt to gain control of the medications through control of the doctor. The patient no longer tells the doctor the relevant truth, but instead presents a distorted symptom picture coupled with urgent displays of affect that are intended to coerce the doctor into prescribing a medication regimen that the patient feels is within his or her control (Koenigsberg, 1991). The patient may opt to supplant the doctor, receiving the doctor's prescription but taking the medications according to his or her own whim— either too little, too much, or in dosing schedules that are dangerous or ineffective.

In cases where the doctor manages to maintain control of the medication regimen (see Brockman, 1990, for a compelling clinical description of such an encounter), or when the patient is so ill that all he or she can do is submit to the prescriber, the emergence of nocebo phenomena (Hahn, 1997; Mintz, 2002) may occur. The nocebo effect, which is the inverse of the placebo effect, occurs when the expectation of harm is translated into actual harm in the form of new somatic or psychological symptoms. Although any patient may experience a nocebo reaction, it may be especially prevalent in psychiatric populations (Mintz, 2002), whose members commonly experience their position as disadvantaged and unavoidable—factors known to be nocebogenic (Hahn, 1997). Nocebo-prone patients become treatment resistant when medication trials are repeatedly interrupted by intolerable side effects, or therapeutic doses of medications are never achieved as a result of the patient's exquisite sensitivity to side effects.

> Be aware of the nocebo effect—a negative placebo effect—in which expectation of harm leads to experience of harm.

For example, Mr. B, a college-age male, entered treatment for depression and anxiety. He complained particularly of chronic insomnia related to nightly panic attacks. Extensive medication trials had been repeatedly unsuccessful or intolerable. He came from at least three generations of irritably obsessive people, but was misattuned to his family, who regarded him as cranky and demanding from infancy, projectively locating the family pathology in the patient. Consequently, he felt that his family was always trying to "hush" him.

Mr. B was begun on a trial of a selective serotonin reuptake inhibitor (SSRI) for depression and panic and soon began to complain of "emotional deadness," a known SSRI side effect. The therapist-prescriber experienced the patient as less overwhelmed and more able to engage productively in self-exploration, but the patient found the experience intolerable and argued that he was too cut off from his emotions to use therapy. He wanted to stop the medication. It became clear that Mr. B feared that his emotionality was intolerable to the doctor, whom he felt wanted to "hush" him, as had his family. He experienced the medication as a rejection. Once this meaning was engaged in the psychotherapy, they were able to negotiate a more genuine alliance.

Treatment Resistance from Medication

Patients may also develop treatment resistance in relation to medications that they neither fear nor resist. These patients ask for medications and experience them as valuable and effective. The prescriber may observe that the medication produces a reduction in symptoms, but the patient does not get better. In these cases, treatment resistance may derive *from* the medication or some meaning ascribed to the medication. Acting out with medications, as occurs when a patient makes repeated small overdoses or uses a medication "recreationally," is one way that potentially beneficial medications are turned toward a countertherapeutic effect. Unfortunately, in most cases where treatment resistance is promoted by medications, the dynamic is not obvious, and the prescribing doctor may become an unwitting participant in the development of resistance, colluding with defensive structures in the patient that act counter to the therapeutic intervention of the psychotherapy.

Medications can, for example, play a role in undermining a patient's ability to trust in and learn from his or her feelings. Emotions have an important role in directing learning and in motivating growth and change in relation to the inevitable disappointments of human relationships. This is one reason they become a central focus of psychotherapy. When "pain" or "bad feelings" are defined as part of a "disease" process, the patient's ability to trust and use emotions as necessary data for evaluating the accuracy of perceptions and for decision making is impaired. When medications signify that a patient has symptoms rather than feelings, meaningful opportunities for self-understanding are lost.

Affect competence is the capacity, developed over time, that enables a person to experience and use emotions as a tool to understand himself and others. From it, a patient creates an internal working model of him- or herself and others as relates to what his or her emotions might mean. Affect competence is a developmental achievement that cannot be taken for granted. The culture of the family of origin teaches attitudes toward emotions that become a template for the patient's interpretation of his or her own feelings and those of others (Tomkins, 1995). An aggressive temperament may be encouraged as a sign of competitiveness and strength in one family, whereas in another, the same temperament is pathologized and treated as dangerous. These templates transmit intergenerational learning about the meaning and use of feelings. At times the templates families offer their children bear the scars of a family trauma (see Chapter 5) that cannot be faced. This may manifest itself, for example, in a family that "only looks at the bright side" in an effort to put a trauma behind them, thus leaving children ill equipped to deal competently with sadness or anger. Psychopharmacological interventions for patients who have learned that feelings are useless or inaccessible may reinforce this notion and further undermine their ability to use feelings productively.

People can lose affect competence when they become reliant on a drug to sooth emotional discomfort. A substance-abusing adolescent may develop the attitude that emotions are to be titrated and tightly controlled. He or she might not learn from dysphoric feelings that offer valuable information about the negative effects of his or her actions. Some people use psychopharmacologists in the same way.

Patients who mistrust themselves and their capacities may make decisions that defer development while waiting for medications to solve problems. The patient, thus regressed, can only surrender authority, turning him- or herself over to the doctor, who is presumed to have the ability and tools to interpret and control the patient's feelings. This surrendering risks deepening a sense of incompetence. Entering a vicious cycle, such a patient may lose potentially supportive social roles and may even find that relationships are less likely to support personal growth as the technical language of diagnoses replaces understanding and working through of complex emotional dilemmas. In this way medications may contribute to treatment resistance.

Patients may also use medications in a defensive manner that hinders insight and change. Research into nonpharmacological effects of medications (e.g., the placebo effect) suggests these effects serve defensive functions to manage intrapsychic conflicts (Fisher & Greenberg, 1997). For example, Gibbons and Wright (1981) found that subjects with greater sexual guilt experienced more pronounced sexual disinhibition in response to a placebo than subjects with fewer conflicts about sexuality.

Patients who rely on splitting and projective defenses may manage their "badness" by locating it outside themselves, often in another person. When these patients receive a medication, it may come with an explicit or implicit diagnosis from the doctor that serves as an inexact interpretation (Glover, 1931; Nevins, 1990) signifying, "Your behavior is not you, it is your disease." This explicit or implicit message supports a defensive disavowal of agency and a split in the patient, who attributes his or her badness to the illness while the remaining goodness resides in him- or herself. When this happens, there is often an initial decrease in his distress. Treaters may be tempted to interpret this response as confirmation of the diagnosis and unwittingly collude with the defense because the decrease in the patient's excruciating self-hatred is so relieving (for both the patient and doctor). Unfortunately, the final result is often a worsening in the patient's overall functioning, as the patient no longer feels responsible for destructive behaviors and allows them free rein. The result may be worsening social problems, alienation from self, and treatment resistance.

A similar splitting dynamic can unfold at the interpersonal or family level. The patient and family members may collude in projecting responsibility for negative or conflictual feelings into the illness in order to avoid awareness of family dysfunction. The "badness" of the illness becomes something the family *suffers from* along with the patient. Whereas illness is projected into the patient, hope is projected into the doctor and his or her "cure." If the doctor colludes with this biologically reductionistic perception, the patient may be hampered in his or her recovery in several ways. First, the patient cannot learn from a family that has disavowed any relevance of family patterns to the symptom. Second, this perception may support the family's defensive effort to continue to view the patient as the container of disavowed family problems. Medication may interfere with the family's ability to address and work through developmental impasses by locating the problem in the patient and the solution in the doctor.

Another situation in which medications may cause treatment resistance occurs when people are defensively replaced by medications in patients' psychic lives. These patients, who have often come to experience human relationships as unreliable, may turn to medications to avoid the risk of frustration when seeking comfort from people. In some cases a medication becomes a fetish, more important to these patients than the health it was supposed to generate. These patients may be unconsciously motivated to stay ill to secure certain medications and resist efforts to switch to more appropriate medications.

Patients may use medications to avoid appropriate affect and healthy developmental steps. For example, Mr. C requests treatment of depression and attention-deficit/hyperactivity disorder (ADHD). He complains of inattention and inability to meet work demands that may endanger his employment. Investigation of his situation reveals that Mr. B is working 16-hour days to meet unrealistic job demands. He hopes that a stimulant will allow him to function normally under these extreme circumstances. He cannot admit that the demands of the job may be too much. If the psychopharmacologist colludes with the patient's wish to use medications to erase normal and healthy limits, his depression is unlikely to remit, no matter what medications are used.

Patients' efforts to master past trauma or important developmental failures may lead to a compulsion to repeat the scenario of past failures. This compulsion becomes especially complicated in enactments (see Chapter 2), when an aspect of the treater's life history resonates with and is "hooked" by an aspect of the patient's life history. The requirement to act (prescribe), often under time pressure and with limited information about the patient's dynamics, provides fertile ground for enactments by prescribers.

Consider Mr. D, a patient who experienced repeated early failures in caregiving. He manages feelings about these failures and attempts to preempt future disappointments by ragefully devaluing caregivers. Mr. D's focus on his doctor's failures bolsters a defensive "sour grapes" position or provides vengeful pleasure from exposing the caregiver's inadequacy. The psychopharmacologist, who sought medical training out of a personal need to feel helpful related to a childhood family role as everyone's helper, experiences feelings of inadequacy with this patient, which he counters by more zealous and aggressive prescribing, leading to an ever more complicated but ineffective medication regimen. The patient, covertly motivated to experience caregivers as failures, does not tell the prescriber about worsening side effects. In this enactment the patient's negative transference expectation is actualized as, ultimately, medications produce more harm than good. Until the prescriber appreciates that the patient may have perverse motivations for treatment (either consciously or unconsciously) and understands his own countertransference to the patient, enactments of this sort can be difficult to detect, formulate, and engage interpretively in the treatment.

This case also suggests a source of treatment resistance other than treatment resistance *to* or *from* medications, namely, treatment resistance originating from the prescriber's countertransference. Sometimes it is not the patient who is treatment resistant, but the treatment itself. When the patient's dynamics intersect in particular ways with the prescriber's vulnerability or needs, prescribers may be led to prescribe irrationally. The resulting irrational regimens may not work because they address the prescriber's unconscious needs more than the treatment needs of the patient.

PHILOSOPHICAL UNDERPINNINGS OF PSYCHODYNAMIC PSYCHOPHARMACOLOGY

A psychopharmacologist practicing a biological approach to mental illness tends to make fundamentally different assumptions about the patient, the doctor–patient relationship, and the purpose of treatment than does a psychiatrist who practices with a prominent psychodynamic approach (Roose & Johannet, 1998; Sandberg, 1998). We believe there are several fundamental philosophical positions in psychodynamic psychopharmacology that can help the doctor and patient avoid falling into positions that promote treatment resistance. These positions are (1) the importance of mind–body integration, (2) the value of learning from experience, and (3) the centrality of patient authority.

Though we know that mind and brain are interconnected (Kandel, 1999), with meaning, learning, and experience affecting the physiology of the brain, and physical changes in the brain structuring possibilities of experience, it can be difficult to hold a complex model of mind that avoids a mind–body split. Such a split is embedded deep within our worldview, both historically (Goodman, 1991) and also in the context of a contemporary culture in which we have "lost our mind," with an increasing tendency to see problems in living as problems of biology. The "scientific" way of thinking about medications is concrete (Gutheil, 1982), stripped of subjectivity (Docherty, Marder, van Kammen, & Siris, 1977), and insidiously fosters biological reductionism in our thinking. When a patient receives a new prescription, then returns a week or two later reporting improved mood, how often does the prescriber doubt that the medication is the reason? Ultimately, however, we do not know if a medication or *its meaning* is what is healing our patient.

Patients may also promote a mind–body split to serve their own needs. This stance may, in turn, influence the thinking of psychiatric caregivers, particularly if the patient defensively (albeit unconsciously) presents his or her symptoms or side effects in the form of an argument for a predominantly biological or psychodynamic etiology. A psychodynamic psychopharmacologist recognizes these sources of bias and works to understand how symptoms are manifestations of both meaning and biology.

For example, Mr. E, a middle-age man with a panic disorder comorbid with a personality disorder and a history of suicide attempts, sought treatment for unremitting depression. Mr. E was in a split treatment, with psychotherapy from one provider and psychopharmacology from another, and he was requiring larger, but ineffective, doses of anxiolytics. He was unaware of any reason for his anxiety. Ultimately the psychopharmacologist informed the patient that he would prescribe no more anxiolytics, instructing the patient to call when having a panic attack so that they might meet and try to understand what precisely the medication was meant to treat. In the urgently scheduled meeting with the prescriber that followed at the time of the next panic attack, it became apparent that the patient felt angry at his therapist and was planning suicide. The thought of dying, however, made him extremely anxious. The patient observed that his anxiety commonly emerged after psychotherapy hours, and that he had not told the therapist of his frustration or anger. The psychopharmacologist reflected back to the patient that he appeared to be requesting anxiolytics so that he could plan suicide without anxiety—which hardly seemed like an appropriate use of medications. The patient agreed to discuss his anger with the therapist. The patient, his therapist, and psychopharmacologist met together to review the dynamic in which the negative transference had been split out, "biologized," and left to the psychopharmacologist to detoxify. They agreed that further anxiolytics were not warranted at that time. The patient's "treatment-resistant" anxiety remitted when the negative transference was identified and engaged in the therapy.

In a psychodynamic approach to psychopharmacology, learning is of central value. Medications may support treatments by supporting learning (if defensive uses of medications can be identified and worked through). Medically treating severe depression, anxiety, or psychosis may allow patients to learn better in psychotherapy (Klerman, 1975). However, the optimal level of distress that promotes learning (Yerkes & Dodson, 1908) is not zero. A patient who feels no anxiety, but is too sedated to think, engage in the world, and develop a sense of mastery will not likely recover. Learning, rather than symptom elimination, may take precedence in a psychodynamic approach to pharmacotherapy.

In our approach to psychodynamic psychopharmacology, recognition and respect for patient authority is of fundamental importance. In a biologically reductive approach, the patient tends to be viewed as a victim of genes or of "chemical imbalance." In psychodynamic psychopharmacology the patient, who may be struggling with significantly disordered biology (Cooper, 1985), is understood to have a subjectivity that interacts with the biological substrate and he or she is seen as having internal resources that can be recruited to address problems. The patient is not a passive battleground between the doctor and the disease. Instead, he or she is an important ally, or adversary, and the outcome of pharmacological treatment depends largely upon recognizing and using this stance.

> In psychodynamic psychopharmacology recognition and respect for patient authority is of fundamental importance.

This position in relation to patient authority has implications for the nature of the therapeutic alliance. Alliance, first of all, is not simply treatment compliance (Gutheil, 1978; see Chapter 8). The goals of the patient may not necessarily be congruent with the a priori goals of the psychopharmacologist. As in a psychotherapeutic contract, the alliance and goals of treatment must be negotiated with the prescriber.

For example, Ms. F, manifestly a high-functioning medical student, presented for treatment of depression and weight loss from somatized gastric pain. Her habitual efforts at becoming what others wanted her to be had left her feeling empty, with almost no sense of agency. One of her medications promoted weight loss, whereas the alternatives would likely promote weight gain. The pharmacologist, feeling that his first duty was to "do no harm," wanted to change the medication to avoid colluding with further weight loss, but the patient objected. The doctor could have discontinued the medication, but chose first to explore the patient's resistance, with the aim of helping the patient understand her resistance and its connection to broader struggles in her life. It became clear that the patient feared that, if she gained weight, she would not know if this represented her action or the action of the medication. The psychopharmacologist was persuaded not to change the medication, as this served the patient's declared therapeutic goals of differentiating her true self from false self adaptations. The patient was able to incorporate her subsequent weight gain into an experience of her own emerging agency.

One potential countertransference risk is that a greater understanding of the patient's dynamics can be used in ways that diminish patient authority. When an understanding of the patient's vulnerabilities is used primarily to persuade compliance with a particular course of action (e.g., to take medications), this "manipulation" (Bibring, 1954; Niven, 1990) undermines agency. Such manipulation may at times be an unavoidable part of the psychopharmacological intervention, but prescribers working within a psychodynamic frame consider these dynamics and their potential consequences. Manipulation, even if it pushes a patient into making "healthy" choices, can undermine the patient's authority, foster reactive aggression toward the prescriber, and thereby undermine the therapeutic alliance.

TECHNICAL IMPLICATIONS OF
PSYCHODYNAMIC PSYCHOPHARMACOLOGY

From the preceding discussion of sources of treatment resistance and the philosophical underpinnings of psychodynamic psychopharmacology, we have derived six basic technical principles for pharmacological practice with treatment-resistant patients. The first, and overarching, principle is to avoid a mind–body split in thinking about patients and their symptoms. Much of this work is internal, done in the mind of the treater, though there are clear technical and framework implications that follow. The second technical principle, following from the first, is that it is essential to know your patient. It is not sufficient to collect a list of symptoms and apply corresponding medications. To adequately care for treatment-resistant patients, one must respect and address the larger meanings for the patient of medications, illness, and treatment. This leads to the third principle, which is to attend to any ambivalence on the part of the patient about loss of symptoms. Fourth, treaters should be aware that many patients hold, consciously or unconsciously, negative feelings about medications and/or doctors. It may be essential to address negative transferences and resistance *to* medications in order to promote positive outcomes. Fifth, treaters should also be aware of countertherapeutic uses of medications (resistance *from* medications). Patients may misuse medications in a myriad of subtle ways, often unconsciously, undercutting either treatment effectiveness or larger developmental aims. Sixth and finally, it is necessary to identify and address the effects of countertransference enactments on prescribing when working with difficult-to-treat patients.

It may be important to note that, while these principles are useful in the treatment of all patients, their application can also be labor intensive and impractical in a busy practice. However, the price of ignoring these principles is high in work with patients who are treatment resistant.

Six technical principles for pharmacological practice with treatment resistant patients:

- Avoid a mind–body split.
- Know your patient.
- Attend to the patient's ambivalence about the loss of symptoms.
- Address negative transferences and resistance *to* medications.
- Be aware of countertherapeutic uses of medications (resistance *from* medications).
- Identify and contain countertransference enactments involving prescribing.

Avoid a Mind–Body Split

The work of avoiding a mind–body split proceeds on two fronts: (1) the development of an integrated treatment frame and (2) subsequent work with the patient to negotiate a realistically complex appreciation of symptoms and how they function for him or her.

In initial meetings with the patient, negotiating an integrated frame may involve clarifying the task of psychodynamic psychopharmacology, which is primarily that of maximizing the patient's capacity to engage in psychotherapy. When this frame is negotiated with the patient, it may counter his or her hope that symptoms can be eradicated without examining developmental struggles and making necessary compromises. To the extent that medications serve primarily to support the therapy, resistances to the productive use of medications can be understood by the therapist as resistances to the therapy and as manifestations of the transference, linked in important ways to the patient's underlying struggles. Interpretations aimed at elucidating the dynamics of resistance can then support the work of the psychopharmacologist, just as the psychopharmacology aims to support the psychotherapy.

In split treatments, with a separate therapist and prescriber, communication between providers is essential. Just as the therapeutic alliance is a core factor in producing positive treatment outcomes in psychotherapy (Martin, Garske, & Davis, 2000) and psychopharmacology (Krupnick, Sotsky, Simmens, Moyer, Elkin, et al. 1996), a "triadic alliance" (Kahn, 1991), or a sharing of goals between the patient, the therapist, and the prescriber, may enhance treatment outcomes when there is a split treatment arrangement. A collaborative treatment relationship (Ellison & Harney, 2000), with good interdisciplinary communication between the therapist and prescriber, may be critical in work with treatment-resistant patients, particularly those who have difficulties in integration or who use primitive defense mechanisms such as splitting.

Given that neither the therapist nor the psychopharmacologist will see all the transference implications of medications, communication between treaters may expose ways that the treatment arrangement allows transference to be split off and disguised, as in the case of Mr. E, whose negative transference was expressed as anxiety. When interdisciplinary disagreements are apparent, as when a patient complains about one treater to the other (Gould & Busch, 1998), or when one treater has made an intervention that encroaches on the role of the other (e.g., when a therapist suggests that the patient consider a medication change or when a prescriber interprets to the patient a resistance to medication use), communication between treaters can be especially important.

For patients who see themselves as troubled simply by disordered genes or neurotransmitters, an integrated approach, sometimes even with the therapist and prescriber meeting together with the patient (if in a split treatment), may provide an opportunity to negotiate a treatment agreement that explicitly considers the dimension of meaning in pharmacological care. This process might take the form of describing an evolving understanding of the ways that psychology impacts medication responsiveness (alliance factors, readiness to change, placebo and nocebo responses), and also a beginning exploration of the underpinnings and implications of a patient's devotion to a reductionistic biological self-understanding. Although it may not be possible to clearly distinguish biologically disordered responses from expectable responses to difficult situations, this conundrum may usefully be left for the patient to struggle with. After all, the process of identifying where one has agency and how feelings are related to choices and context is central to human development and maturation.

Just as it may be useful to question the notion that the entire problem lies in the patient's biology, it may also be helpful to question the notion that all of the healing is in the doctor's medications. This questioning may be especially important when patients have lost affect competence in the face of psychiatric treatments. When patients who have already been failed by countless medical treatments develop magical expectations of cure (sometimes promulgated by previous prescribers), it can be important for the doctor to make a realistic assessment of the likely limitations of medications and to include this information in the patient's informed consent to treatment. This was the case for Mr. C, who sought stimulants in an effort to negate fundamental and healthy limitations in his abilities. With Mr. C the recognition of limitations modeled an accommodation to reality that reformulated the question of hope in achievable terms, such as the possibility that he might live with and adapt to the ways that he was ordinarily human, neither perfect nor so flawed that he could not help himself.

Know Your Patient

When it comes to the treatment-resistant patient, we concur with the valuable observation attributed to Sir William Osler, the father of modern medicine, that "It is much more important to know what sort of patient has a disease than what sort of disease a patient has." Taking a thorough history can provide a foundation for a psychodynamic approach to the patient's medication use. This history is not simply a detailed history of symptoms and medication trials, but also a developmental history that identifies important life experiences, basic relationship patterns, areas of intrapsychic conflict, and likely transference configurations.

The process of taking a careful developmental history plays an important role in establishing a treatment alliance. When patients are already inclined to experience people as uncaring and narcissistically preoccupied, a prescription given after a brief interview can feel like a rejection (Winer

& Andriukaitis, 1989), providing fertile ground for nocebo reactions and hostile enactments around medication use. Taking a thorough developmental history reminds the patient that the prescriber is interested in him or her as a person, and not just in his or her symptoms, and gives the prescriber ways of understanding and addressing problematic psychosocial factors that may contribute to treatment resistance.

Attend to the Patient's Ambivalence about Loss of Symptoms

The initial history might include tactful questions about what the patient might stand to lose if this symptom were successfully alleviated. It is important to contextualize this question by noting that patients may desperately want to get well, but, as is true for all humans, have a dynamic unconscious and are ambivalent beings. Raising for discussion the question of unconscious ambivalence educates the patient to this possibility, which then becomes included in the work. Mrs. A, whose psychosis protected her from the overwhelming grief over the loss of her child, needed a space to grieve her loss in the context of a secure and reliable therapeutic relationship. She needed to see how her psychosis deepened her loneliness before she was ready to change and accept more effective antipsychotic medications. Highlighting the patient's ambivalence and exploring the costs of the present solution may motivate him or her to use medications more productively.

Address Negative Transferences and Resistance to Medications

Having obtained a thorough history, the prescriber will have some ideas about likely transference paradigms and modes of resistance. Questions concerning the patient's feelings about medications may, in particular, help predict future problems. Anticipating forms of resistance with the patient (Marcus, 1990) may fortify an alliance with his or her healthier aspects before unconscious resistance emerges. For example, a patient with a repeated history of medication noncompliance and deep conflicts about dependency might be alerted to the fact that emerging fears of dependency on medications should be brought to the prescriber's and/or therapist's attention promptly so that they might be addressed rather than acted out through medication noncompliance.

The information gleaned from the developmental history provides an interpretive context so that transference assumptions that have promoted treatment resistance can be brought to consciousness. The patient's authority may then be mobilized to support rather than hinder treatment effectiveness. This was the case with Mr. B, who felt that effective medications were a rejection and a sign of his doctor's intolerance of his emotionality. The therapist was able usefully to interpret the patient's concern about medications as a concern that the psychopharmacologist was using medication to "hush" him, as had been his experience in his family of origin. Acknowledging that this expectation might be contributing to side effects of numbness and neurasthenia, the patient agreed to continue the medication. The side effects, which turned out to be a nocebo response, resolved quickly, and Mr. B became panic free and able to sleep for the first time in his adult life.

Attend to Countertherapeutic Uses of Medications (Resistance from Medications)

Countertherapeutic uses of medications may be addressed interpretively, as in the case of Mr. E, who was using anxiolytics to avoid the anxiety associated with planning his suicide. In this case making the source of the anxiety conscious was sufficient to motivate the patient to make changes that led to a resolution of his treatment-resistant anxiety. In other cases, such as Mr. D, who used medications to manage feelings and exact revenge on caregivers, the countertherapeutic use of the medication proved too gratifying for him to give up. In these cases, the prescriber need not feel compelled to collude with a patient's demand for a medication that the doctor cannot, in good conscience, prescribe. In these cases, the pharmacologist may negotiate the discontinuation of the medication, or, if the countertherapeutic use of the medication is dangerous or entrenched enough, may make the discontinuation of the medication a condition of continuing pharmacological treatment. This approach also holds true when medications have fetishistic qualities. It may be necessary for the psychopharmacologist to negotiate the discontinuation of the medications so that the patient can learn about their pathological uses and recover some personal authority (Swoiskin, 2001). However, one must also be aware that these patients may be prepared to leave treatment to protect access to their chosen drug.

Identify and Contain Countertransference Enactments Involving Prescribing

The treatment of characterologically disturbed patients often includes a goal of containing impulsive action, but not necessarily only the impulsivity of the patient. When patients struggle with overwhelming dysphoric affects, they often elicit corresponding affects in their prescribers. If the doctor misses the point that these feelings communicate something about the patient's inner life and must be contained and translated into words, an important opportunity for empathy, alliance building, and deepening the work is missed—and the doctor is left anxious and predisposed to action. If the doctor prescribes from this countertransferential state, he risks failing to address the patient's symptoms, given that the intervention is aimed more at addressing *the doctor's* own distress. The patient, sensitive to the doctor's needs, may respond to the medication with a masochistic surrender that impairs the emergence of his or her own authority, or if his or her resistance is sparked, power struggles may ensue.

Monitoring for and using countertransference beneficially remains a significant aspect of work with treatment-resistant patients for both therapist and prescriber. As was the case for Mr. B, who wanted to stop a medication that was unconsciously experienced as a rejection, the patient's request for a change in medications should alert the doctor to consider transference aspects of the request (Busch & Auchincloss, 1995). Similarly, when the doctor contemplates making a change in treatment, he or she might usefully wonder if his or her motivation stems from countertransference.

The issue of countertransference highlights the importance of consultation with colleagues in work with treatment-resistant patients. These patients often cannot be treated in isolation because they push us to the limits of our pharmacological knowledge and our therapeutic and relational creativity. Treatment-resistant patients often push us to emotional limits as well, leading to countertransference-based prescribing. Colleagues can hold the standards of rational prescribing in mind, at a distance from the transference–countertransference tangle, allowing them to function as a valuable "Third" (see Chapter 6), and helping the prescriber avoid becoming lost in the intense feelings evoked in the doctor–patient dyad.

CONCLUSION

Psychodynamic psychopharmacology is a way of approaching the task of prescribing that is distinct from, but complementary with, a conventional approach to prescribing, which relies primarily on population-based studies for guidance. A straightforward, "scientific" approach to prescription establishes a "rational" basis for treatment choice, but runs the risk of neglecting the unique impact of the patient's subjectivity, failing to attend to the patient's authority, and missing the importance of relationships and of meaning to cure. Given evidence for the importance of these factors in treatment effectiveness, treatments that neglect these factors may inadvertently foster treatment resistance. Psychodynamic psychopharmacology offers a potential antidote to those forms of treatment resistance that may have more to do with subjective factors than with biology.

Despite cultural and psychodynamic influences that promote a mind–body split in our thinking, psychiatric caregivers must remain open to considering the myriad of possible sources of pharmacological treatment resistance, including those of psychosocial origin. The psychodynamic psychopharmacologist appreciates that treatment resistance emerging from the level of meaning is likely to be addressed successfully only at that level. To address such treatment resistance, in split as well as in combined treatments, therapists and psychopharmacologists are wise to attend to the patient's history and dynamics. By practicing a psychodynamic approach to psychopharmacology the doctor is positioned to comprehend and address reasons why a patient may be ambivalent about the loss of symptoms, may react to medications as instruments of harm, or may turn potentially useful medications to countertherapeutic ends. The perspective of psychodynamic psychopharmacology is that patients are not simply victims of biology, but also exercise agency through the way they and their treaters approach their illness. This stance creates the possibility for a deeper alliance in which patients can claim authority for their treatment, and within which the doctor can work with patients to help effect lasting changes in a manner and at a pace that respect patients' unique developmental needs and the significance of their conflicts.

REFERENCES

Beitman, B.D., Beck, N.C., Deuser, W.E., Carter, C.S., Davidson, J.R.T., & Maddock, R.J. (1994). Patient stage of change predicts outcome in a panic disorder medication trial. *Anxiety, 1,* 64–69.

Bibring, E. (1954). Psychoanalysis and the dynamic therapies. *Journal of the American Psychoanalytic Association, 2,* 745–770.

Brockman, R. (1990). Medication and transference in psychoanalytically oriented psychotherapy of the borderline patient *Psychiatric Clinics of North America, 13*(2), 287–295.

Brody, H. (1977). *Placebos and the philosophy of medicine.* Chicago: University of Chicago Press.

Busch, F.N., & Auchincloss, E.L. (1995). The psychology of prescribing and taking medication. In H.J. Schwartz (Ed.), *Psychodynamic Concepts in General Psychiatry* (pp. 401–416). Washington, DC: American Psychiatric Association.

Cooper, A. (1985). Will neurobiology influence psychoanalysis? *American Journal of Psychiatry, 142,* 1395–1402.

Docherty, J.P., Marder, S.R., Van Kammen, D.P., & Siris, S.G. (1977). Psychotherapy and pharmacotherapy: Conceptual lenses. *American Journal of Psychiatry, 134,* 529–533.

Ellison, J.M., & Harney, P.A. (2000). Treatment resistant depression and the collaborative treatment relationship. *Journal of Psychotherapy Practice and Research, 9*(1), 7–17.

Fisher, S., & Greenberg, R.P. (1997). The curse of the placebo: Fanciful pursuit of a pure biological therapy. In R. P. Greenberg & S. Fisher (Eds.), *From placebo to panacea* (pp. 3–56). New York: Wiley.

Forrest, D.V. (2004). Elements of dynamics: II. Psychodynamic prescribing. *Journal of the American Academy of Psychoanalysis and Dynamic Psychiatry, 32*(2), 359–380.

Gibbons, F.X., & Wright, R. A. (1981). Motivational biases in causal attributions of arousal. *Journal of Personality and Social Psychology, 40,* 588–600.

Glover, E. (1931). The therapeutic effect of inexact interpretation: A contribution to the theory of suggestion. *International Journal of Psycho-Analysis, 12,* 397–411.

Goodman, A.G. (1991). Organic unity theory: The mind–body problem revisited. *American Journal of Psychiatry, 148*(5), 553–563.

Gould, E., & Busch, F.N. (1998). Therapeutic triangles: Some complex clinical issues. *Psychoanalytic Inquiry, 18*(5), 730–745.

Gutheil, T.G. (1978). Drug therapy: Alliance and compliance. *Psychosomatics, 19,* 219–225.

Gutheil, T.G. (1982). The psychology of psychopharmacology, *Bulletin of the Menninger Clinic, 46,* 321–330.

Hahn, R.A. (1997). The nocebo phenomenon: Scope and foundations. In A. Harrington (Ed.), *The placebo effect: An interdisciplinary exploration* (pp. 56–75). Cambridge, MA: Harvard University Press.

Havens, L.L. (1968). Some difficulties in giving schizophrenic and borderline patients medication. *Psychiatry, 31,* 44–50.

Kahn, D. (1991). Medication consultation and split treatment during psychotherapy. *Journal of the American Academy of Psychoanalysis, 19,* 84–98.

Kandel, E.R. (1999). Biology and the future of psychoanalysis: A new intellectual framework for psychiatry revisited. *American Journal of Psychiatry, 156*(4), 505–524.

Khan A., Warner, H.A., & Brown, W.A. (2000). Symptom reduction and suicide risk in patients treated with placebo in antidepressant clinical trials: An analysis of the Food and Drug Administration database. *Archives of General Psychiatry, 57,* 311–317.

Kirsch, I., Moore, T.J., Scoboria, A., & Nicholls, S.S. (2002). The emperor's new drugs: An analysis of antidepressant medication data submitted to the U.S. Food and Drug Administration. *Prevention and Treatment, 5,* Article 23.

Kirsch, I., & Sapirstein, G. (1998). Listening to Prozac but hearing placebo: A meta-analysis of antidepressant medication. *Prevention and Treatment, 1.*

Klerman, G.L. (1975). Combining drugs and psychotherapy in the treatment of depression. In M. Greenblatt (Ed.), *Drugs in combination with other therapies* (pp. 67–82). New York: Grune & Stratton.

Koenigsberg, H.W. (1991). Borderline personality disorder. In B.D. Beitman & G.L. Klerman (Eds.), *Integrating pharmacotherapy and psychotherapy* (pp. 271–290). Washington, DC: American Psychiatric Association.

Krupnick, J.L., Sotsky, S.M., Simmens, S., Moyer, J., Elkin, I., Watkins, J., et al. (1996). The role of therapeutic alliance in psychotherapy and pharmacotherapy outcome: Findings in the National Institute of Mental Health Treatment of Depression Collaborative Research Program. *Journal of Consulting and Clinical Psychology, 64,* 532–439.

Marcus, E. (1990). Integrating pharmacotherapy, psychotherapy, and mental structure in the treatment of patients with personality disorders and depression. *Psychiatric Clinics of North America, 13*(2), 255–263.

Martin, D.J., Garske, J.P., & Davis, M.K. (2000). Relation of the therapeutic alliance with outcome and other variables: A meta-analytic review. *Journal of Consulting and Clinical Psychology, 68*(3), 438–450.

Mintz, D. (2002). Meaning and medication in the care of treatment-resistant patients. *American Journal of Psychotherapy, 56*(3), 322–337.

Mintz, D. (2010, May 25). Psychodynamic psychopharmacology: An introduction. Presented at the Annual Meeting of the American Psychiatric Association, New Orleans, LA.

Moerman, D.E., & Jonas, W.B. (2002). Deconstructing the placebo effect and finding the meaning response. *Annals of Internal Medicine, 136,* 471–476.

Nevins, D.B. (1977). Adverse response to neuroleptics in schizophrenia._*International Journal of Psychoanalytic Psychotherapy, 6,* 227–241.

Nevins, D.B. (1990). Psychoanalytic perspectives on the use of medications for mental illness. *Bulletin of the Menninger Clinic, 54,* 323–339.

Prochaska, J.Q, & DiClemente, C.C. (1983). Stages and processes of self-change in smoking: Toward an integrative model of change. *Journal of Consulting and Clinical Psychology, 5,* 390–395.

Roose, S.P., & Johannet, C.M. (1998). Medication and psychoanalysis: Treatments in conflict. *Psychoanalytic Inquiry, 18*(5), 606–620.

Sandberg, L.H. (1998). Analytic listening and the act of prescribing medication, *Psychoanalytic Inquiry, 18*(5), 621–638.

Swoiskin, M.H. (2001). Psychoanalysis and medication: Is real integration possible? *Bulletin of the Menninger Clinic, 65*(2), 143–159.

Thase, M.E. (1996). The role of axis I comorbidity in the management of patients with treatment-resistant depression. *Psychiatric Clinics of North America, 19*(2), 287–309.

Tomkins, S.S. (1995). Script theory. In E.V. Demos(Ed.), *Exploring affect: The selected writings of Silvan S. Tomkins* (pp. 312–388). Cambridge, UK: Cambridge University Press.

Winer, J.A., & Andriukaitis, S.M. (1989). Interpersonal aspects of initiating pharmacotherapy: How to avoid becoming the patient's feared negative other. *Psychiatric Annals, 19,* 318–323.

Yerkes, R.M., & Dodson, J.D. (1908). The relation of strength of stimulus to rapidity of habit-formation. *Journal of Comparative Neurology and Psychology, 18,* 459–482.

———◆◇◆———

Chapter 4
Working with the Negative Transference

Eric M. Plakun, MD

Although there are few systematic studies of the implications of failing to engage the negative transference in difficult treatments, two studies suggest the relevance of doing so. In her study of a series of therapies that resulted in sexual misconduct between therapist and patient, Celenza (1998) found that therapists' intolerance of the negative transference was the single most ubiquitous feature associated with boundary transgressions. Second, in her unpublished study of patient suicide during psychotherapy, Rubenstein (2000) reports that problems tolerating or engaging the negative transference were common in the therapists of patients who died by suicide.

THE NEGATIVE TRANSFERENCE, HATRED, AND TREATMENT RESISTANCE

My own experience over the course of 30 years and in performing well over a thousand in-depth preadmission consultations with treatment-resistant patients also suggests that a problem engaging or tolerating the negative transference is one of the most frequent phenomena associated with treatment resistance. Here I am suggesting that in these instances the actual "resistance" to treatment may unwittingly be located in the therapist in the form of a resistance to engaging the patient's aggression and hate in the transference and to becoming aware of his or her own hate and aggression in the countertransference. Winnicott (1949, p. 74) addresses this issue when he notes that in some analyses the patient "cannot be expected to tolerate his hate of the analyst unless the analyst can hate him." Maltsberger and Buie (1974, p. 628) make a similar point when they note: "Without exception the transference of borderline and psychotic suicidal patients will involve the denouncement of the therapist as a cold, uncaring person," whereas "certain therapists are heavily invested in an image of themselves as unfalteringly all-encompassing in their love for the patient," and that "all therapists, seasoned and unseasoned, find hating a distressing experience, and all are inclined unconsciously to mobilize defenses against it." Writing about countertransference hate, they add (p. 632), "The best protection from antitherapeutic acting out is the ability to keep such impulses in consciousness." They advise therapists to gain comfort with their countertransference hate through the process of "acknowledging it, bearing it, and putting it into perspective" (p. 632). In his paper on the therapeutic value of hate in the countertransference, Epstein (1977, p. 460) concludes that "the extent to which the patient's ego becomes integrated over the course of the therapy will depend on the therapist's confidence in the potential therapeutic value of his countertransference hate and *on his recognition of those instances when the patient needs to receive it*" (italics added).

> Engaging the patient's transference hate, in the context of awareness of reciprocal countertransference hate, has often been missing in the prior therapies of patients with treatment-refractory disorders

The patient who develops a difficult-to-tolerate negative transference is, after all, only doing his or her job in mobilizing, in the here and now of the therapeutic relationship, central past object relationships that communicate, without yet remembering in words, central affectively laden struggles in their lives. These patients often suffer at least as much from too much hate that cannot be tolerated by others, including treaters, as they do from insufficient love. Engaging the patient's transference hate, while acknowledging, bearing, and putting into perspective (and sometimes using judiciously) the therapist's countertransference hate, offer an opportunity to deepen therapeutic work with treatment-refractory patients through engagement of core features that make them refractory to treatment. This notion must be tempered by the recognition that I am not here encouraging impulsive and injudicious sadism toward patients, but, rather, thoughtful, balanced, and relatively infrequent use of counter-transference hate in the context of a strong positive transference and strong alliance.

Therapists often recoil from intense negative affects in the transference and countertransference, though learning to tolerate such feelings is one of the reasons supervision and a personal analysis are essential aspects of training to do intensive psychodynamic psychotherapeutic work, and that consultation is so useful in clinical practice. One can think of Riggs in some ways as a system for managing negative transference. Patients have the opportunity to disperse transferences among multiple clinicians involved in their treatment, without having to face prematurely their hatred and anger toward the therapist on whom they also feel powerfully dependent. This is illustrated in the case example later in this chapter, when the patient first becomes aware of anger at his social worker. For Riggs therapists and other clinicians facing and trying to bear difficult negative transferences, the program offers a kind of support system through team and clinical staff meetings, as will become clearer in the chapter on working in a psychodynamic treatment team. Therapists working in other settings are advised to consider the comparable resources available to them in work with such patients, such as individual and group supervision and consultation.

One of the ways negative transferences may become intolerable is through the countertransferences they mobilize in the therapist. A bit of the patient's life history, embedded in his or her character structure, becomes activated in the transference in the form of hate, anger, or contempt. In such instances the therapist may have trouble taking such a distasteful transference while remaining in a technically neutral stance.

The patient's negative transference projects into the therapist aspects of the patient's own character and life history. This projective identification into the therapist may engage a bit of the therapist's own character vulnerability in the countertransference. The resulting intolerable countertransference feelings may lead the therapist to engage in a projective identification into the patient based on aspects of the therapist's own character and life history (Shapiro, 1997). This kind of mutual and complementary projective identification involving therapist and patient has already been identified as the definition of an enactment in a previous chapter. In my experience, enactments involving negative transference and negative countertransference issues are frequently associated with treatment resistance.

NEGATIVE TRANSFERENCE ENGAGEMENT IN
A TREATMENT-REFRACTORY PATIENT

The following patient material from a case treated by a senior colleague illustrates a number of the foregoing points.

Joe was a married father of three in his 40s with a treatment-refractory major depressive disorder and relentless suicidality that made his outpatient treaters, and even his insurance company case manager, feel hopeless, despairing, and fed up with him. After multiple hospitalizations, failed medication and electroconvulsive therapy (ECT) trials, and multiple failed outpatient therapies, Joe's psychiatrist recognized that they were at a dangerous impasse, always fending off the next crisis or recovering from the last. The psychiatrist felt defeated, frustrated, frightened, and overwhelmed, and suggested to Joe that he might need a different kind of treatment, referring him to Riggs.

When Joe accompanied the Riggs admissions officer into the admission consultation, the admissions officer asked what was going on in his life that led to their meeting about the possibility of treatment at a place like Riggs. Joe responded that he thought it would simply be better to commit suicide and be dead than to meet with him or come to Riggs. The admissions officer felt jolted, anxious, challenged, and began to become aware of hating Joe for putting him in a tough spot immediately, but swallowed and hunkered down, determined to pick his way through what he was presented with. Recognizing that a lot would depend on this patient's capacity to take up his own agency and authority in treatment, the admissions officer replied to Joe by wondering what the purpose was of their meeting, then, and offered to stop if he wished. After a pause Joe decided to stay, and the consultation unfolded.

During the course of the consultation session they gradually deepened the intimacy of the discussion, delineated Joe's authority and the doctor's, while learning a bit more about each other. It emerged that Joe was a bright and capable man who had grown up feeling neglected and abandoned within a large, rigid, competitive family. He had always tried to be very good, but this never seemed recognized by his clinician parents, whom he experienced as critical and absent during his childhood. Joe married a cold, emotionally unavailable, anxious and narcissistic woman with whom he had three difficult preteen children. Joe loved his children but was overwhelmed whenever he tried to care for them, as they joined their mother in seeing him as inadequate. Joe began to fail at his job, and then became depressed and relentlessly suicidal, with failure to respond to treatment that included multiple medications, outpatient psychotherapy, and multiple hospitalizations. He kept a noose, a lethal supply of pills, and a revolver at hand for eventual suicide. Joe viewed himself as a bad spouse, bad parent, and bad patient who could not get better, and thought everyone would be better off if he died, including his children.

Joe was clearly a formidable treatment-resistant patient, with a view of himself as deserving death, and at high risk for suicide. The admissions officer felt daunted by Joe's capacity to use suicide and failing in treatment as weapons, but he was also concerned that Joe, the son of clinicians, seemed unaware of his aggression, which appeared to have a component intended to defeat clinicians. The admissions officer was aware of liking Joe and feeling empathy for his difficult life circumstances. He was also aware of early countertransference dislike of Joe in response to Joe's unconscious aggression, but contained this feeling. The admissions officer suggested that Joe might be right about being better off dead, but it also seemed worth considering that he might also be reacting to a life in which he had never had the experience of recognition or of his needs being met, despite trying so hard to be good. He went on to suggest to Joe that suicide might have something to do with feeling terribly hurt and quite furious about the way he had been failed. Joe looked startled and acknowledged that this was right, and then took from his wallet a well-worn suicide note he kept there. He allowed the admissions officer to read its secret message of ashamed rage at his parents, at his ex-wife, and at his children. Joe said he had never shown the note to anyone or spoken about his rage with his treaters, and that they had never asked. By the end of the consultation Joe said he wanted to pursue treatment at Riggs and felt he could meet the admissions officer's two conditions. First, although he did not have to relinquish his suicidal wishes, he would have to take responsibility for containing them and for speaking to staff if he felt unable to refrain from acting. Second, he would have to get rid of the gun, the rope, and the pills stockpiled for suicide, and give to his Riggs therapist the suicide notes he always carried with him. Joe accepted these conditions, and when a bed became available, he was admitted to Riggs.

The admissions officer was heartened that, despite Joe's initial stance that he was more interested in dying than in a consultation about admission to Riggs, Joe had been able to claim authority for the meeting continuing, and they had been able to use their developing relationship to find the meaning hidden beneath suicidality—that is, his previously unacknowledged anger. Further, beneath the anger lurked shame and hurt related to childhood experiences of abandonment and neglect in an environment he experienced as made up of rigid rules from his parents and his church. The admissions officer had also found elements of countertransference hatred related to Joe's formidable use of suicide and treatment failure as weapons. At the same time he was aware of a certain fondness for Joe based on the way he joined a process that noticed his authority and responsibility for staying alive, the limits of any doctor's authority over him, and Joe's apparent gratitude for being offered a space to speak about his anger and hate. In the outpatient work that preceded the consultation, Joe's treaters had focused on suicide as a symptom of a mood disorder, but had found no way to bring its meaning into the work or the relationship.

Joe met the conditions set for admission to Riggs. Recognizing his situation, Joe's insurance case manager agreed to support treatment at Riggs for the full 60 days available that year, but he would have to use his own resources if he wished to stay longer, and these were enough for just another few months.

Joe was assigned to work with the doctor who had first met him in the role of admissions officer. This psychiatrist provided four-times-weekly psychotherapy and prescribed medications. Their goal was to do enough therapeutic work in the residential setting on Joe's pattern of repeatedly being in crisis to allow Joe to return to more productive outpatient functioning. Although psychopharmacological treatment was also provided to Joe by the therapist, including continuation of two antidepressants Joe was taking at admission, Joe had been on virtually all classes of agents by the time he entered treatment at Riggs. The only significant medication change during Joe's treatment was the reduction of an atypical neuroleptic that did not seem to help, and appeared to have been prescribed by previous treaters out of a desperate wish to be helpful, but without any demonstrable response or benefit.

A couple of weeks after admission to the fully open setting, Joe became suicidal and revealed to his therapist that he was considering implementing a suicide plan. In one session he menacingly voiced the realization that, since his doctor was holding his suicide notes, if Joe killed himself the therapist was in a position to deliver them to his children and other relatives to whom they were addressed. Other therapists had always refused to take his suicide notes to avoid being put in precisely this spot. Joe, however, said he had decided not to kill himself in order to give the treatment a chance.

Again aware of his own hatred of Joe for this provocation, the therapist said he was both pleased and not so pleased to hear what Joe was saying. Giving the treatment a chance was Joe's choice, and the therapist was glad to work with him. The therapist knew that at some point the pain of the work would get quite bad, as it apparently had recently, so bad that Joe would wonder if it was worth it. It was not giving the treatment a chance that would matter then, but whether or not Joe meant to keep the terms of their agreement. The therapist also reminded Joe of the circumstances under which he took the suicide notes, which was to hold them because they might be useful sources of information. The therapist pointed out that Joe had unilaterally revised these terms and had used holding the notes to put the therapist over a barrel. He added that he didn't much like being put over a barrel by anyone. Joe smiled and came to life, saying he would not have thought that, but when it was pointed out, he could see it. He realized this was something he had done before, as when he had once hung up on a crisis worker with whom he was speaking about suicide plans, and to whom he had given only his first name. He realized he did things he was not fully aware of; he also realized that what he did had something to do with anger.

Initially Joe's awareness of anger was experienced only as uncomfortable agitation, with any conscious angry feelings directed only toward himself. Over time, though, he became aware of anger at others, including his social worker, who was willing to work with him toward an early discharge date at his request. Joe was outraged that she was willing to let him leave before he had accomplished enough to allow him to use outpatient treatment more productively. It reminded him of his mother, who seemed so busy with her clinical work and his siblings that she paid no attention to his individual needs within a large family. Negotiations with his family about loaning him more money to support the treatment had gone poorly. In fact, one parent, frustrated by years of worry over the risk Joe would die by suicide after draining family resources, stated on the basis of "clinical experience" that sometimes it was better to let a hopelessly ill patient die.

Joe reported he left a social work session early to buy a rope to hang himself, but settled for an extension cord when the store had no rope. His therapist observed that this time Joe had picked as a means of suicide an extension cord, the purpose of which is to make something that is too short, longer, which was how Joe seemed to be feeling about his treatment. They explored the new development of Joe's ability to get angry at someone besides himself, though much of his anger seemed like a black hole. It never really escaped the event horizon, always getting pulled back into himself.

Joe wanted his therapist to forget about the extension cord and allow him to keep it, but his therapist said it was not helpful to turn their backs on something so important. Joe turned in the extension cord. Joe also became increasingly angry in group and community meetings. As his anger emerged and was survived, Joe realized that something important and useful was happening. He realized that his anger was often directed at others, usually others on whom he must depend, like his parents and his therapist. It seemed like a dangerous time, though, as he felt pulled to act and to make a decision about whether to leave Riggs soon or continue treatment longer. Joe wondered if he could possibly stay long enough to learn what he needed to. Joe pressed the therapist to tell him what to do about continuing his stay at Riggs, which was now being paid for from his own resources and some borrowed money from his parents. Joe felt confused and unable to think, experiencing his therapist's avoidance of a direct recommendation about what to do as evasive. He felt his therapist did not care what he did. The therapist told Joe that he did not think he had been hired to make decisions about how long Joe should stay in treatment at Riggs or how to live his life. The therapist reminded Joe that he had, in fact, offered a plan about Joe's treatment, and that it was one they had discussed the first time they met. It had to do with there being an important connection between unexpressed feelings, like anger, and Joe's suicidality and treatment resistance. The connection was mostly out of his awareness, but its effect had been devastating and might still kill him. What the therapist had to offer was an opportunity for Joe to become aware of these feelings and to take charge of what he currently couldn't see and, thus, wasn't yet in charge of. Beneath Joe's demands that the therapist tell him what to do, they discovered worry about whether or not the therapist cared about him. He feared he was just another number and that their work together was experienced by the therapist as "just a job." Joe thought that he needed more time for treatment before he could be a more successful outpatient, but he feared becoming resourceless and dependent, and was afraid to ask for help.

Joe's anger at the therapist for not giving him a plan persisted, but there was more than anger in their relationship. Joe spoke of awareness that while one experience of the therapist was as his greatest adversary, and as uncaring, critical, and distant like his father, another was of the therapist as his greatest ally, also a feeling he had sometimes felt toward his father while growing up. Joe was finding ways to be more honest than he ever had been with anyone in his life. Eventually Joe was able to make his own plan, deciding he could afford 2 more months in the highest-level residential program, and then wanted to move to the less expensive day treatment program for several months before transitioning to outpatient therapy with the Riggs therapist.

Here it is worth noting the way in which the relationship and a stance that recognized Joe's own authority, not as a patient, but as the agent in charge of his life, began to show tentative signs of engaging Joe's lost agency. They were not out of the woods, though.

As Joe struggled to make sense of the way the therapist was working with him, he reported a dream of being in a class that was taught entirely in Greek and thus utterly incomprehensible to him, so he couldn't learn anything. He wanted to do well in the class, but there were no tests because the class was for mental patients. This dream illuminated Joe's difficulty making sense of the way the therapist was working with him, which in some respects seemed incomprehensible, as in "It's all Greek to me." And what was incomprehensible was not something he, as a mental patient, could be tested on or held accountable for.

Joe spoke of seeing treatment as helpful, but it wasn't clear if it was helpful enough to keep him alive. He reported another dream of being underwater with his children. There was a tunnel he had to swim through with them to escape, but he wasn't sure he could hold his breath long enough or bear the weight of his children on his back while swimming through it. At the time the therapist thought this was a dream related to the time limitation for treatment. However, subsequent events suggested that the dream also related to something else besides his breath that Joe was not letting out concerning his children.

Over a weekend Joe visited his family, but the visit went badly. Joe reported he had driven back to Riggs recklessly and at high speeds, passing every car he could on narrow two-lane roads, hoping to lose control of the car and crash. The therapist told Joe that it sounded like he needed to knock off the dangerous driving and instead find a way to bring what he was feeling into the sessions in words. Joe became more disorganized and quite angry in the session, speaking about being nasty, about being fed up with being nice in some fake candy-coated way to everyone in his life, about wanting to kill himself and his kids, and knowing he was not the kind of patient the therapist expected, who was fully honest, able to manage feelings, and able to keep the agreement perfectly. The therapist suggested that if he could do all that, they could stop work. The therapist wanted to hear more about the angry parts of Joe, in response to which Joe said he couldn't believe that the therapist really wanted to help someone like him. The therapist told Joe he was right; he didn't want to help him. He wanted to be his therapist, which meant offering a relationship in which Joe could grapple with who he was, what he felt and what he wanted, with all its anger and nastiness. Being his therapist had no more to do with some kind of fake, candy-coated niceness in the therapist than it did in Joe.

In the next session Joe apologized for the previous one, feeling that he had been awful and had brought the wrong stuff into the last session, but the therapist declined to accept the apology. The therapist told him his view was that Joe hadn't brought the wrong stuff at all, but had responded to the suggestion that he bring his road rage into the office, where it wouldn't kill someone. The therapist suggested that Joe had taken a step toward bringing his rage into their relationship, where it could be examined, rather than acting it out on the road. With this in mind, the therapist commented that Joe had taken the risk of bringing in what he felt, with all its nastiness, including his dread about his wish to kill his children. Joe blanched, looked away, and said he hoped the therapist had forgotten that. He avoided eye contact as he spoke of deep shame, guilt, and self-loathing about his murderous feelings toward his own children. A murder–suicide involving them sometimes seemed like the best solution. He felt evil and crazy and thought the therapist must see him that way. Raised in a strict religious tradition, Joe felt it was a sin to have bad thoughts. These were the kind of thoughts he may have needed to hold his breath about in the dream of being underwater. He wondered if the therapist couldn't see now why suicide made sense. The therapist said that he could see there was an altruistic component to his wish to die as well as a murderous one.

Joe went on to say that his increased awareness of anger gave him a greater sense of himself as capable of taking action. Suicide did not feel very far away. He said menacingly that he took consolation in knowing that the therapist couldn't stop him from suicide. Joe gradually revealed awareness of a part of him that wanted to defeat all his treaters. He wanted to be too sick and disturbed to be helped, and then just to die in the face of their neglect. After all, no one in his life had noticed his needs or cared for him as he needed. Joe acknowledged that he had become aware of intensely angry, hateful, and aggressive fantasies toward the therapist, who replied that he was glad Joe now knew that—because the therapist had felt Joe's anger and hate since the first time they had met. Now it was on the table and in the room, where it belonged.

The therapist also told Joe that it sounded like he had come to an important crossroads in treatment. In one direction Joe was closer than ever to action and might attempt suicide. The therapist said he would do everything in his power to stop that, but he wasn't God. Joe was right in the certainty that the therapist couldn't stop him from dying by suicide. They had to consider that he might need a different kind of treatment if he were too close to taking that action. In another direction at the crossroads, though, was the recognition that Joe had taken the considerable risk of revealing his secret murderous thoughts and the associated shame and self-loathing. This is what the therapist had asked him to do, and he was doing it. That could be a hopeful sign. Joe voiced fear that the therapist couldn't bear what he was being told and was just pretending to, as this was just a job. The therapist spoke gently about how much Joe wanted to believe that he (the therapist) was there for him in ways that went beyond a job, and Joe wept in agreement.

Joe's enraged driving reemerged as a concern. While driving his car with his children, Joe "accidentally" drifted across the double yellow line and had a close call with an oncoming car. In the sessions that followed, they explored Joe's wish to die and to kill his children in a murder–suicide. Joe struggled painfully as he acknowledged these feelings as part of his close call, recognizing that this incident was more than "just a lapse" in which he had momentarily drifted off. With great pain, Joe was able to speak of the guilt and self-loathing he felt about accepting what he knew deep down: that he wanted to kill his children and himself. The close call led to a thorough review of the treatment. A decision was made that a report to the state department of child services was necessary. Joe accepted the suggestion that he report himself to the agency, with a staff member listening, but a case was not opened by the state agency, as no one was injured.

The therapist told Joe candidly that he felt jerked around by the invitation into increasingly intimate conversations at the same time as Joe was secretly toying with carrying out his suicide and the murder of his children. This was not what the therapist had agreed to be part of. Joe said that he felt he had to avoid these thoughts because of fear that the therapist wouldn't want to work with him and would impulsively quit. The therapist told Joe that getting him to quit was an achievable goal, but they ought to notice that *Joe* was the one who seemed to be considering making that choice. Joe's goal of defeating the therapist and treatment was neither unrealistic nor unfamiliar in his treatment history. The next session brought a contrite and genuine-sounding apology from Joe. This time the therapist decided to accept it. As this event was explored further, the therapist learned that Joe was struggling with terror about how utterly needy of and dependent on the therapist he felt, when he had never wanted to need anyone. He was fearful of losing the therapist whether he got better or died, and he thought the latter option might be more bearable. The therapist took some reassurance that they seemed to have decreased the time it took to translate the "Greek" of Joe's actions into understanding of what he felt in words, but realized that they were not out of the underwater tunnel yet.

Over the next few months, as his resources for treatment dwindled, Joe moved through step-down programs, returned home, and then was discharged to once-weekly outpatient therapy with the Riggs therapist. Suicide and murder became less an issue as Joe struggled to put his feelings of rage, hatred, shame, hurt, and self-loathing into words, and as he struggled with his longing for a reliable attachment to the therapist. Interpretive work was also done about the way Joe's enraged failure to respond to treatment by clinicians mirrored his feelings toward his clinician parents.

A year later Joe terminated outpatient treatment with the therapist, switching instead to a geographically more convenient therapist within his insurance plan's network. Termination was difficult, with an upsurge in suicide risk over the last few weeks, and some missed appointments that included an invitation to the therapist to give up on holding the last few sessions. The therapist declined to accept this invitation, taking a stance about the importance of recognizing the significance of their work by making time to say goodbye. Joe worried about giving up their relationship and was not sure he had the emotional resources to manage without the therapist, but the transition occurred uneventfully.

In their final session Joe wondered if his new therapist would recognize how important the Riggs therapist had been to him and that Joe was capable of keeping an agreement, of being a competent adult, and of working deeply in therapy even in the face of suicidal ideation. Joe said that he felt the therapy had saved his life, and that he was close, but not fully out of, the underwater tunnel in that sense. Joe said that he had found the therapist tough, but what he needed, and that he was aware he both hated and liked things the therapist did. He offered as an example the therapist's insistence on seeing driving across the double yellow line toward an oncoming car as an indication of wishes to carry out murder and suicide. Joe offered that it was awful to have to face the ways he was not just a nice person, but also potentially a murderer. Joe guessed it was best that he knew, though knowing this was very hard for him to endure.

CASE DISCUSSION AND CONCLUSION

The case of Joe illustrates several key points in working with treatment-refractory patients. First, from the initial engagement Joe was treated as a competent agent with authority over his own life and his decisions, without the clinician abdicating his own role or relinquishing the authority to set the terms of admission and of treatment. Second, in Joe's individual therapy and other treatment relationships at Riggs, the continuity of relationships over time and their importance were recognized and emphasized. Third, in spite of his presentation with symptoms of a treatment-refractory mood disorder, Joe was engaged at the level of the meaning of his symptoms, particularly in terms of their link with his character and his life history, and the ways these were connected to suicide and to treatment resistance. The therapist used his awareness of Joe's aggression and of his own countertransference hate to keep himself more or less adequately in a therapeutic, technically neutral stance, while containing the countertransference of which he was aware. Over time, the therapist helped Joe become aware of Joe's own aggression and hatred, and did not let this painful awareness elude them, once stated. The therapist also made interpretations that let Joe know about and feel some of the therapist's anger and hatred in manageable, situation-specific, limit-setting ways, as when he let Joe know that he didn't like being "put over a barrel by anyone" or that he felt "jerked around" by Joe's dangerous acting out while driving instead of bringing his murderousness and rage into the therapy in words. Joe appeared able to tolerate, use, and learn from his experience of his therapist's countertransference.

Principles from Joe's therapy for working with negative transference:

- From the initial engagement Joe was treated as a competent agent with authority over his own life, even as the therapist maintained his own authority to set the terms of admission and of treatment.
- Joe was engaged at the level of the meaning of his symptoms in terms of his character and life history, and how this meaning was connected to suicide and to treatment resistance.
- Within a mutually agreed-upon alliance with clear terms, the therapist used his awareness of Joe's transference hatred and his own countertransference hatred to stay in a therapeutic, technically neutral stance.
- The therapist made judicious interpretations that let Joe know about and feel some of the therapist's anger and hatred in manageable, situation-specific, limit-setting ways.

REFERENCES

Celenza, A. (1998). Precursors to therapist sexual misconduct: Preliminary findings. *Psychoanalytic Psychology, 15,* 378–395.

Epstein L. (1977). The therapeutic function of hate in the countertransference. *Contemporary Psychoanalysis, 13,* 442–466.

Maltsberger, J.T., & Buie, D.H. (1974). Countertransference hate in the treatment of suicidal patients. *Archives of General Psychiatry, 30,* 625–633.

Rubenstein, H. (2000, December). *What can we learn from patient suicide?: The dilemma of the therapist's availability.* Paper presented at the winter meeting of the American Academy of Psychoanalysis, New York.

Shapiro, E.R. (1997). The boundaries are shifting: Renegotiating the therapeutic frame. In E.R. Shapiro (Ed.), *The inner world in the outer world: Psychoanalytic perspectives* (pp. 7–25). New Haven, CT: Yale University Press.

Winnicott, D.W. (1949). Hate in the counter-transference. *International Journal of Psychoanalysis, 30,* 69–74.

Chapter 5
Transmission of Trauma and Treatment Resistance

M. Gerard Fromm, PhD

Writing in this 150th anniversary year of Freud's birth, I would like to bracket this chapter with two of his statements. The first famously outlines the clinical trajectory of psychoanalysis: "Where Id was, there Ego shall be" (1923/1964, p. 80). In a sense, this description of psychoanalysis launched the field of ego psychology, leading to a rich set of theoretical concepts and a point of view about clinical technique. The conceptual contributions included the potential neutralization of the drives, and the technical approach emphasized supporting the ego in its all-important efforts at synthesis and mastery.

As part of his radical "return to Freud," Jacques Lacan drew on Freud's original German and retranslated the above foundational quote as "Where It was, there I must come to be" (1977, p. 129). He thereby shifted the field of discourse from one of forces and their control—Freud's proverbial horse and rider—to the dimension of subjectivity. He recognized that it had been Freud's genius to discover a model of psychological treatment that reversed the ordinary positions of doctor and patient. Within a traditional medical model, the patient was to make himself the object of the doctor's knowledge and ministrations. But Freud, though he sometimes struggled with his startlingly new paradigm, set up a clinical situation in which *he* was to become the object of the patient's unconscious strivings. As this transference from the past was gradually interpreted, Freud would return to the patient his or her own formerly inchoate knowledge about the sources of the illness.

Lacan drew attention to a different task for clinical psychoanalysis: Pathology reflected a position of objectification, and treatment facilitated a subject's coming into being. For Lacan, the essence of being human is our immersion in meanings—first of all, what we mean to the other person—and the essence of human activity is our effort to grasp meaning for ourselves. The psychoanalytic situation was set up for exactly this purpose: to discover, within a therapeutic relationship, the unconscious meanings the patient was carrying, much to his or her psychic discomfort. The technique of clinical psychoanalysis was organized around this profoundly different understanding of the locus of authority within the treatment. In an earlier paper (Fromm, 1989), I outlined the analyst's role in setting the frame for the treatment, which reflects his or her authority, and the patient's role in using the analyst as a medium for emotional communication, which reflects the patient's authority.

TREATMENT RESISTANCE AND PATIENT AUTHORITY: RESISTING AUTHORITY TO FIND AUTHORITY

This point regarding patient and analyst roles bears directly on the problem of treatment resistance. By the latter term, I mean something more specific than resistance in the usual psychoanalytic sense. I do not mean resistance to experiencing anxiety or to unacceptable thoughts or feelings or resistance as a specific transference to the analyst. Nor do I necessarily mean a negative therapeutic reaction, though, if space permitted, it would be useful to review this concept as an important form of treatment resistance. Rather, by *treatment resistance* I simply mean negative treatment results over time and across a number of treaters.

My point of view in this chapter is that treatment resistance can be considered the response of some patients to treatments that do not take into account the critical issue of subjectivity—that is, of the core meaning-making dimension of human experience. And, of course, many treatments do not include the issue of subjectivity, for reasons that make sense within their frames of reference. Psychopharmacology operates within a traditional medical model and aims toward an objective assessment of symptoms, to be followed by a therapeutic action upon them. Cognitive–behavioral treatment invites the patient to isolate self-defeating thoughts and apply a more constructive way of thinking in those situations of anxiety where habitual, maladaptive thoughts arise.

These ordinary, nonpsychodynamic approaches rely on patients' lending themselves as both partners and objects to the treatment process.

These approaches may work well for those people who can take themselves for granted as subjects and take the good intentions of the doctor for granted as well. But, assuming both good intentions and expertise on the doctor's part (and treatment resistance makes a different kind of sense when either of those cannot be assumed), it may be that many patients who eventually come to be regarded as treatment resistant can do neither. Instead, they cannot fully use treatments that do not address the role of meaning in their symptoms and of relationships in the origin of their disturbances and in their efforts to get well. They cannot surrender to the authority of the doctor if their own confused or disabled sense of authority is not recognized.

Freud's ideal clinical course, as reframed by Lacan, is about patient authority—the "I" that must become able to stand in the place where "It" was: "It," I would suggest, means unintegratable affective experience, regardless of its source in impulse life or external impingement. To the degree that such affective experience overwhelms the ego's capacities, we enter the realm of trauma, the variations of which open up a vast area for exploration. For the purpose of this discussion, suffice it to say that experience that may not be traumatic for a person who has developed a cohesive sense of self may be quite traumatic for a person who has not. For the latter patient, fantasies related to the trauma are concretized and lived out in and as reality. Patients' ability to use words to symbolize experience is compromised, and they need an interpersonal space to play out and thereby learn about their internal experience through the responses of others and the interpretive work of their therapy.

TRAUMA AND ITS TRANSMISSION

It was, in fact, the issue of trauma that led Freud, after his encounter with the psychological casualties of World War I, to reconsider the ego and its operations "beyond the pleasure principle." Trauma studies have burgeoned in the last several years and moved clinical understanding beyond a narrow focus on posttraumatic stress disorder to a broader appreciation of states of extreme arousal, both sudden and sustained, in which the adaptive coping mechanisms of a person shut down in favor of massive organismic dissociation. This is a vast literature, which I cannot review here. Suffice it to say that, in the Austen Riggs Center's Follow-Along Study of over 200 patients followed over more than a decade, an early finding documents the prevalence of trauma in the life histories of treatment-resistant patients and the effect of specific kinds of trauma on later relationship patterns (Drapeau & Perry, 2004).

In this chapter I focus on one aspect of the issue of trauma, namely, its transmission from one generation to the next. The seminal paper on this subject, "Ghosts in the Nursery" by Fraiberg, Adelson, and Shapiro (1975), describes vividly and painfully a mother who could not hear her baby's cries because, it turned out, she could not hear her own cries within her original family, just as her parents could not hear her as a child either. At the time this paper was published, the problems of the children of Holocaust survivors were coming to light and systematically studied for the first time. Though we have subsequently learned all too well the crude fact that abuse to one generation often begets abuse upon the next, Fraiberg's paper and the study of second-generation Holocaust survivors opened a new field of investigation—one that, I argue, adds to our understanding of treatment resistance.

More than 30 years before Fraiberg's groundbreaking paper, Anna Freud and Dorothy Burlingham wrote their influential book, *Children in War* (1943). In it, they showed that during the London Blitz, children whose mothers were traumatized by the experience developed trauma symptoms themselves, whereas this was not the case for children whose mothers were able to serve as "protective shields" despite the dire nature of the threat. Freud and Burlingham thus demonstrated that the potential effects of trauma were mediated by human relationships.

Since September 11, 2001, a number of clinician-researchers have taken up similar studies of the traumatic consequences of the attacks on the World Trade Center. Susan Coates (2003) argues persuasively that trauma and human bonds may be inversely related: That is, trauma is often a phenomenon of aloneness and, on the other hand, going through a terrible situation with other people sometimes mitigates its traumatic effects. In this same volume, Schecter (Coates et al., 2003) tells the story of a little girl who seems to be holding not only her own terrifying experience, but her father's too. She drew in red, yellow, and black the burning buildings she had seen on TV and in which she, and her family too, had thought her father had died. But he had not been at the World Trade Center that day; he was doing errands, having exchanged his shift at its top-floor restaurant with a friend who did indeed die in the catastrophe. He was shocked to realize that his daughter believed he was nearly killed by the fire. Suffering agonizing survivor guilt about his friend and recurrent nightmares envisioning how he had died, this father had lost touch with his little girl.

"So your daughter is drawing your dreams," Dr. Schechter said. His intervention put father and daughter back in conscious emotional touch with each other. Dr. Coates and her colleagues (2003) illustrate powerfully the unconscious attunement between children and parents, especially in situations of potential trauma. Dr. Schechter's clinical vignette shows how child and parent can be both in unconscious resonance with, but also dangerous isolation from, each other. As I wrote elsewhere (Fromm, 2004):

> Parents *mind* children. That verb connotes the holding-in-mind of the total child, including the developing mind of the child. When parents lose their minds under circumstances of extreme distress . . . *children mind their parents*. The critical question is whether the parent can hear the child's interpretation, an interpretation delivered in a drawing, a nightmare or disruptive behavior. (p. 9)

Fonagy and Target (2003) have developed the concepts of reflective functioning and the interpersonal interpretive function, both describing the minding function. They call this function *mentalization*. Their research takes up the relationship between the state of these capacities in a child and that child's proneness toward, or resilience in the face of, traumatization.

In another recent study, Davoine and Gaudillière (2004) present findings from their psychotherapeutic work over many years with traumatized and psychotic patients. They are convinced that the psychotic patient is madly conducting a research into the rupture between his or her family and the social fabric, a rupture brought about through trauma and betrayal. They suggest that the unthinkable traumatic experience of the preceding generation lodges itself in highly charged but chaotic fragments in the troubled mind of the patient. In a sense, these patients are attempting to give a mind to that which has been cut out of the social discourse that surrounds them.

Davoine and Gaudilliere's work powerfully links the clinical arena with the historical and the political. Like Freud, their encounter with World War I, particularly through the work of the military psychiatrist

Thomas Salmon, has led them to realize a remarkable similarity between his principles of treatment for traumatized soldiers and theirs with psychotic patients. One of their major points is embedded in the subtitle of their book: "Whereof one cannot speak, thereof one cannot stay silent." The experience of trauma must be communicated, or at least communicable, if the traumatized person is to carry on as a whole person. When it cannot be communicated in words that carry genuine emotion, it is transmitted through action, a kind of unspoken, unspeakable speech, and, like Dr. Schechter's 3-year-old little girl, someone is listening.

Vamik Volkan's recent work (2002, 2004) argues cogently that the transmission of trauma from one generation to the next takes many forms. For example, anxiety or other feeling states may be passed from parent to child; or, unconscious fantasies about the cause, nature, and effects of the trauma may be passed on. Or sometimes an unconscious task is deposited in the child, for example, to avenge a parent's humiliation or to make up for a terrible loss. Holocaust studies and our clinical experience at Austen Riggs show that the effects of trauma are carried forward, not only into the next generation, but also into the second generation and perhaps succeeding generations as well. Indeed, Volkan (2004) has powerfully illustrated the political mobilization of a society's ancient "chosen trauma" to fuel contemporary ethnic conflict.

THE BIG HISTORY AND THE LITTLE HISTORY

The theorists discussed in the preceding section examine the intersection between the big history of wars, atrocities, diaspora, and social upheaval and the little history of a person in a family in a particular time and place. It has proven to be such a clinically compelling perspective to me that, if I find myself without the time to read the full case abstract at Riggs case conferences, I begin with the story of the grandparents and the earliest part of the patient's life history. The following clinical vignette illustrates the intersection of the big history and the little history as well as a patient's unconsciously assigned task of making up for a parent's experience of loss.

A young woman brought up in London reported a dream after her therapist's vacation. "There were some ruined buildings. They were destroyed by fire. One was a pet shop. There were some guinea pigs in a cage, doing something sexual with each other." The next day, she remembered that the buildings were not destroyed by fire, but by rain. Spontaneously, as though it were more her thought than his, her therapist said: "There is a kind of rain that brings fire." The patient said, "Bombing," and suddenly remembered, for the first time, an event from her childhood.

Night after night, her father would watch newsreels of the bombing of London. He seemed to be looking for something. His 8-year-old daughter sat anxiously beside him and repeatedly asked him why he was looking at these films again and again. He made no reply. This took place just after the father's mother had died, with whom he had been quite close. In fact, mother and son had long since been left by the grandfather, so that when her son moved away to be with his own family, the patient's grandmother became desperately lonely and seemed to will herself into debilitation and death. The patient was named for this grandmother. She was later to learn that her father had lost his childhood home in the bombing of London when he was 8 years old.

After his mother's death and the phase of searching newsreels for his destroyed home, the patient's father entered a long, subtle depression that his adoring daughter's liveliness and flirtatiousness were designed, though not destined, to cure. As she grew into adolescence, this former "pet" of her father felt that she had lost her father's presence and love completely. She became vulnerable to rejection in love relationships, deeply conflicted about sexuality, determinedly involved with wounded, remote men, and increasingly convinced that no one could stand the anger, borne of hurt and humiliation, that she felt inside her. Eventually, she became recurrently and seriously preoccupied with death. Multiple near-fatal suicide attempts were interspersed with both outpatient treatments and short-term inpatient treatments, none of which led to sustained improvement. From one angle, she seemed to be following in her namesake's suicidal footsteps, as though to replace her grandmother as the object of her father's mourning. Perhaps, if she could not have access to his liveliness, she could at least access his depression.

There is a great deal that could be said about this case. Life stories are always complex, and psychopathology is always multidetermined. Here I suggest that this vignette illustrates the way that trauma to one generation falls out upon or is, in a sense, given to, the next. There is a paradox within this transmission. On the one hand, silence is a recurrent feature in the transmission of trauma, silence about something both terribly confusing and absolutely urgent. This 8-year-old experienced an urgent speechlessness from her father at the core of his trauma. Had it been possible for her father to speak, his choosing to be silent might have been designed to protect her. But, in her experience, it deprived her, and the subsequent, ongoing deprivation she felt from her father led to a retaliatory, deeply depriving motive within her suicidal actions.

From another angle, the unspeakability of her father's trauma spoke in different and very powerful ways to his daughter. It spoke with images, which, like their content, bombarded the little girl with affect-laden stimulation. She was saturated with her father's unspeakable grief, and, of all her siblings, she was the one to stay with him through it. This special place—the woman in the next generation with the same name as the lost woman from the preceding generation—may have meant that the patient had already been spoken to through her name, as though this naming was her father's unconscious act of encoding the past for the purpose of future recovery.

There is an Oedipal dimension to this special place. The patient was stimulated by her father's experience without the containment that would have been provided by his explaining to her that he was looking for his lost home in those films. An essential perspective was missing, which would have functioned as a Third (see Chapter 6; and Muller, 1996), structuring, containing, and providing meaning to the patient's childhood affectivity and interpretations. Instead, like the patient's father, who had been left alone by his father to deal with, and perhaps cure, his mother, the patient was left alone with the arousing, terrifying, and ultimately futile task of curing her father.

To put the situation in slightly different terms, the loss of his mother, and all that she had meant to him in the traumatic history of his original family, led the patient's father to lose his mind in grief. But he had a daughter who—in her name, in her 8-year-old-ness, and in the dissociated experience he shared with her—*re-minded* him, for better or worse, of these losses. And indeed, it may have been for worse. One finding from the 9/11 studies (Coates et al., 2003) is that traumatized parents cannot bear the reminders of loss that their children bring to them in the most innocent and ordinary ways. To the degree that the patient's father could not bear what his daughter represented for him, she may have become the unconscious repository for a crucial bit of dissociated history—and, as children do, she took it personally. To her great peril, she misinterpreted the subsequent rupture with her father as the consequence of her Oedipal claims on him and her adolescent badness. More basically, she identified with the dissociated history she had shared with him. It was not that experience of his past or of his mother that he could not bear to see; it was *her*! Her suicide would not only have been a depriving retaliation, but the burial, once and for all, of her father's trauma.

Sometimes a child's fulfillment of this kind of role for a traumatized parent represents a form of mission, and naming is one way such missions are unconsciously assigned. This patient felt a charge from her father in the dual sense of that word—that is, in the energy invested in his relentless searching of those images of destruction and, through their silent togetherness, an unconscious assignment that implicated her in his trauma. This goes beyond a patient's having a designated unconscious role in his or her family, in which he or she receives the unwanted projections of its members, though that too was part of this patient's experience. Rather, I mean to emphasize an unconscious sense of duty and authorization in the patient through which she is to represent and live out a dynamic at the intersection of her family's and the society's history. Especially if the family's issues are interwoven with societal trauma, the child's mission is not so much the restoration of the family's well-being, but the representation of its painful and dissociated history in language.

Treatment resistance in patients like this has to do with the unconscious task they are living out on behalf of their family. This patient was not only bringing her suicidal depression to treatment, but her father's and her grandmother's as well. Unconsciously, she was not seeking relief from her symptoms. In fact, she would experience efforts to provide her with relief as a current attempt at further dissociating a crucial bit of history, and she would experience actually feeling relief as a deep disloyalty. Instead, she seemed to be seeking in treatment a relational venue for bringing into discourse what I have come to think of as her "unconscious citizenship" (Fromm, 2000) in her family.

In a sense, the patient played out the transmission of trauma in the transference relationship to her therapist by allowing herself to react to his vacation with the feelings and images of abandonment in her dream. These nodal points of condensed meaning Lacan calls "signifiers." The dream image of buildings ruined by a fire-rain—and perhaps the history of images she had "bombarded" her therapist with over the course of her treatment—opened up a crucial bit of the patient's and her father's history and gave a completely new context of meaning to the sexuality about which she had been in such conflict. Sex now seemed like an effort to bring life into a context of death. Indeed, the work in her therapy following her dream and the de-repression of the memory of watching newsreels with her father led to major changes in her treatment-resistant symptoms. She became far less given to the blindly passionate pursuit of damaged, inaccessible men, and thus far less prone to the self-destructiveness that regularly followed.

The act of dreaming this dream represented the patient's effort to formulate and take authority for what these images had meant in her family's life. Originally she was, to some degree, an object in the presence of her father's trauma, but in treatment she attempted to become a subject in relation to it. Her actual access to her father as someone who could, in a sense, bear witness to her witnessing, helped her build the emotional narrative of her family's life. This process of inscribing a dissociated history is not without peril for a patient, who may feel an inexpressible fear of destructiveness in speaking the formerly unspeakable. Speaking separates the patient from a person she needs and who needed her. It discharges the mission she has been carrying for someone she loves. Something life-defining and deeply intimate is over. In addition, she is speaking something that her father could not or would not speak. In this way, too, she leaves him. This real and painful separation may get to what Lacan means by his statement that the symbol is "the murder of the thing" (1977, p. 104) and is another source of treatment resistance for patients carrying the trauma of preceding generations.

"SOMETHING OPENED UP"

"A year ago, something closed and something else opened up, and I can't close it again, and the person who could isn't here to." This person was a patient's father, who had died the year before her treatment at Riggs. His death precipitated an intractable and volatile, treatment-resistant depression, including cutting and suicide attempts. The patient was a young, highly accomplished and driven lawyer whose father had also been a very successful lawyer as well as her mentor. She experienced his death as an unbearable abandonment. A story from her treatment is a more ordinary example of the unconscious transmission of trauma and its contribution to treatment resistance.

Immediately after telling her therapist that she needed to speak with him about things she had done that she considered bad, she became extremely conflicted about speaking at all. She then came to her session having cut herself while in the woodworking area of the hospital's Activities Department. This was a major violation of a community norm against acting out in any way in this creative space. She felt she was showing her "badness" and perhaps trying to provoke her therapist into agreeing with this definition of herself and punishing her. This would have alleviated her guilt, but also protected her from having to say the things she felt she needed to say. Eventually her therapist said to her that she might be communicating something else to him in this act: "Cutting yourself in the Activities Department desecrates what people here consider to be a sacred space. Cutting can be seen as desecrating your body. Maybe you are trying to tell me about desecrating your body in a way that I can feel."

After the patient and her therapist worked through her defensive reactions to this interpretation, she got to what she had been afraid to say. She spoke in detail and in a tone of great seriousness about a complicated and ultimately destructive romantic entanglement with an older man who had "opened up the world" to her. She felt extremely guilty for the consequences of this relationship and had kept it to herself for years.

At this point in the therapy, the ongoing, agitated lament about her father changed completely into a quieter, deeper, and more alive anger at her mother, who had drifted into low-key but chronic medication abuse during the patient's early childhood. As she developed this material, the patient found, to her surprise, that she no longer wanted to cut herself and that she could look at pictures of her father again. She was no longer angry with him; instead she missed him but felt she had him with her in a new way. The transference shifted from a paternal constellation to a maternal one, and, after further work in this area, the patient took the frightening step of asking her mother if they could speak frankly about their relationship. She also asked her therapist to take part in this meeting.

At the meeting, the patient spoke with her mother about how angry she had been at her for being emotionally absent during her childhood. She went into detail and spoke with feeling. Her mother replied: "You're right; I wasn't there; I'm so sorry." In the course of reflecting on the early years of her marriage, the patient's mother revealed to her daughter an early complicated and ultimately destructive romantic entanglement of her own. Its traumatic ending had been quite public and so terribly shameful and crushing to the mother that she had completely withdrawn from a promising and already accomplished artistic career. The patient's father came along at this time and rescued her from this catastrophe. She became pregnant with the patient soon after they married. But the shame and grief persisted, symptoms related to physical stress developed, and she medicated herself to deal with the strain of raising a lively child and responding to an ambitious husband. She did, however, devotedly encourage her daughter in the arts.

The patient's mother realized in this conversation the true extent of her grief at losing her artistic career. Performing had been for her "the most meaningful experience of my life, a glimpse of something beyond ordinary human experience. It needed concentration. I was in it. I wasn't really myself anymore." It had also brought "a special joy" to her sad and withdrawn father. "He didn't talk about it, but we could meet there."

After this remarkable conversation, the patient felt she had rediscovered her mother as both a person and as a resource in her effort to get well.

This also seems to be a story about the transmission of trauma. In a family session, the patient's mother remembered, and disclosed to her daughter for the first time, a critical traumatic event in her early adulthood, an event remarkably similar to the traumatic relationship the patient eventually confesses in her therapy. Her mother's traumatic experience involved a love relationship that she felt to be enormously exciting but illicit. It had led to great shame and to a series of terrible losses, including of her artistic career. The latter represented the creative place where a wounded father and a loving, very talented daughter could "meet," and so, embedded in this young-adult disaster was also the mother's despair at losing her own father.

In the next generation, the patient as a child felt this loss of her mother, but this painful experience was hidden behind the more overtly passionate relationship with, and eventual loss of, her father. Once the patient made emotional contact with this earlier loss in her therapy, she discontinued her cutting. She then began to recognize how she had attributed the early loss of her mother to her own badness. She had become convinced that her anger at her mother's absence would only lead to the further loss of this fragile person. It came to seem to her that it was in response to this conflict with her mother that she had directed her vitality toward her father, a move that felt both rescuing and illicit.

The patient's mother's willingness to open her own trauma to her daughter gave the patient a new context for her trouble. The parallels were remarkable even if totally unknown, at least consciously, by the patient. Like her mother, she had become entangled with a man in a way that led to shame, guilt, and painful losses. Both women shared a devotion to their fathers, and, like her mother, the loss of her father was cause for despair. Indeed, it seemed likely that the patient's mother had unconsciously sponsored the kind of relationship between father and daughter that she had had with her own father and then lost. She certainly sponsored her daughter's artistic interests and talents. All of this suggests the intricacies and the subtlety of a trauma's transmission.

The window into this transmission was opened by a major piece of acting out in the patient's treatment. She cut herself in the Activities Department. From one angle, this was the kind of assault on the treatment setting that provokes the designation "treatment resistant." But, from another, this action brought into the treatment two aspects of the trauma in her life and in her mother's. First, it enacted (as it simultaneously attempted to stay silent about) what she felt to be the illicit use of her body, just as her mother felt that her illicit use of her body had led to such humiliation and loss. Accompanying this in the transference was the wish for a punishing father, who would relieve the guilt of a sexually transgressing daughter and restore a damaged relationship.

Second, this action brought into the treatment the patient's assault on the creative life of other patients and staff in the Activities Department, precisely replicating a childhood role she felt herself to have occupied. Her birth had indeed sealed her mother's decision to withdraw from creative life, and her anger at her mother's relative unresponsiveness compounded her sense that she was the destroyer of her mother's vitality. There was both painful irony and liberating understanding in this part of her analysis. The patient was certainly acting out an Oedipal issue. She secretly wanted her therapist to pair with her and forgive her attack on the creative space of other people, just as she wanted her father to take her side in the battle with her mother. But her action carried an echo from another generation. In fact, it replicated the trauma of her mother's early adulthood: It enacted shameful sexuality in displaced form, and it had major consequences for the creative space she also loved. This is the kind of sobering realization that links the patient's symptoms with the family's history of trauma and frees a patient to use, rather than resist, treatment.

THE UNCONSCIOUS AS INSTRUMENT

My second and closing quote from Freud is his remarkable, mysterious, and completely unelaborated declaration that "Everyone possesses in his own unconscious an instrument with which he can interpret the utterances of the unconscious in other people" (1913/1958, p. 320). Trauma seems to be transmitted from one generation to the next through this unconscious instrument, however much we still do not know about the specifics of its operation. Erikson noticed similar phenomena. He wrote about "the subtler methods by which children are induced to accept . . . prototypes of good and evil" and the way that "minute displays of emotion . . . transmit to the human child the outlines of what really counts" (1959, pp. 27–28).

My argument in this chapter is that treatment resistance for some patients reflects a complex authority issue. The experience of some children has been "authored," if you will, by the unspeakable traumas of their parents. Some have been especially, if unconsciously, "authorized" to carry their parent's trauma into the future. This "unthought known," in Christopher Bollas's apt phrase (1987), must come into being as emotional understanding if the patient is ultimately to take authority for his or her own life as distinct from that of the traumatized parent. Treatments that threaten to further dissociate this experience or threaten the unconscious mission to which the patient is deeply loyal will be resisted to the death, no matter how valuable they have objectively been for other patients.

In more practical terms, I am suggesting that the therapists of apparently treatment-resistant patients consider the nature of the trauma those patients might be carrying from the preceding generation. This would mean that the therapist would be interested in the life stories of the patient's parents and grandparents; that the therapist would develop some sense of the social–historical context, especially its upheavals, in which these stories were taking place; that he or she would develop an "ear" for potential "signifiers" and perhaps be especially curious about the names people are given; that he or she would notice areas in the patient's life that are blanketed by silence; and that he or she would trust that his or her associations to the patient's material have potential meaning about the larger story the patient is trying to tell and come to know.

In the examples above, these larger meanings are told through a dream and an acting out. The therapists' responses are relatively spontaneous associations, but I would argue that they are, in fact, brought about by the patient's material. In other words, people to whom trauma is transmitted unconsciously must transmit it to the therapist and must use the same channel of unconscious communication that was used with them. Freud invited us to investigate this "instrument." Some treatment-resistant patients invite us to use it to understand how it has been used with them.

I offer the following clinical principles to guide clinicians in work with treatment-resistant patients who may have multigenerational trauma histories:

Treatments may work best when we:

- Consider the nature of the trauma suffered by preceding generations that the patient might be carrying on their behalf. This requires learning about the stories of the patient's parents and grandparents, putting them into social–historical context, and facilitating the patient's interest in them.
- Develop an "ear" for words or images that resonate as carrying meaning, albeit not yet understood. Let the patient's language "work on you" in this way. Pay particular attention to the meaning and story behind names.
- Tune in to areas of the patient's life or discourse that seem blanketed by silence; "spoken" in recurrent, perhaps quirky, images, phrases, or actions; or that convey an uncanny sense to them.
- Trust your associations, feelings, and dreams in working with the patient. Regard them as illuminating communication from the patient, and as potentially meaningful fragments of the traumatic context the patient is struggling to know.
- Respect treatment resistance as a response to the underlying issues of loyalty and identification embedded within it. Recognize that the patient's telling of a story the family has been unable to speak is an act of differentiation and separation, and the potential beginning of useful mourning.

REFERENCES

Bollas, C. (1987). *The shadow of the object: Psychoanalysis of the unthought known*. London: Free Association Books.

Coates, S. (2003). Introduction: Trauma and human bonds. In S. Coates, J. Rosenthal, & D. Schecter (Eds.), *September 11: Trauma and human bonds: Vol. 23. Relational Perspectives Book Series* (pp. 1–14). Hillsdale, NJ: Analytic Press.

Coates, S., Rosenthal, J., & Schecter, D. (Eds.). (2003). *September 11: Trauma and human bonds: Vol. 23. Relational Perspectives Book Series*. Hillsdale, NJ: Analytic Press.

Davoine, F., & Gaudillière, J.-M. (2004). *History beyond trauma: Whereof one cannot speak, thereof one cannot stay silent* (S. Fairfield, Trans.). New York: Other Press.

Drapeau, M., & Perry, J. (2004). Childhood trauma and adult interpersonal functioning: A study using the Core Conflictual Relationship Theme method (CCRT). *Child Abuse and Neglect, 28*(10), 1049–1066.

Erikson, E. (1959). Part I: Identity and the life cycle: Selected papers (with a historical introduction by D. Rapaport). In G. Klein (Ed.), *Psychological issues: Identity and the life cycle; studies in remembering; on perception and event structure and the psychological environment; cognitive control* (pp. 5-171). New York: International Universities Press. (Original work published 1946, 1950, 1953, 1956 [Erikson]; 1958 [Rapaport])

Fonagy, P., & Target, M. (2003). Evolution of the interpersonal interpretive function: Clues for effective preventive intervention in early childhood. In S. Coates, J. Rosenthal, & D. Schecter (Eds.), *September 11: Trauma and human bonds: Vol. 23. Relational Perspectives Book Series* (pp. 99–113). Hillsdale, NJ: Analytic Press.

Fraiberg, S., Adelson, E., & Shapiro, V. (1975). Ghosts in the nursery. *Journal of the American Academy of Child Psychiatry, 14*, 387–421.

Freud, A., & Burlingham, D. (1943). *Children in war.* New York: Medical War Books.

Freud, S. (1958). The disposition to obsessional neurosis: A contribution to the problem of choice of neurosis. In J. Strachey (Ed. & Trans.), *The standard edition of the complete psychological works of Sigmund Freud* (Vol. 12, pp. 313–326). London: Hogarth Press. (Original work published 1913)

Freud, S. (1964). The dissection of the psychical personality. In J. Strachey (Ed. & Trans.), *The standard edition of the complete psychological works of Sigmund Freud* (Vol. 22, pp. 57–80). London: Hogarth Press. (Original work published 1923)

Fromm, M. (1989). Impasse and transitional relatedness. In M. Fromm & B. Smith (Eds.), *The facilitating environment: Clinical applications of Winnicotts's theory* (pp. 179–204). Madison, CT: International Universities Press.

Fromm, M. (2000). The other in dreams. *Journal of Applied Psychoanalytic Studies, 2*(3), 287–298.

Fromm, M. (2004). Psychoanalysis and trauma: September 11 revisited. *Diogenes, 51*(3), 3–14.

Lacan, J. (1977). *Écrits: A selection* (A. Sheridan, Trans.). New York: Norton.

Muller, J. (1996). *Beyond the psychoanalytic dyad: Developmental semiotics in Freud, Peirce, and Lacan.* New York: Routledge.

Schecter, D. (2003). Intergenerational communication of maternal violent trauma: Understanding the interplay of reflective functioning and posttraumatic psychotherapy. In S. Coates, J. Rosenthal, & D. Schecter (Eds.), *September 11: Trauma and human bonds: Vol. 23. Relational Perspectives Book Series* (pp. 115–142). Hillsdale, NJ: Analytic Press.

Volkan, V. (2002). *The Third Reich in the unconscious.* New York/London: Brunner–Routledge.

Volkan, V. (2004). *Blind trust: Large groups and their leaders in times of crisis and terror.* Charlottesville, VA: Pitchstone Publishing.

Chapter 6
Why the Pair Needs the Third

John P. Muller, PhD

Previous chapters have addressed the value of attending to the meaning of patients' speech and behavior, the importance of developing a therapeutic relationship, and the role of the patient's authority in treatment. When these are neglected, we often find that patients become "treatment resistant" or "treatment refractory." I will join these issues to the notion of the Third as it has been presented in recent psychoanalytic writing. When I refer to the "Third" I use a capital "T" in order to distinguish it from a third object in a series; by "Third" I do not mean any specific object but rather a logical place from which relations are structured.

Patients designated as treatment refractory or treatment resistant often report the life experience of not being recognized or not feeling understood. When this experience is repeated with those providing health care to them, the iatrogenic consequences are clear: Such patients wear their diagnostic labels like armor, hiding behind them and defying the next practitioner to look beyond the paraded diagnoses, thereby participating in the misrecognition process that goes on. Such patients are often touchy about treatment arrangements, have their own expectations about promises made, and insist that an exception on their account is justifiable according to their reading of the terms of the treatment contract. Dyadic treatment itself stirs up in the patient longings based on unmet developmental needs, which therapists frequently misinterpret, as Stolorow and Atwood write: "When the patient revives such a longing within the therapeutic relationship, and the therapist repeatedly interprets this developmental necessity as if it were merely a pathological resistance, the patient will experience such misinterpretations as gross failures of attunement" (1992, p. 106).

Rage reactions to empathic ruptures (Kohut, 1978) are routinely provoked in these patients whenever the psychotherapist makes an error, even inadvertently, unleashing what Cooperman (1983) described as a "defeating process." When these moments occur, both Kohut and Cooperman advise the therapist to avoid a power struggle in which the patient wins by losing, to review the incident, and to acknowledge the error now perceived in retrospect. Earlier Ferenczi (1933/1980b) noted how "the willingness on our part to admit our mistakes and the honest endeavor to avoid them in the future, all these go to create in the patient a confidence in the analyst" (p. 160). By reviewing the empathic failure, the therapist can recognize his or her part in it, and the patient usually not only calms down but also learns something about the process of mutual recognition.

TREATMENT RESISTANCE AND THE THIRD

As I see it, "misattunement" is not simply about the therapist's empathic rupture with the patient, but more precisely the therapist's failure to understand the patient in context—that is, to understand the patient as related to what is beyond the dyad. The patient is not enraged because he or she cannot control the therapist; the reparative resolution works not because the therapist finally gives in to the patient. The therapist's recognition of his or her part in the upset is effective because he or she takes into account a standard of care and/or a social norm from which his or her behavior has deviated, if only inadvertently. That is, what the patient sees is that he or she was right, acting in accordance with the expectations generated by a right rule. This is very different from feeling that he or she simply won. To be right means to be judged according to a standard and found acceptable: The complaint was not a matter of whining but of asking for justice. The therapist, in measuring his or her behavior against the standard, makes a just judgment about this behavior as well as the patient's behavior. It is this implied or at times explicit reference to a Third, beyond the therapeutic dyad, that constitutes the decisive act of reparation.

This implied reference to a shared Third is what makes effective the recommendation by Shapiro and Carr (1991) to ask of the patient, "How is he or she right?" (p. 80), rather than, for example, rigidly holding to procedure, as though staff authority were synonymous with the Third. In their view, reference to a shared Third (or, more precisely, to its representative) is required to ground the dyad in effective treatment (Carr, 1985, speaks of "a transcendent reference," p. 17; see also, Shapiro & Carr, 1987, p. 80). Shapiro writes:

> Bion (1961) described the shared irrationality inherent in any "pairing" disconnected from the larger group's task. The notion of an isolated dyad, however, is an illusion. The therapeutic pair has always been embedded in a larger context: the community, the profession, the managed-care networks, the mental institution. Though we do not always pay attention to this, there is inevitably a "third" that keeps the pair grounded in reality. (1997, p. 17)

Earlier David Rapaport warned of the regressive dangers of the dyad: "The reduction of reality relationships to a single interpersonal relationship . . . impairs the ego's autonomy from the id" (1956/1967b, p. 728). The social theorist Georg Simmel (1908/1964) called attention to regressive features of the dyad. He wrote that in the dyad "each of the two feels himself confronted only by the other, not by a collectivity above him" (p. 123). The dyad, in Simmel's view, is specially aware of its fragility in a way that a group is not, since a group usually survives the death of a member, but the dyad cannot: "It makes the dyad into a group that feels itself both endangered and irreplaceable, and thus into the real locus not only of authentic sociological tragedy, but also of sentimentalism and elegiac problems" (p. 124). Dyads have an intrinsic tendency to regress toward narcissistic illusions of self-sufficiency and are therefore prone to repeated disappointment.

Writing of such regressive dynamics in the dyad, Gentile (2001) warns that

> when a closed dyadic process prevails, instead of impelling therapeutic action toward thirdness and intersubjectivity, agency gets mired in a trapped, perverse state of "twoness"— a state of phenomenological confinement that elides the space of intersubjectivity and symbolic communication. In the collapsed state of twoness, fusion-based dynamics, power relations, and brute force yield a relatedness that looks like, but actually precludes, psychological intimacy. (pp. 623–624)

My main point is that "treatment resistance" is often a product of the practitioner's disregard for the place of the Third, arrogating its authority into his or her relationship to the patient, unwittingly promoting regression, and then narcissistically imposing on the patient what the patient correctly perceives as an arrogant refusal or demand. To put it another way: In these moments the patient is implicitly (sometimes explicitly) appealing to the Third as witness to the truth, witness to reasonableness and to history (even, at times, invoking a religious discourse to do this [Tillman, 1999]). What provokes the patient's rage is the way the therapist eclipses this place of the Third as witness and claims its authority for him- or herself, as if the therapist were the only valid witness. It is not quite precise to say of this moment that the patient feels hurt because he or she isn't being recognized: The patient, rather, is enraged, disappointed, disillusioned, and hurt because his or her *relation* to the Third—the Third as witness to the true and the reasonable—is not being recognized, and, in this failure to recognize, the therapist does not appreciate his or her *own relation* to this place of the Third. By the eclipse of the Third, the therapeutic relation has collapsed into a dyadic struggle.

CLINICAL FUNCTIONS OF THE THIRD

We can see the place of the Third operating in earlier chapters. When Fromm emphasizes the shared authority of patient and therapist, he is invoking the Third as the principle distributing the shared authority and thereby governing the relation each has to his or her own proper authority. Betrayal of this principle by parents, teachers, priests, police, government officials, and therapists, as representatives of the Third who cross boundaries, is intrinsic to the transmission of trauma. Ferenczi (1931/1980a) also noted the role of such betrayal in making traumatic experiences pathogenic: "Probably the worst way of dealing with such situations is to deny their existence, to assert that nothing has happened and that nothing is hurting the child. Sometimes he is actually beaten or scolded when he manifests traumatic paralysis of thought and movement. These are the kinds of treatment which make the trauma pathogenic" (p. 138).

When, as the authors of Chapter 1 state, "resistance to treatment may be the only way left for a patient to exercise authority" (p. 16), they also invite us to think about the Third as the principle that apportions proper authority to both patient and therapist. Here we are developing an additional role for the Third in treatment, one that rests on the notion of the treatment alliance, the treatment contract or pact. At the end of his life,

Freud (1940/1964, p. 173) wrote, referring to himself and the patient, "We form a pact with each other" (*"Wir schliessen einen Vertrag mitein-ander,"* 1940b, p. 98). The pact functions as representative of the Third, governing the speech of both participants. Freud elaborates:

> The sick ego promises us the most complete candour—prom-ises, that is, to put at our disposal all the material which its self-perception yields it; we assure the patient of the strictest discretion and place at his service our experience in interpret-ing material that has been influenced by the unconscious. . . . This pact constitutes the analytic situation (1940/1964, p. 173). (*"In diesem Vertrag besteht die analytische Situation,"* 1941, p. 98.)

It is the pact that establishes the analytic context by defining the treat-ment and authorizing each of the speakers to take up his or her speaking role in relation to his or her task in treatment. The pact is not just some third item in a series (therapist, patient, pact) but the very vehicle that transforms a dyadic into a triadic structure. The pact is a performative speech act (Muller, 1999c) committing one subject in relation to another, like speaking wedding vows or saying "I forgive you." The pact does not simply describe the situation—the pact brings it about, it "constitutes the analytic situation," it creates the ethical demand on both participants to act in accordance with the standard they thereby embrace.

The Third as pact governs much of the work done with Joe, as de-scribed by Plakun in Chapter 4. The therapist points out how "Joe had unilaterally revised" the terms of the treatment pact (p. 72), how Joe's suicidal and murderous plans were "not what the therapist had agreed to be part of" (p. 77), and Joe, in turn, by disclosing his thoughts, was doing "what the therapist had asked him to do" (p. 76), since "Joe was capable of keeping an agreement" (p. 78). The treatment pact as norm was invoked in other ways as well: When Joe stated that "no one in his life had noticed his needs or cared for him as he needed" and therefore he wanted "to de-feat all his treaters" (p. 76) by committing suicide, his therapist made a triple reference to the Third: (1) by affirming that he would try to prevent the suicide, in accordance with his commitment to the treatment pact; (2) by disclaiming an identity with God, in effect, saying, "I am not the Third" but functioning instead as its representative; and (3) by consider-ing whether Joe "might need a different kind of treatment" (p. 76), based on the assessment of his needs in relation to the standard governing the provision of care as represented by the pact. In examples like these we can see how the appeal to the Third, by either patient or therapist, acts to give necessary ballast to the dyad, performing a "righting" function and helping to contain the work of the dyad. As Aron states, "the notion of the third is particularly useful in understanding what happens in and in resolving clinical impasses and stalemates" (2006, p. 349).

CONCEPTUALIZING THE THIRD

How are we to understand this place of the Third? I will suggest that the Third is the structure of signification grounding the position of each (therapist and patient) in an evolving contextualized relationship, serving as the basis for any interpretive speech act (Muller, 1996). In order to unpack this complex notion, it helps to examine its range of formulations, as presented, for example, in a special 2004 issue of *The Psychoanalytic Quarterly*, in which Gerson delineates "three different usages of the concept of thirdness—namely, the *developmental third*, the *cultural third*, and the *relational third*" (2004, p. 65, emphasis in original). He describes these as follows:

> For some, this something called a *third* that transcends individualities is thought of as a product of an interaction between persons; others speak of it as a context that originates apart from us even as it binds us together; and there are some for whom the third is a developmental achievement that creates a location permitting reflective observation of lived experience, be it singular or communal. (2004, p. 64)

I have found this delineation very helpful in resolving some of my earlier inconsistencies about the Third, which Crastnopol (1999) has rightly pointed out. I modify Gerson's three categories or types of theories of the Third and use them to ground what this book articulates as primary values: attending to meaning, the value of relationships, and the role of patient authority.

The *developmental* Third is the individual's psychological achievement of a triadic perspective, opening the capacity for symbolization and thereby finding meaning in experience; for the analyst, finding meaning requires the development of a model or conceptual space for thinking about the clinical process. The *relational* Third is the dyadic intersubjective field generating the shared history of representations required for the developmental Third to emerge in the psychic life of the individual through a relationship with another human being. In treatment such dyadic work essentially consists in co-creating (by conscious and unconscious collaborative efforts) the transference–countertransference matrix whose interpretation is required for the Third to emerge as an effective psychic structure in the individual. Precisely because of its regressive potential, the dyadic transference–countertransference matrix acts as a "solution" in which previously undecipherable somatic ailments become accessible and can then become interpretable symbolic symptoms. The *structural* Third precedes and authorizes the participants in their dyadic roles (mother and child, therapist and patient) so that they can have a shared authority in creating and interpreting a common representational history.

In the semiotic terms of the American philosopher Charles Sanders Peirce (1887–1888/1992), the Third is whatever functions as a sign to relate a Second (a dyadic process) to a First (a psychic quality). To refer to the dyadic matrix itself as "the Third" is to take a part for the whole, is to eclipse all the other more basic structural conditions (such as culture and language), and to reduce the structural Third to a product rather than a cause of the analytic work.

The Third is commonly taken to mean one of three units, such as the third person whose presence sets up a triangle, usually described in Oedipal terms. The Third is also commonly viewed as any object—physical, social, or mental—that is not encompassed by each member of a dyad. Such thirds include a transitional object brought into a therapy session, a psychoanalytic theory, the family, the community, therapeutic groups, the treatment team, the state licensing board. Of course any community or group can become a mob in collapsing internal differentiations and eclipsing the role of the Third in response to a dominating leader. One could say that such group eclipse of the Third is precisely what defines fascism. In such times of eclipse the leader identifies with being the Third, claims to speak as the Third, in covert opposition to any notion of (imperfectly) representing the Third.

I am arguing that as the basis for all common representatives of the Third, we must consider a structural Third in the logic of relations—a necessary logical place, which Lacan calls "the Other" to distinguish it from others (other persons or objects). I and my patient can be in a therapeutic relationship because our roles and positions are already specified by the cultural and linguistic forms that are not "others" to us, as if added on to us, but rather antecedent to us, forming us, already partially determining our possibilities—"the Other with a capital O," states Lacan, "the very foundation of intersubjectivity" (1956/1987, p. 35), "the guarantor of Good Faith" (2004, p. 164) and "Truth's witness" (2004, p. 293). The Other as structural Third works primarily at an unconscious level, as Felman notes:

> The Other is in a position of a Third, in the structure of the psychoanalytic dialogue: it is a locus of unconscious language, sometimes created by the felicitous encounter, by the felicitous structural, verbal coincidence between the unconscious discourse of the analyst and the unconscious discourse of the patient. (1987, pp. 125–126)

This structural Third is readily grasped in its effects (both positive and negative) through a wide range of normative aspects of context that function as representatives of the Third. These include:

1. Law, ethical code, government, religious authority, and police—who may (and are likely to) misrepresent the Third through ignorance, neglect, or malice.
2. Elements of the treatment situation beyond the treatment dyad, including other functions and other practitioners (psychopharmacologist, medical internist, administrators, nurses, therapeutic community staff, the team, substance abuse group, etc.), each of which can usefully function as delegate of the Third (but not to be identified with it) or may rather imperfectly misrepresent it, especially when staff members engage in their own countertransference power struggles with patients and with one another.
3. Aspects of the patient's history and life situation, including family members, the family system and its history (much of which may be obscured, foreclosed, or unconscious), teachers, and friends, representing what is beyond the patient's current treatment relationship, providing a witnessing perspective to the patient's current behavior in the dyadic transference, and establishing a context for understanding repetition.
4. Varieties of sublimatory activities producing a historical record of achievement, as in athletics, or an artistic product that serves as a witness to the patient's previous state of mind and behavior; these

can provide a corrective function for present misrepresentations of the patient's mind and behavior.

5. Norms of objectivity and evidence that govern logical inferences and lead to correct judgments about others, situations, and oneself.

The Developmental Third

This set of formulations calls attention to aspects of thinking and attending to meaning—thinking as a developmental achievement for the patient and thinking as a requirement for the analyst. As Aron states: "It is the analyst's reflexive self-awareness, a dialogue with oneself, that creates a third point within what was a simple dyad, a triangular space where there was only a line" (2006, p. 361). For the analyst, the Third may function as "the analyst's deployment of a working model of a dynamic unconscious" (Brickman, 1993, p. 905; see also, Muller, 1999a, p. 474). Such deployment of the Third includes respectful silence before the not-yet-manifest, an appreciation of the meaning of one's own unconscious processes, a humility on the part of the ego in facing the ongoing "unmasterability" of human life. Bion's model of the mind offers a notion of triangular space functioning as a set of coordinates and therefore as representative of the Third for the analyst's mind (Schoenhals, 1995). For Zwiebel (2004), "the central analytic task is *to survive* the relationship with the analysand," and this requires the Third: "I propose that, in order for the analyst to survive that relationship, a *third position* must be developed, which has to be drawn out from the internal working processes of the analyst, over and over again" (p. 216, emphasis in original). Any mapping of psychic space can represent the Third insofar as it functions to mediate, for the analyst, between impulses and ideas, feelings and thoughts, the unsayable and the imaginable, and thereby provide means to mediate for the patient what the patient presents as commingled, confused, merged—or conversely, what persists as conflicted, distant, disavowed, or delinked (Muller, 2005).

An example of the Third as standing for a developmental achievement is offered by Minolli and Tricoli (2004) when they write: "We think the third was born as an attempt to recall the human being's special capacity to grasp himself reflexively" (p. 143). They relate this capacity to reflective functioning, mentalization, and metacognition as presented by Fonagy, Steele, Moran, Steele, and Higgit (1991), but in place of the Third they prefer the Hegelian term "self-consciousness." In their view self-consciousness "depends exclusively on a personal developing process: it cannot be dependent on anything other than itself" (2004, p. 144). Speaking to the contrary, Britton (2004) asserts that the developmental achievement at stake here depends precisely on the child's experience of mother and father in triangularity. Britton writes: "The closure of the oedipal triangle by the recognition of the link joining the parents provides a limiting boundary for the internal world. It creates what I call a 'triangular space,' i.e., a space bounded by the three persons of the oedipal situation and all their potential relationships" (2004, p. 47). In Cavell's view, thinking requires "triangulation" (1998, 2003), namely "two creatures in communication with each other" and "an object outside them both to which they refer"—and she asserts: "It is triangulation that makes room for the normative distinctions between the true and the false, how things *appear* to any one of us and how they objectively *are*" (2003, p. 807, emphasis in original). The intersubjective aspects of triangulation as a developmental achievement are apparent: "The essential condition is not merely that infant and caretaker can point to the same object, but that they can observe each other making this reference" (2003, p. 810).

Benjamin (2004) refers to this developmental achievement as "the Third in the One," to distinguish it from what she calls "the One in the Third." In this way she formulates a more integrative framework: "I think in terms of thirdness as a quality or experience of intersubjective relatedness that has as its correlate a certain kind of internal mental space; it is closely related to Winnicott's idea of potential or transitional space" (p. 7). She elaborates:

> In my view of thirdness, recognition is not first constituted by verbal speech; rather, it begins with the early nonverbal experience of sharing a pattern, a dance, with another person. I . . . have therefore proposed a nascent or energetic third—as distinct from the one in the mother's mind—present in the earliest exchange of gestures between mother and child, in the relationship that has been called *oneness*. I consider this early exchange to be a form of thirdness, and suggest that we call the principle of affective resonance or union that underlies it the *one in the third*—literally, the part of the third that is constituted by oneness. (2004, pp. 16–17, emphasis in original)

There is some imprecision here, as I read it: First, if there is an "exchange of gestures between mother and child," then the "oneness" is not a fusional state but rather a state of relatedness, a state of "we-ness" of two semiotic agents—hence I would alter the formulation in order to address the developmental Third, the emerging psychic structure, as constituted not in oneness but in resonance and relatedness. Secondly, if the exchange of gestures is meaningful—if there is a pattern, a dance—it is because the participants are behaving according to some code that informs their actions, a code they do not invent from scratch but that is an aspect of their culture or even their DNA. Elsewhere I have summarized data from infancy research (1996) indicating that as early as 4 weeks of age the infant is functioning as a semiotic partner in mutual gazing play and shows displeasure when the mother violates the rules of play.

The Relational Third

Gerson (2004), along with Aron (2006), Benjamin (2004), and Ogden (1994, 1999, 2004), are in the forefront of those attempting to conceptualize a relational perspective that includes the Third. For example, Gerson writes: "The notion of thirdness as arising from within the dyad is what I am referring to as the *relational third*, and it is this usage of the concept of thirdness that is most frequently associated with an intersubjective perspective" (2004, p. 79, emphasis in original). Gerson's thoroughly relational viewpoint, however, eventually leads him to give up the notion of thirdness when he states that "the concept of the relational unconscious is, I believe, preferable to that of concepts invoking thirdness because it signifies a dynamic process that belongs fully to the human participants" (2004, p. 81). In Gerson's terms the analytic process seems capable of grounding itself.

Ogden, taking some cues from Green (2005) about the analytic object, describes an intersubjective framework within which "the analytic third" both takes shape and also, in time, affects the dyadic participants who co-create it. He defines the analytic third as follows:

> This third subjectivity, the intersubjective analytic third, is the product of a unique dialectic generated by/between the separate subjectivities of analyst and analysand within the analytic setting. It is a subjectivity that seems to take on a life of its own in the interpersonal field, generated between analyst and analysand. (2004, p. 169)

Ogden presents a paradox, for while he emphasizes that the relational Third is co-created by the participants, he also asserts that "there is no analyst, no analysand, and no analysis in the absence of the third" (1994, p. 17). Mills (2005), in his extended critique of relational theory, finds a contradiction when Ogden "nebulously introduces the notion that the analytic dyad is 'generated' through the process of 'creating' the analytic third, hence overshadowing his previous claim that the 'third' is 'created' by the intersubjective dyad, a convoluted thesis that begs for misinterpretation" (p. 171). Mills's criticism calls attention to the obscure status of the structural Third in the relational paradigm. Benjamin (2004) names such a structural feature of the Third when she states: "Analytic work conducted according to the intersubjective view of two participating subjectivities requires a discipline based on orientation to the structural conditions of thirdness" (p. 42). These conditions are both determining and freeing, for "we might say that the third is that to which we surrender, and thirdness is the intersubjective mental space that facilitates or results from surrender" (2004, p. 8). Yet, in a move that parallels Mills's point, Benjamin also states: "By making a claim on the potential space of thirdness, we call upon it, and so call it into being" (2004, p. 33). In my view it is the other way around: We do not call "thirdness" into being, for it is what enables us to speak and grounds us in our roles and tasks. Thus when Benjamin writes: "The only usable third, by definition, is one that is shared" (2004, p. 13), I too would underline the role of the Third in establishing relationships and therefore I would emend this to read: "The only usable Third, by definition, is one that is *already* shared *before it is experienced as shared.*"

Some of the inconsistency noted by Mills can be resolved if we view the relational Third as the history of the transference–countertransference responses in the intersubjective field, a history that becomes established in an intelligible and usable manner because it follows the semiotic rules of discourse—that is, because it is held by the structural Third and can then function as a representative of the Third. Half a century ago Erikson, although not referring to the semiotic dimension, already presaged the relational viewpoint when he wrote that the treatment must include

> a wider view of the complaint, and entail corresponding *inter-*
> *pretations* of the symptom to the patient, often making the
> "patient himself" an associate observer and assistant doctor.
> This is especially important, as subsequent appointments
> serve a *developing treatment-history*, which step by step verifies
> or contradicts whatever predictions had been made and put

to test earlier. . . . To put it briefly, the element of subjectivity, both in the patient's complaints and in the therapist's interpretations, may be vastly greater than in a strictly medical encounter. . . .

Indeed, there is no choice but to put subjectivity in the center of an inquiry into evidence and inference. . . . I shall claim that there is a core of *disciplined subjectivity* in clinical work—and this both on the side of the therapist and of the patient. . . . How the two subjectivities join in the kind of disciplined understanding and shared insight which we think are operative in a cure—that is the question. (1958, pp. 52–53, emphasis in original)

I believe it is Erikson's question that Ogden attempts to answer when he offers us "the analytic third" and states: "The analytic process reflects the interplay of three subjectivities: that of the analyst, of the analysand, and of the analytic third" (1994, p. 3). When this "third subjectivity" is experienced as "subjugating" the participants, it can be "superseded" by "an act of mutual recognition that is often mediated by the analyst's interpretation of the transference–countertransference and the analysand's making genuine psychological use of the analyst's interpretation" (2004, pp. 193–194). I read this as saying that the analytic third is essentially the history of the transference–countertransference field.

Benjamin is especially aware of the need for the Third based on the propensity of the dyad to become stuck in the impasse of treatment resistance:

One of the most common difficulties in all psychotherapeutic encounters is that the patient can feel "done to" by the therapist's observation or interpretation; such interventions trigger self-blame and shame, which used to be called by the misnomer "resistance." . . . There may be no tenet more important to overcoming this shame and blame in analytic work than the idea that recognition continually breaks down, that thirdness always collapses into twoness, that we are always losing and recovering the intersubjective view. (2004, pp. 28–29)

Her means of resolution when such an impasse occurs relies on what she terms "the moral third," as when she writes: "The notion of the moral third is thus linked to the acceptance of inevitable breakdown and repair, which allows us to situate our responsibility to our patients and the process in the context of a witnessing compassion" (2004, p. 40). This moral third functions as a standard for "certain principles of responsibility": "This is what I mean by the moral third: acceptance (hopefully within our community) of certain principles as a foundation for analytic thirdness—an attitude toward interaction in which analysts honestly confront the feelings of shame, inadequacy, and guilt that enactments and impasses arouse" (2004, p. 41).

The Structural Third

Benjamin's invocation of the psychoanalytic community's "principles" as representing the Third is an affirmation that such a Third is not co-created by the analytic dyad but precedes it, authorizes its participants, and hopefully functions well beyond it. As Zeddies states: "The psychoanalytic community as a third presence keeps the relational process in check, sometimes in spite of the wishes of the dyad, and in so doing allows for a special kind of interpersonal connection to develop" (2001, p. 134). Professional standards as representative of the Third have received attention in terms of an ethics of practice (Aron, 1999; Crastnopol, 1999; Spezzano, 1998), as well as an ethics of discourse (Muller, 1999b; Widlöcher, 2004). Aron's explicit emphasis "extends to the wider professional, social, and historical culture in which the dyad is embedded" (1999, p. 6). As a contemporary anthropologist has put it: "The signifying chain, the Symbolic [yes]order, culture, and grammar, we might say, serve to stabilize the relations between self and other by functioning as a Third" (Crapanzano, 1982, p. 197).

Others find within the dyadic relationship itself the structuring presence of the Third. The philosopher Emmanuel Levinas writes that when two people are speaking, there is "an irreducible movement of a discourse which by essence is aroused by the epiphany of the face inasmuch as it attests the presence of the third party, the whole of humanity, in the eyes that look at me" (1969, p. 213). For Levinas the human face is a signifying presence that cannot be encompassed conceptually and makes an ethical claim on me that joins me to humanity. In his 1944 lectures, David Rapaport noted that "a trichotomy is given . . . in the encounter of two human beings"—an encounter he names the "psychoanalytic constellation"—and "there appears to be within this 'constellation' itself a triadic structure which may have more to do with the triadic concepts of psychoanalysis than meets the eye" (1944/1967a, pp. 197–199). Such triadic structure minimally includes (as Cavell also noted) the following: "there is some-body who communicates, something that is communicated, and some-body to whom it is communicated" (1944, p. 203).

Contrary to many contemporary psychoanalysts who label Freud's work a "one-body psychology," Rickman, more than a half-century ago, as Lacan noted (1953–1954/1988, p. 11), pointed to "Freud's three-body theory," stating: "A three-body psychology deals with all of the derivatives of the Oedipus complex" (1957a, pp. 166–167; 1957b, p. 220). Hanly (2004) agrees with Rickman that psychoanalysis for Freud "is a three-person psychology that requires the analyst to be able to observe the dy-adic analytic relation from the position of a third person" (p. 280). Lacan translates this position into a triadic structure, insisting that: "There is no two-body psychology without the intervention of a third element. If, as we must, we take speech as the central feature of our perspective, then it is within a three- rather than two-term relation that we have to formulate the analytic experience in its totality" (1953–1954, p. 11).

The analytic discourse, Lacan later stated, "solders the analysand—to what?"—"not to the analyst": instead, "it solders the analysand to the cou-ple analysand–analyst" (1975, p. 187, my translation). Lacan here formu-lates the analytic structure not as a dyadic object relation but as a relation to a relationship mediated by speech—that is, as inclusive of a third posi-tion from which the analysand–analyst relationship can be observed. This is another way of describing Freud's statement about the pact as a speech act positioned in relation to the treatment relationship that it specifies by defining the relative authority of both patient and analyst.

Although these triadic aspects of the structural Third serve to repre-sent it by structuring the context of our work, the structural Third is not a determinate subject or object but rather a logical structure, shaping our thinking and our relationship to each other and to the world. Hanly shows us that "it is necessary to differentiate threesomes, triangular relations, and the use of the metaphor of 'triangular space' or 'triangulated space' from the third as such, although important linkages with them may be found" (2004, p. 276). He calls it "an *epistemological* third" that releases us from our "irreducible subjectivity" (2004, pp. 270–271, emphasis in original), and he locates its psychological genesis to Freud's notion of representa-tion and the distinction made between the image of the satisfying object and the object itself: "At the heart of this experience is the first rudimen-tary awareness that images represent but do not duplicate, that they point beyond themselves to the needed, real, need-satisfying object" (2004, p. 276).

The primary-process satisfaction through images becomes inhibited by submission to what we may call the "as-structure" of signs: Images as well as perceptions are taken *as* standing for something else. Bass (1997) discusses the problem of concreteness in the type of patient for whom "seeing is believing," for whom things are just as they are found in one's perception, and therefore interpretations (e.g., of dreams) are rejected along with the claim that one thing might mean another (both in the world and in oneself). Bass writes:

> The typical countertransference danger for the analyst in such situations is to share the patient's conviction that "seeing is believing." The analyst would then attempt to convince the patient that what *he or she* sees has to be believed. Both patient and analyst would operate from within the assumption that perception guarantees objectivity. (1997, p. 665, emphasis in original)

I find this an excellent description of how the eclipse of the Third leads to impasse. Both patient and analyst insist that the iconic aspect of perception—perception as a form of imaging—no longer functions to mediate experience as sign but is to be taken identical with experience, in the grip of the primary-process feature of "the temporal immediacy of perceptual identity" (Bass, 1997, p. 660). The as-structure of perception as sign, what Heidegger called the "existential-*hermeneutical* 'as'" (1927/1962, p. 201, emphasis in original), and what for Freud became, as Hanly noted, the key to reality testing, is disavowed. Instead, writes Bass (1997), a "conviction about the indisputable self-evidence of perception is maintained in the intrinsically regressive state of consciousness that uses perception to bypass reality testing" (p. 660) and thereby "to use undoubted perceptions to conflate fantasy and reality" (p. 671). What has been eliminated in this regressive conflation of fantasy and reality is the as-structure of perception as sign, as representation. This is why, for Green, "the concept of representation is, without a shadow of a doubt, the cornerstone of Freud's conception of the psychic apparatus" (2004, p. 110).

A representation functions when we take something as standing for something else in some respect. The representation points beyond itself, and by doing so it opens up the world, allowing for play, mediation, and substitution. This as-structure grounds the sign in its capacity to represent the object in some respect—not in its totality, but only in some respect.

This grounding guarantees that the sign does not equate the object but only represents it, thereby generating the partial, probabilistic, and indefinite nature of human knowing in which signs lead to signs in an unending process of semiosis. Because of the uncertain, tentative, fallible efforts to achieve knowledge, Bakhtin tells us that when we attempt to communicate we frame our words not just in terms of our actual addressee, but with reference to an ideal listener, that our speech "presupposes a higher *superaddressee* (third), whose absolutely just responsive understanding is presumed" and often takes the form of "various ideological expressions (God, absolute truth, the court of dispassionate human conscience, the people, the court of history, science, and so forth)." Bakhtin continues: "Each dialogue takes place as if against the background of the responsive understanding of an invisibly present third party who stands above all the participants in the dialogue (partners). . . . The aforementioned third party is not any mystical or metaphysical being (although, given a certain understanding of the world, he can be expressed as such)—he is a constitutive act of the whole utterance" (1986, p. 126).

This superaddressee is, I think, the nearest we can come to personifying the Third as the locus of immense transference longings. The effort to be understood, given the as-structure of the sign, invokes such an ideal listener who contains the entire field of signification and therefore understands, since our actual listeners (and readers) do so only imperfectly. But this Other does not exist, Lacan reminds us, and so we have to settle for the Other, the Third, as "the locus of signifying convention," that is, "a third locus which is neither my speech nor my interlocutor" (2004, p. 164). This locus of signifying convention, the field in which the things we take to be signs function as signs, is the zone of mediation, the as-structure of the sign, in-between the sign and the object it represents, enabling us to take the sign as standing for something else. This zone is the Third to the sign and its object, opening the potential space of reference, meaning, and interpretation between sign and object. Gentile (2001) favors this semiotic emphasis, for "psychoanalysis is increasingly establishing itself, in part, as a semiotic enterprise in which access to a third space between symbol and symbolized creates the possibility for an intersubjective agent and subject to come into being" (p. 625).

In psychoanalysis and in life, we are the primary signs to each other—child to parent, patient to analyst—and our living response to one another constitutes the various meanings of (and to) one another as signs (Muller, 2005). We live our interpretation, show it paraverbally, and only confound the other when we deny this. Our signed status as human subjects begins with the naming of our place in a lineage. At the dawn of our Western literature we learn about this place in the symbolic order. In Book One of Homer's *Odyssey*, Athena, in disguise, asks Telemachus if he is the son of Odysseus (who has not yet returned from the Trojan War). Telemachus answers: "My mother says that I am his child; but I know not, for never yet did any man of himself know his own parentage" (1919, lines 215–216, p. 19). Until the development of DNA technology (i.e., for thousands of years), the father—the father as known—is the father as named by the mother. The name of the father is first spoken by the mother, and this speech act clears a space for the Third through the provision of the father as symbolized by a name. By naming the father, by taking this man *as* father of her child, the mother inscribes the triangulation necessary to provide a holding context for the life of the child, a fixed place in a lineage and network of kinship relations. Naming the father introduces mediation into psychic structure. Through the father's name the community is now capable of taking the child *as* the child of the mother *and as* child of the father, as subsequent to the relation of mother and father, therefore as representative of each, as a complex sign of their union, and as the most recent expression of their separate lineages. My relation to my mother is now related to my father's relation to my mother, and each relation is now related to my relation to my father. We now have triangularity not as three units but as a complex relation of relations.

The father's name mediates a network of relations, giving us our "relatives" who take us as a sign of our parents and, because the relatives each have a place in the network of kinship, they are thereby authorized to bear witness to our place. The family lineage as a system of relations marked out by signs holds our history, often unconsciously, and, as Fromm notes in an earlier chapter, transmits the family experience of trauma. When a parent treats the child as a part of him- or herself and precisely not as a sign for others of a new person, separate from the parents, we have one of the conditions for severe pathology, due to what Lacan (1977) called the failure of "the Name-of-the-Father" in its structuring of the patient's unconscious (Friedlander, 2000).

CONCLUSION

The widespread phenomenon of "treatment-resistant" patients may be a result of the eclipse of the Third. Much of the published psychoanalytic work on the Third can be usefully classified as (1) monadic formulations that emphasize the crucial developmental achievement called "mentalization," "triangulation," "oedipalization," or "mediation," essential for the symbolizing capacity that enables us to find meaning in experience; (2) dyadic formulations that emphasize one-to-one interaction as co-creating an intersubjective field and shared context within which meaning can develop in relationships; and (3) triadic formulations that address the formative context specifying tasks and roles and establishing places from which each member of the dyad can speak with the authority that derives from the structural properties of the treatment context.

The Third is understood here not as a person or thing but as a logical principle grounding and mediating differentiated positions, as a standard defining behavior in terms of tasks and roles, and as a shared code providing the means for human subjects to sustain a common perspective. Typical representatives of the Third include the law and founding constitutions, authority figures, organized guilds, dictionaries, differentiated groups and communities, the unconscious transmissions of shared history (especially family history), and the shared formulations dealing with the observation of facts.

The Third is likely to be misrepresented through ignorance, neglect, malice, and narcissistic illusion. When therapist and patient reach an impasse in treatment, one can usefully look to see how the Third has been eclipsed, often by the therapist's failure to recognize the patient's position and the patient's relation to the Third. Betrayal by a representative of the Third, with its associated eclipse of the Third, is an essential feature of psychological trauma.

The following clinical principles from the perspective of the Third are useful in working with treatment resistant patients:

Treatment resistance is often a product of one or more therapists' disregard for the place of the Third, acting as if able to claim that authority as their own, and unwittingly promoting regression. To use the concept of the Third in clinical work with treatment-resistant patients:

- Be mindful of the terms of the "pact" or alliance that authorize the work.
- Be aware that the pair doing individual psychotherapy can become lost in a narcissistic bubble that, when it bursts, often turns into a power struggle that the patient wins by losing.

- To mitigate the emergence of power struggles, be alert for opportunities to remind the patient that the treatment framework is binding on both of you, and not just the patient.
- When the patient gets angry, it may help to understand the anger in terms of standards of care and how the patient feels about their possible violation.
- In cases of trauma, look for the double-beat effect: namely, that after the initial traumatic assault there is usually a second trauma involving a betrayal by a representative of the Third (e.g., a parent, a teacher, a priest, an officer of the law, a health service provider). This second trauma must be addressed in an effort to reconstitute a viable Third as container of the affects and the basis of credible social links. Frequently, a comparable experience of something akin to trauma will also arise within the transference.

REFERENCES

Aron, L. (1999). Clinical choices and the relational matrix. *Psychoanalytic Dialogues, 9*, 1–29.

Aron, L. (2006). Analytic impasse and the third: Clinical implications of intersubjective theory. *International Journal of Psychoanalysis, 87*, 349–368.

Bakhtin, M. (1986). *Speech genres and other late essays* (C. Emerson & M. Holquist, Eds., V. McGee, Trans.). Austin: University of Texas Press.

Bass, A. (1997). The problem of "concreteness." *Psychoanalytic Quarterly, 66*, 642–682.

Benjamin, J. (2004). Beyond doer and done to: An intersubjective view of Thirdness. *Psychoanalytic Quarterly, 73*, 5–46.

Bion, W.R. (1961). *Experiences in groups.* London: Tavistock.

Brickman, H. (1993). Between the devil and the deep blue sea: The dyad and the triad in psychoanalytic thought. *International Journal of Psychoanalysis, 74*, 905–915.

Britton, R. (2004). Subjectivity, objectivity, and triangular space. *Psychoanalytic Quarterly, 73*, 47–61.

Carr, A.W. (1985). *The priestlike task.* London: SPCK.

Cavell, M. (1998). Triangulation, one's own mind, and objectivity. *International Journal of Psychoanalysis, 79*, 449–467.

Cavell, M. (2003). The social character of thinking. *Journal of the American Psychoanalytic Association, 51*, 803–824.

Cooperman, M. (1983). Some observations regarding psychoanalytic psychotherapy in the hospital setting. *The Psychiatric Hospital, 14,* 21–28.

Crapanzano, V. (1982). The self, the third, and desire. In B. Lee (Ed.), *Psychosocial theories of the self* (pp. 179–206). New York: Plenum Press.

Crastnopol, M. (1999). The analyst's professional self as a "third" influence on the dyad: When the analyst writes about the treatment. *Psychoanalytic Dialogues, 9,* 445–470.

Erikson, E. (1958). On the nature of clinical evidence. *Daedalus, 87,* 65–87. Revised in *Insight and responsibility* (pp. 49–80), 1964, New York: Norton.

Felman, S. (1987). *Jacques Lacan and the adventure of insight: Psychoanalysis in contemporary culture.* Cambridge, MA: Harvard University Press.

Ferenczi, S. (1980a). Child analysis in the analysis of adults. In M. Balint (Ed.), E. Mosbacher (Trans.), *Final contributions to the problems and methods of psycho-analysis* (pp. 126–142). New York: Brunner/Mazel. (Original work published 1931)

Ferenczi, S. (1980b). Confusion of tongues between adults and the child. In M. Balint (Ed.), E. Mosbacher (Trans.), *Final contributions to the problems and methods of psycho-analysis* (pp. 156–167). New York: Brunner/Mazel. (Original work published 1933)

Fonagy, P., Steele, H., Moran, G.S., Steele, M., & Higgit, A. (1991). The capacity for understanding mental states: The reflective self in parent and child and its significance for security of attachment. *Infant Mental Health Journal, 13,* 200–217.

Freud, S. (1941). Abriss der Psychoanalyse. *Gesammelte Werke, 17,* 63–138. London: Imago.

Freud, S. (1964). An outline of psycho-analysis. In J. Strachey (Ed. & Trans.), *The standard edition of the complete psychological works of Sigmund Freud* (Vol. 23, pp. 144–207). London: Hogarth Press. (Original work published 1940)

Friedlander, S. (2000). The "third" party in psychoanalysis. In K. Malone & S. Friedlander (Eds.), *The subject of Lacan: A Lacanian reader for psychologists* (pp. 141–156). Albany, NY: SUNY Press.

Gentile, J. (2001). Close but no cigar: The perversion of agency and the absence of thirdness. *Contemporary Psychoanalysis, 37,* 623–654.

Gerson, S. (2004). The relational unconscious: A core element of intersubjectivity, thirdness, and clinical process. *Psychoanalytic Quarterly, 73,* 63–98.

Green, A. (2004). Thirdness and psychoanalytic concepts. *Psychoanalytic Quarterly, 73*, 99–135.

Green, A. (2005). Configurations of thirdness. In A. Weller (Trans.), *Key ideas for a contemporary psychoanalysis: Misrecognition and recognition of the unconscious* (pp. 187–201). New York: Routledge.

Hanly, C. (2004). The third: A brief historical analysis of an idea. *Psychoanalytic Quarterly, 73*, 267–290.

Heidegger, M. (1962). *Being and time* (J. Macquarrie & E. Robinson, Trans.). New York: Harper & Row. (Original work published 1927)

Homer. *The odyssey*, vol. 1 (A.T. Murray, Trans., 1919). Cambridge, MA: Harvard University Press.

Kohut, H. (1978). Thoughts on narcissism and narcissistic rage. In P. Ornstein (Ed.), *The search for the self* (pp. 615–658). New York: International Universities Press.

Lacan, J. (1974). "La troisième." Septième congrès de l'école Freudienne de Paris, Rome. *Lettres de l'École Freudienne*, No. 16. Paris, 1975, pp. 178–203.

Lacan, J. (1987). Seminar on "The purloined letter." In J. Muller & W. Richardson (Eds.), *The purloined Poe* (pp. 28–54). Baltimore, MD: Johns Hopkins University Press. (Original work published 1956)

Lacan, J. (1988). The seminar of Jacques Lacan. Book 1: Freud's papers on technique (J.-A. Miller, Ed., J. Forrester, Trans.). Cambridge, UK: Cambridge University Press. (Original work presented 1953–1954)

Lacan, J. (2004). *Écrits: A selection* (B. Fink, Trans.). New York: Norton.

Levinas, E. (1969). *Totality and infinity: An essay on exteriority* (A. Lingis, Trans.). Pittsburgh: Duquesne University Press.

Mills, J. (2005). A critique of relational psychoanalysis. *Psychoanalytic Psychology, 22*, 155–188.

Minolli, M., & Tricoli, M. (2004). Solving the problems of duality: The third and self-consciousness. *Psychoanalytic Quarterly, 73*, 137–166.

Muller, J. (1996). *Beyond the psychoanalytic dyad: Developmental semiotics in Freud, Peirce, and Lacan*. New York: Routledge.

Muller, J. (1999a). The Third as holding the dyad. *Psychoanalytic Dialogues, 9*, 471–480.

Muller, J. (1999b). The ethics of speech in psychoanalysis. *Psychoanalytic Review, 86*, 513–528.

Muller, J. (1999c). Consultation from the position of the Third. *American Journal of Psychoanalysis, 59*, 113–118.

Muller, J. (2005). Approaches to the semiotics of thought and feeling in Bion's work. *Canadian Journal of Psychoanalysis, 13*, 31–56.

Ogden, T. (1994). The analytic third: Working with intersubjective clinical facts. *International Journal of Psychoanalysis, 75*, 3–20.

Ogden, T. (1999). The analytic third: An overview. In S. Mitchell & L. Aron (Eds.), *Relational perspectives in psychoanalysis: The emergence of a tradition* (pp. 487–492). Hillsdale, NJ: Analytic press.

Ogden, T. (2004). The analytic third: Implications for psychoanalytic theory and technique. *Psychoanalytic Quarterly, 73*, 167–195.

Peirce, C. (1992). A guess at the riddle. In N. Houser & C. Kloesel (Eds.), *The essential Peirce: Selected philosophical writings* (Vol. 1, 1867–1893, pp. 245–279). Bloomington, IN: Indiana University Press. (Original work published 1887–1888)

Rapaport, D. (1967a). The scientific methodology of psychoanalysis. In M. Gill (Ed.), *The collected papers of David Rapaport* (pp. 165–220). New York: Basic Books. (Original work published 1944)

Rapaport, D. (1967b). The theory of ego autonomy. In M. Gill (Ed.), *The collected papers of David Rapaport* (pp. 722–744). New York: Basic Books. (Original work published 1956)

Rickman, J. (1957a). The factor of number in individual- and group-dynamics. In W. Clifford M. Scott (Ed.), *Selected contributions to psycho-analysis* (pp. 165–169). New York: Basic Books.

Rickman, J. (1957b). Number and the human sciences. In W. Clifford M. Scott (Ed.), *Selected contributions to psycho-analysis* (pp. 218–223). New York: Basic Books.

Schoenhals, H. (1995). Triangular space and the development of a working model in the analysis. *International Journal of Psychoanalysis, 76*, 103–113.

Shapiro, E. (1997). The boundaries are shifting: Renegotiating the therapeutic frame. In E. Shapiro (Ed.), *The inner world in the outer world: Psychoanalytic perspectives* (pp. 1–25). New Haven, CT: Yale University Press.

Shapiro, E., & Carr, A.W. (1987). Disguised countertransference in institutions. *Psychiatry, 50*, 72–82.

Shapiro, E., & Carr, A.W. (1991). *Lost in familiar places: Creating new connections between the individual and society*. New Haven, CT: Yale University Press.

Simmel, G. (1964). The isolated individual and the dyad. In K. Wolff

(Ed. & Trans.), *The sociology of Georg Simmel* (pp. 118–144). New York: Free Press. (Original work published 1908)

Spezzano, C. (1998). The triangle of clinical judgment. *Journal of the American Psychoanalytic Association, 46,* 365–388.

Stolorow, R., & Atwood, G. (1992). *Contexts of being: The intersubjective foundations of psychological life.* Hillsdale, NJ: Analytic Press.

Tillman, J. (1999). Religious language in psychotherapy: Dyadic and triadic configurations. *Psychoanalytic Psychology, 16,* 389–402.

Widlöcher, D. (2004). The third in mind. *Psychoanalytic Quarterly, 73,* 197–213.

Zeddies, T. (2001). On the wall or in the ointment?: The psychoanalytic community as a third presence in the consulting room. *Contemporary Psychoanalysis, 37,* 133–147.

Zwiebel, R. (2004). The third position: Reflections about the internal analytic working process. *Psychoanalytic Quarterly, 73,* 215–265.

Chapter 7
System Pressures, Ethics, and Autonomy

Marilyn Charles, PhD

At the Austen Riggs Center we rely on patient authority to preserve the open setting. Our patients' willingness to take on the challenges and responsibilities of citizenship in the therapeutic community—and the larger community in which it is embedded—enables us to work together without bars or locks. Patients arrive often having been labeled "treatment resistant." This label can connote noncompliance, but it can also mark the complexity of the trouble and a resistance to being objectified in ways that are dehumanizing. The process of failing to derive benefit from treatment can itself be discouraging and disheartening, at times adding to a view of self as victim rather than encouraging an interest in understanding one's own participation in the persistence of the distress. Such patients pose a different problem than those who more actively seek assistance for a problem they designate as their own (Barker, 2001).

For those for whom outpatient and inpatient treatments have failed, it is likely that the problems are complex. Coming from a psychodynamically informed systems perspective, we assume that these problems can be best understood in the context of the life narrative in which they are embedded. As we attempt to consider more broadly the contexts in which the individual has become mired, we at times come up against ideas regarding current "standards of care" that define and prescribe certain ways of viewing patients and of attending to their distress that may be too simplistic to facilitate the growth and development of that individual. In this chapter I discuss how current ideas about standards of care may insufficiently take into account the importance of the patient's authority—and the therapist's own standards—in helping an individual to make sense of life and experience, and how facing this dilemma head on can reduce resistance.

IS THE STANDARD OF CARE A FLOOR OR CEILING?

As psychodynamic health care providers, we find ourselves at a critical juncture in which we are enjoined to practice in accord with the standards defined by our various guilds. In an era of concern about cost of treatment, however, managed care drives pressures to provide minimum treatment, and also a preference for evidence-based practice. Such standards often represent a floor rather than ceiling in terms of our own ideas regarding best practice. Efforts to oversee the quality of psychological services and to provide standards and accountability have proved problematic in a field in which diversity of practice has been the norm, and the variables are complex and difficult to quantify. As demands for financial accountability increased, "evidence-based medicine" became the buzzwords, and randomized controlled trials (RCTs) began to be valued over other types of evidence that were pejoratively viewed as anecdotal or unscientific. Countering the tendency to view RCTs as the gold standard of evidence in health care, some voices have cautioned against favoring this type of evaluation research over modes of observational study that may be closer to the actual events and behaviors under consideration (Sacks, Chalmers, & Smith, 1982; Westen, Novotny, & Thompson-Brenner, 2004; White & Stancombe, 2002).

More pointedly, Borkovec and Castonguay (1998) suggest that the attempt to validate such complex questions may, in and of itself, be misguided. These authors encourage researchers to think in terms of validation of basic questions regarding the nature of psychological problems and of therapeutic change mechanisms to build a body of data that can inform the larger questions regarding the potential efficacy of one treatment versus another in a given instance. Similarly, Westen et al. (2004) advocate a move away from research focused on validating treatment packages and toward the empirical testing of intervention strategies and theories of change that can be *integrated* "into *empirically informed treatments*" (p. 658, italics in original). Research sponsored by the National Institute of Mental Health (NIMH) has shown that some of the major assumptions guiding current efforts toward identifying types of treatment are flawed, and that type of treatment and symptom reduction are not the most useful measures of efficacy (Blatt & Zuroff, 2005). Rather, these authors' data show that the primary mutative factors in brief outpatient treatment of, for example, serious depression are the quality of the therapeutic relationship established very early in treatment and the personality characteristics of the patient pretreatment. Regarding outcome measures, these authors suggest that "evaluation of therapeutic gain, in addition to symptom reduction, should include assessments of the reduction of the vulnerability to depression and the development of resilience as expressed in increased adaptive capacities in the ability to manage stressful life events" (p. 479).

Empirically *informed* treatment may be our best goal (Marquis & Douthit, 2006). However, with rising health care costs and the increasing presence of managed care in the United States, the trend is increasingly toward evidence-based practice and toward prescriptive practice guidelines (Nathan, 2004). This tendency toward reductionism in health care can be short-sighted and costly if we are not attentive to the longer-term sequelae of interventions that may offer the type of resilience suggested by Blatt and Zuroff's (2005) findings. As clinical practice is increasingly impacted by external pressures that invite short-term solutions and quick fixes, the demands of the systems created to enforce accountability can conflict with clinicians' standards regarding quality of care, as our idealization of science threatens to obscure more humanistic values (Peterson, 2004).

> In managing tensions between scientific and humanistic aims and values, attention to the authority of the patient is crucial to optimize outcomes with treatment-resistant patients.

Although scientific and humanistic values at times seem to oppose one another, psychology is inevitably pluralistic, according to Peterson (2004), such that the resolution of tensions between science and practice is furthered by valuing the knowledge offered by science while also "acknowledging that some problems confronting practitioners are inaccessible to rigorous inquiry and require alternative, primarily humanistic approaches" (p. 196). McWilliams (2005) endorses the importance of *humanity* as a core value in psychotherapy practice. She suggests that this core value is in danger of becoming lost under the weight of current tendencies to frame psychotherapy not in terms of understanding or accommodating to painful realities, but rather the attempt to "medicate, manage, reeducate, control, and correct the irrational behavior of people whose suffering is inconvenient to the larger culture" (p. 140). At Riggs we are mindful of how attempts to manage patient behavior may not only be dehumanizing, but may also interfere with the patient's competent self-management. We can see this type of tension in relation to self-destructive behaviors, such as substance abuse, where the therapist's movement into a managerial position can invite the patient to focus on opposing this management rather than to reflect on the meanings of this stance and the consequences in terms of his or her own well-being.

> With treatment-resistant patients the standard of care is a floor and not a ceiling.

The press from evidence-based practice is toward models that are more easily validated but may be simplistic and miss important elements relevant to an individual's well-being. In this era of increasing bureaucratic regulation of health care, one hazard is that the important regulatory functions of dialogue are threatened as we move toward dichotomous thinking regarding empirical support or empirical validation as a greater than warranted endorsement of efficacy (Westen et al., 2004). The divergence between ideas about best practice that are culled from research versus those culled from clinical experience may pose particular problems for the clinician who works with individuals with complex symptom pictures and multiple comorbid disorders, such as those labeled treatment resistant. For such individuals, there is no easy match between problem and solution. Rather, the problem marks the need for further inquiry to achieve greater understanding of where the trouble lies. In this way the therapist moves from the role of problem solver into a less defined but more expansive attitude that acknowledges both the complexity of the problem and the importance of the patient's agency and authority to any viable long-term resolution. As noted in Chapter 1, transformation of a highly comorbid treatment-resistant patient into an individual who can take charge of his or her life requires a relationship in which the psychological meaning embedded within symptoms and character structure can be deciphered. This translation process requires what Muller refers to as the Third: a triadic structure that grounds the therapeutic dyad within a system of rules.

Although we might contest any particular facts within a given system, the system itself, in Muller's view, comes to represent the possibility of an absolute truth that can be appealed to and affirmed. In some ways, the current trend toward evidence-based practice is an appeal to just such a Third to provide basic standards to help us ground our work. And yet, our need for the Third that can stand for a universal truth at times stands in uneasy relation to our need to be in dialogue with any individual truth. This means that, as professionals, we cannot abdicate our responsibility to remain in active dialogue with whatever standards are in place. For those of us who work intensively with small samples of highly comorbid treatment-resistant patients, the evidence from our practice may at times be at odds with research evidence culled from trials that carefully select patients with more responsive disorders and no comorbidity. If we are lax in our obligation to actively and reflectively weigh a range of evidence—including contextual factors and patient values—in our professional decisions, our standards may then be increasingly impacted by research based on clinical populations that bear little relation to the more complex symptom pictures often encountered in clinical practice (Levant, 2004; Westen et al., 2004).

The evidence from practice with treatment-resistant patients may be at odds with research evidence from trials that carefully select patients with more responsive disorders and no comorbidity.

THE IMPACT OF LITIGATION

The view from within clinical practice can be very different from an outside view. Without active dialogue with practitioners, professional regulatory boards may develop standards that have more relevance to fears ensuing from litigation than to the actual practice of the profession. One practitioner who spent many years on a professional ethics board noted that evidence tended to be weighed very differently depending on the observer's perspective. Whereas an overabundance of material in a complaint might signal to a clinician the possibility of an Axis II disorder affecting the perspective of the complainant, for nonclinicians this same weightiness of the file might suggest legitimacy. The practitioner's experience, along with others who have felt caught up in systems that seemed unrelenting, unreflective, and unresponsive, was of a growing tendency to apply standards arbitrarily. This tendency seems to be opposed by efforts, such as those of Bennett and his colleagues (2006), to encourage clinicians to *recognize* sources of risk rather than necessarily avoid them. This type of handbook encourages clinicians to think about how they might work with more complex symptom pictures, such as those offered by patients labeled "treatment resistant," without feeling as though that very work might put them in undue jeopardy. Because there can be different vantage points that may at times be difficult to reconcile, it is increasingly important for clinicians to find ways to articulate their knowledge in dialogue with researchers or regulatory agents who may be less grounded in clinical facts.

Litigation also plays a role in encouraging reductionism in health care. Tensions between legal and ethical injunctions or between an external standard and an internal one can result in what Austin, Rankel, Kagan, Bergum, and Lemermeyer (2005) have termed "moral distress." These authors use this term to "describe one's reaction when one believes one knows the right thing to do but does not do it" (p. 198). This type of situation can result when there are competing values that are not easily recognized and worked through—as, for example, when a clinician is in the position of possibly recommending the care an insurance company will cover rather than advocating for alternative treatment that is not likely to be covered. When guidelines for care are created with research based on samples excluding treatment-resistant individuals with comorbid disorders, the guidelines for care may seem clearer and more straightforward than they are in practice with these patients.

In a phenomenological research study designed to encourage more reflective action, Austin and her colleagues (2005) interviewed mental health practitioners about their experiences of moral distress. Previous research had shown that psychologists may be even more deeply embedded in their ethical code when considering moral dilemmas than are physicians (Hadjistavropoulos, Malloy, Sharpe, & Fuchs-Lacelle, 2003). And yet, as the study by Austin and her colleagues highlights, our ethical codes cannot resolve all of our difficulties for us, particularly in our work with highly comorbid, treatment-resistant patients with complex symptom pictures.

As we work with patients with greater comorbidity, we can also run into differences of perspective between the various guilds involved in a case. Medication, for example, might be very differently viewed by the psychiatrist versus the psychologist, making dialogue within treatment teams critically important to avoid splitting and exacerbating whatever dilemmas are already in place regarding the patient's relationships to medication, diagnosis, and identity (see Chapter 3). Even within guilds, increasingly we are seeing guidelines such that diagnosis can dictate treatment rather than guide it. One of the strengths of the approach at Riggs is the provision of a space within which patients can consider questions that might be difficult to entertain without such a holding environment. One example of this dilemma at Riggs occurs when a patient with a history of psychosis desires a trial off medication. The idea of stopping medication that has helped to relieve highly problematic symptoms can and should raise the anxiety and concern of staff members who have worked with the patient through difficult times. The treatment team, then, can provide a space in which patient and staff concerns can be considered collectively and respectfully. This type of dialogue both encourages and models greater reflectivity at times when affect is mobilized, the type of important adaptive function that the independent practitioner models in her or his determination to talk through difficult issues with the patient rather than preemptively foreclosing such conversations by setting a limit prematurely.

One patient, for example, had a history of psychosis that included alarming levels of suicidal ideation and hopelessness. As the patient improved over time and became increasingly coherent, reflective, and goal-directed, she wondered whether or not she still needed the medications that had been extremely helpful, but also carried deleterious side effects. One aspect of this question seemed to be the extent to which she could trust and rely on her own mind. She came to her treatment team asking for a trial without medication while she still had the resources of Riggs available to her. This request raised anxiety, particularly from nursing staff who had seen this patient through troubled times, but also from psychiatrists, for whom taking a previously psychotic person off medication potentially opposed the standard of care in work with such patients. Ongoing discussion ensued as we tried to grapple with the competing values of standard of care, past difficulty with adherence to medication trials that was part of the reason she was referred to Riggs, some uncertainty about her diagnosis, and the strong value we place on patient authority. Was a negotiated trial off medication a foolhardy flirtation with the risk of relapse or suicide? Was such a trial while she was still at Riggs a useful way to form an alliance with the patient to explore the legitimate question of her diagnosis and the need for the medication indefinitely? Were there really clear benefits to continuing the medication indefinitely that outweighed the associated adverse effects of weight gain and cognitive and emotional numbing? Was it the best way to work within an alliance that respected the patient's voice and the reality that, if her preference were ignored, once discharged she might arbitrarily conduct a trial off medication on her own? Resolving these questions in a way that satisfies and respects the input of all members of a treatment team, including the patient, requires faith and a relational matrix within which a decision can be made about whether stopping medication is a viable choice of the patient or an unacceptably risky one with which the treatment team cannot agree. A patient might competently choose to reject the team's treatment recommendation, but that would inevitably signal the need for discussion about whether the patient were choosing to end the treatment with the treatment team, and choose treatment elsewhere with other providers. Ongoing dialogue is an important facet of the process of internalizing the ambivalence about two courses of action that each carries risks and benefits. Treatment teams at Riggs are the loci of such dialogues, as Krikorian and Fowler note in Chapter 13, much as private practitioners may develop formal or informal consultative processes comparable to teams, depending on their treatment settings.

As is evident from the previous example, in our increasingly complex world, our desire for simple solutions may not well serve our patients or our profession in the long run. Fear tends to mobilize affect at the expense of cognition, further exacerbating the urge to find simple solutions to the challenges we face. This type of fear might result, for example, in another patient surreptitiously refusing to take his medications, thereby avoiding the type of open discussion and supporting structure the patient in the previous example was able to utilize as she explored her questions regarding the extent to which antipsychotic medication was or was not of benefit to her. We face real risks in our work. To the extent that we can face them together with our patients, we develop relational safeguards. In isolation, however, we can become as caught as the patient who hides his or her own true desires, without the benefit of discourse with other professionals to help us perhaps better see what we might be missing.

Another hazard for us as professionals is that of becoming caught in a web in which fear of litigation pushes us toward applying rules simplistically rather than using our professional expertise to guide us in interpreting standards. Concerns over risk management can push us toward actions that may seem to be in line with recognized standards, and yet "whatever general rules may apply in treatment, ultimately you have to make decisions based on sound clinical judgment for the particular patient" (Bennett et al., 2006, p. 169). To the extent that we abdicate our important executive functions as mental health professionals, the legal profession or regulatory agencies may be pulled in to arbitrate differences in ways that further increase our desire to find a set of standards or rules that might keep us safe from such scrutiny.

> In difficult treatments, fear in the treater mobilizes affect at the expense of cognition, exacerbating the urge to find simple solutions to complex challenges.

This desire may set us off on an illusory search that undermines our professionalism. Ethical and legal requirements may collide in ways that require the professional to mindfully make difficult judgments (Knapp, Berman, Gottlieb, & Handelsman, 2007). At times it may be the ethical guidelines themselves that are in competition—as, for example, when the principles of beneficence and nonmalfeasance are at odds with respect for patient autonomy (Knapp & Vandecreek, 2007). It is particularly easy when working with treatment-resistant patients to move toward believing that beneficence has greater value than respect for patient autonomy, and yet this very move may endanger whatever fragile autonomy and ego integrity are nascent within that individual.

> With treatment-resistant patients it is easy to believe that beneficence has greater value than respect for patient autonomy, and yet this tendency endangers whatever fragile autonomy and ego integrity are nascent within the individual.

Not only are we at risk to become caught between differing values across belief systems, we also can become mired in disputes over petty differences that may obscure rather than illuminate the essential dilemmas. In spite of theories that warn of the hazards of fragmentation and splitting, psychodynamic clinicians have found it difficult to work together to enhance our understanding of the perils and pitfalls of being a professional—and of being a patient—in these trying times. Increasingly, psychodynamic psychotherapy itself becomes marginalized as we fight over small differences rather than unify around common goals and values. Opposing this tendency, researchers are rising to a growing challenge to provide data that might affirm what clinicians have learned in the consulting room about the benefits of long-term psychodynamic therapy. And yet, in spite of extensive data validating not only psychodynamic therapeutic approaches (Fonagy & Bateman, 2007; Levy et al., 2006; Milrod et al., 2007), but also the greater effectiveness of long-term over short-term treatment (Leichsenring & Rabung, 2008), somehow we have not managed to put forward this information in convincing ways in American culture. As a result, we not only see psychodynamic therapy being undervalued, we also see psychodynamic training being increasingly undervalued in our training programs (Downing, Greenlee, & Luria, 2007; Plakun, 2006; McWilliams, 2005).

To counter these deficits, clinicians are reaching across fragmented lines of communication to offer views affirming the benefits of psychodynamic understanding. In this book we are attempting to speak to some aspects of this complexity, noting the importance not only of the therapeutic dyad, but also of the supporting structures in which those dyads are embedded and the histories and traditions being articulated through complex symptom pictures.

We are well advised to think about our own professional and personal identities and the impact on identity of the multiple layerings of systems in which we are embedded. The stakes are high when working with highly comorbid, treatment-resistant patients, increasing anxiety and burden not only for the treater but also for the supporting structures of relationships in which he or she is embedded. The better we understand the various perspectives and the ways in which anxiety is triggered or mobilized from those positions, the more competent we become at navigating difficult terrain. In this work, respect is a key issue, not only respect for the patient's perspective, but also respect for whatever anxieties are being triggered among treaters that might offer useful information.

One arena in which our desire to be respectful of the patient's autonomy may put us up against some of the standards promoted by findings of research from more traditional evidence-based practice is in relation to substance use disorders. In this area, Melnick, Wexler, and Cleland (2008) assert that not only is there a strong presumption from some quarters of the substance abuse field that abstinence is an essential component of well-being, but also that acknowledgment of disparate views regarding the importance of abstinence may actually be detrimental for those who have had substance use disorders. To the extent that this characterization is true and representative of the standard of care in the field, the standard of care with respect to substance use disorders may be oversimplified. At Riggs, in contrast, we rely on open discussion of varying points of view as a means for encouraging the individual to make better choices with regard to his or her well-being. This view is in line with Tucker and Roth's (2006) review of that literature: "Given its developmental status, the substance abuse field cannot afford a view of evidence that is overly restrictive in focus and methodology. We should resist following the narrow dictates of the early EBP [evidence-based practice] movement and the surrounding 'experimental culture' that elevated treatment outcome research using the RCT and the standardized treatment manual above all else" (p. 929). In line with others who have argued against the privileging of RCT data (Concato, Shah, & Horowitz, 2000; Westen et al., 2004), Tucker and Roth argue for a broader view that includes attention to the wider intra- and interpersonal contextual influences affecting behavior over time.

At Riggs we try to leave room for individuals to learn about the behaviors that have plagued them. Thus, although we ask patients to be substance abstinent for 30 days before admission, and we have a strict rule prohibiting the sharing of substances with other patients with substance use disorders, when it comes to the use of substances by patients at Riggs, we recognize that people may well exhibit the behaviors that have brought them here. Our hope is that the individual will utilize the resources at Riggs and in the larger community (e.g., AA meetings) to learn something about these behaviors and their meanings, and so begin to put their feelings into words rather than continuing to act them out in self-destructive ways. Coming up against the edge of one's own ambivalence regarding giving up self-destructive behavior can be a crucial fulcrum that makes real change possible. If one cannot come up against one's own edge, it is easy to displace the dilemma and oppose whatever force is mandating change. One of the essential tenets of the open setting is that to the extent that individuals can encounter, over time and in treatment, the consequences of their actions, they are in a better position to use whatever resources might be needed in order to change. A second tenet, of course, is that patients cannot be prevented by us from destroying their chance for treatment at Riggs, including through substance use, and we may come to the limit of our ability to watch the above-described struggles unfold.

Given these tenets, we inevitably come up against our own edges in relation to a culture in which hospital-level care tends to signify locked units to which individuals are admitted precisely *because* they cannot be expected to keep themselves or others safe—a culture with increasingly codified ideas regarding best practice. As psychodynamic practitioners we spend a good portion of our lives firmly ensconced in psychic reality and are, to some extent, out of touch with a culture that tends to favor quick fixes and biological models. Psychodynamic practitioners, however, also tend to see a certain subsection of the population for whom biological psychiatry and short-term treatment have not been sufficient. Collectively, we know a great deal about what does and does not work for those more treatment-resistant patients. Translating that knowledge into terms accessible to the larger culture, however, has not been easy. To the extent that we believe we have something of value to offer, it behooves us to increase our efforts at constructive dialogue, not merely with those who already agree with us but, more importantly, with those with whom we might have a useful cross-pollination of ideas.

Having spent most of my professional life in private practice, being part of a therapeutic community has afforded the opportunity to extend my knowledge and challenge my assumptions. At Riggs we rely on the principle of "examined living" to promote growth in the individual and in the community as a whole. Being part of a community in which all members are working at achieving greater understanding and attempting to articulate what they know means that one is continually coming upon conjectures and certainties different from one's own. Experiencing how projections can take on a life of their own, mobilizing affect and action, is a powerful reminder to monitor one's own level of arousal and to pause most deeply exactly when one feels most mobilized to speak. Community living gives a powerful reference point for the principles and theories we learn from Bion, Klein, and others who write of unconscious, at times psychotic, mechanisms within individuals and within groups (Bion, 1961, 1967; Klein, 1935/1975a, 1946/1975b, 1952/1975c; Obholzer & Roberts, 1994). Lest one think that these forces are only or most particularly at work in a therapeutic community, my colleagues who work in business or academic settings report similar phenomena, but fewer opportunities to speak to group dynamics or resolve them.

Pulling out to the larger frame of the position of psychodynamic practitioners in relation to current culture, it is important to note that we are in a minority position. In this way, we tend to be marginalized and to contribute to that marginalization in various ways, as we develop more and more refined and therefore exclusive ways of speaking to one another.

From this position it is easy to feel persecuted and to behave in reactive ways, demonizing the other much as we feel demonized. Much as speech can be impeded as groups get larger, so, too, speech is impeded as projections become amplified. An antidote to this dilemma is to find ways to speak to whomever has become Other, so as to break through the projections and find a common language.

Mental health practitioners have more in common than not. We all inhabit a culture in which our knowledge about the impact of distress on the individual mounts while the resources devoted to attenuating or preventing that distress decrease. If psychodynamic clinicians could pool resources, we might be able to do what our colleagues in Germany, Canada, etc., have managed to do: Articulate the importance of our work sufficiently so that those who manage the resources begin to take notice in ways that have a greater impact systemically on those we are trying to treat. As we become more aware of the diverse factors affecting treatment effectiveness, it will be important to keep open the reflective space in which we can consider alternatives in relation to the individual with whom we are working. This openness and attention to the relational elements may be particularly important in our efforts to help treatment-resistant patients develop greater resilience, thereby enhancing their reflective function and the ability to make constructive sense of life and experience. That particular standard may be one on which we can all agree.

REFERENCES

Austin, W., Rankel, M., Kagan, L., Bergum, V., & Lemermeyer, G. (2005). To stay or to go, to speak or to stay silent, to act or to not act: Moral distress as experienced by psychologists. *Ethics and Behavior, 15,* 197–212.

Barker, P. (2001). The ripples of knowledge and the boundaries of practice: The problem of evidence in psychotherapy research. *International Journal of Psychotherapy, 6,* 11–23.

Bennett, B. E., Bricklin, P. M., Harris, E., Knapp, S., VandeCreek, L., & Younggren, J. N. (2006). *Assessing and managing risk in psychological practice.* Rockville, MD: The Trust.

Bion, W. R. (1961). *Experiences in groups and other papers.* London/New York: Routledge.

Bion, W. R. (1967). *Second thoughts: Selected papers on psycho-analysis.* London: Heinemann.

Blatt, S. J., & Zuroff, D. C. (2005). Empirical evaluation of the assumptions in identifying evidence based treatments in mental health. *Clinical Psychology Review, 25*, 459–486.

Borkovec, T. D., & Castonguay, L. G. (1998). What is the scientific meaning of empirically supported therapy? *Journal of Consulting and Clinical Psychology, 66*, 136–142.

Concato, J., Shah, N., & Horowitz, R. I. (2000). Randomized, controlled trials, observational studies, and the hierarchy of research designs. *New England Journal of Medicine, 342*, 1887–1892.

Downing, D. L., Greenlee, T. M., & Louria, S. (2007). *Psychoanalytical training opportunities in pre-doctoral internships: Opportunities and challenges.* Unpublished manuscript.

Fonagy, P., & Bateman, A. W. (2007). Mentalizing and borderline personality disorder. *Journal of Mental Health, 16*, 83–101.

Hadjistavropoulos, T., Malloy, D., Sharpe, D., & Fuchs-Lacelle, S. (2003). The ethical ideologies of psychologists and physicians: A preliminary comparison. *Ethics and Behavior, 13*, 87–104.

Klein, M. (1975a). A contribution to the psychogenesis of manic–depressive states. In *Love, guilt and reparation and other works, 1921–1945* (pp. 262–289). London: Hogarth Press. (Original work published in 1935)

Klein, M. (1975b). Notes on some schizoid mechanisms. In *Envy and gratitude and other works, 1946–1963* (pp. 1–24). London: Hogarth Press. (Original work published 1946)

Klein, M. (1975c). Some theoretical conclusions regarding the emotional life of the infant. In *Envy and gratitude and other works, 1946–1963* (pp. 61–93). London: Hogarth Press. (Original work published 1952)

Knapp, S., Berman, J., Gottlieb, M., & Handelsman, M. M. (2007). When law and ethics collide: What should psychologists do? *Professional Psychology: Research and Practice, 38*, 54–59.

Knapp, S., & Vandecreek, L. (2007). Balancing respect for autonomy with competing values with the use of principle-based ethics. *Psychotherapy: Theory, Research, Practice, Training, 44*, 397–404.

Leichsenring, F., & Rabung, S. (2008). Effectiveness of long-term psychodynamic psychotherapy. *Journal of American Medical Association, 300*(13), 1551–1565.

Levant, R. F. (2004). The empirically validated treatments movement: A practitioner/educator perspective. *Clinical Psychology: Science and Practice, 11*(2), 219–224

Levy, K. N., Meehan, K. B., Kelly, K. M., Reynoso, J. S., Weber, M., Clarkin, J. F., et al. (2006). Change in attachment patterns and reflective function in a randomized control trial of transference-focused psychotherapy for borderline personality disorder. *Journal of Consulting and Clinical Psychology, 74,* 1027–1040.

Marquis, A., & Douthit, K. (2006). The hegemony of "empirically supported treatment": Validating or violating? *Constructivism in the Human Sciences, 11,* 108–141.

McWilliams, N. (2005). Preserving our humanity as therapists. *Psychotherapy: Theory, Research, Practice, Training, 42,* 139–151.

Melnick, G., Wexler, H. K., & Cleland, C. M. (2008). Client consensus on beliefs about abstinence: Effects on substance abuse treatment outcomes. *Drug and Alcohol Dependence, 93,* 30–37.

Milrod, B., Leon, A.C., Busch, F., Rudden, M., Schwalberg, M., Clarkin, J., et al. (2007). A randomized controlled trial of psychoanalytic psychotherapy for panic disorder. *American Journal of Psychiatry, 164,* 265–272.

Nathan, P. E. (2004). When science takes us only so far. *Clinical Psychology: Science and Practice, 11,* 216–218.

Obholzer, A., & Roberts, V. Z. (1994). *The unconscious at work: Individual and organizational stress in the human services.* New York: Brunner–Routledge.

Peterson, D. R., (2004). Science, scientism, and professional responsibility. *Clinical Psychology: Science and Practice, 11,* 196–210.

Plakun, E. M. (2006). Finding psychodynamic psychiatry's lost generation. *Journal of the American Academy of Psychoanalysis and Dynamic Psychiatry. 34,* 135–150.

Sacks, H., Chalmers, I., & Smith, H., Jr. (1982). Randomized versus historical controls for clinical trials. *American Journal of Medicine, 72,* 233–240.

Tucker, J. A., & Roth, D. L. (2006). Extending the evidence hierarchy to enhance evidence-based practice for substance use disorders. *Addiction, 101,* 918–932.

Westen, D., Novotny, C. M., & Thompson-Brenner, H. (2004). The empirical status of empirically supported psychotherapies: Assumptions, findings, and reporting in controlled clinical trials. *Psychological Bulletin, 130,* 631–663.

White, S., & Stancombe, J. (2002). Colonizing care?: Potentialities and pitfalls of scientific–bureaucratic rationality in social care. *Journal of Social Work Research and Evaluation, 3,* 187–202.

—◄✕✕✕►—

Chapter 8
An Alliance-Based Intervention for Suicide

Eric M. Plakun, MD

Suicide has become an issue with global geopolitical meaning, with suicide bombers an everyday aspect of terrorism, high rates of suicide in parts of the developing world (e.g., among rural women in China), headlines in this country about a high rate of suicide among active duty armed forces or veterans of Middle East conflicts, and an increase in suicide among adolescents and young adults. Globally, close to 1 million people die annually of suicide according to World Health Organization statistics. Yet, beyond these global and epidemiological perspectives lies the reality that each suicide is a human tragedy involving a usually unnecessary death that also affects a network of surviving individuals. Although many emphasize the importance of epidemiological perspectives and public health harm reduction strategies to decrease suicide, our clinical work, focused on intervening to save one life at a time, is congruent with the reality that over 80% of those who die by suicide have mental disorders.

There is no more serious problem faced by mental health clinicians than the risk of the death of a patient by suicide. Suicide is not only a tragedy with a devastating effect on the patient, family members, and friends, but also may have a significantly distressing impact on clinicians. Hendin, Haas, Maltsberger, Szanto, and Rabinowicz (2004) report that 38% of psychiatrists who lost a patient to suicide experienced severe distress. Clinician responses to patient suicide include isolation from colleagues, guilt, shame, fear of litigation, anger, a sense of betrayal, grief, self-doubt, strained relationships with colleagues, withdrawal from other patients, and doubts about continuing to work in psychiatry or with suicidal patients (Hendin et al., 2004; Plakun & Tillman, 2005; Tillman, 2006). In recognition of the significant impact of suicide on psychiatrists, in 2007 the American Psychiatric Association Assembly passed an action paper officially naming patient suicide as an occupational hazard for psychiatrists, and the APA has made resources available on its website for psychiatrists who experience the loss of a patient by suicide. Clinicians from a number of mental health disciplines have begun offering panels at professional meetings to discuss the impact of suicide on clinicians.

A central component of providing adequate clinical treatment to patients who struggle with suicide is treating underlying Axis I and II disorders, such as schizophrenia, mood, substance use, anxiety, or personality disorders. Among the most suicidal patients are those with treatment-refractory mood disorders comorbid with borderline or other personality disorders, for whom most treatment most of the time occurs in outpatient or other unrestrictive settings. For example, Neves, Malloy-Diniz, and Correa (2009) report that in patients with bipolar disorder the presence of comorbid borderline personality disorder is the most significant factor increasing suicide risk, and comorbid alcoholism increases the risk of violent suicide.

This chapter focuses on what we are learning about treating suicidal patients in the open setting of Riggs, with a particular emphasis on extracting central psychotherapeutic principles that may be of use to those treating these patients in outpatient or other unrestrictive settings. The hope is that this will help clinicians improve their ability to work with suicidal patients, while reducing the risk of experiencing the death of a patient by suicide—although this risk is never zero. In fact, the best estimates suggest that psychiatrists face a 50% risk of having the experience of a patient suicide during a career, with the risk remaining at 50% for additional suicides if one has already occurred (Chemtob, Bauer, Hamada, Pelowski, & Muraoka, 1989). It is this reality that underlies forensic psychiatrist Robert Simon's (2004) observation that there are two kinds of psychiatrists: those who have had a patient commit suicide and those who will.

In Chapter 1 we presented data about what we know regarding the effectiveness of Riggs treatment of suicidal patients (Perry et al., 2009). As noted, over 75% of previously suicidal patients recovered from suicidal behavior within 7 years, with a low overall suicide rate in the sample. Although the absence of a control group receiving an alternate treatment confounds our ability to claim that Riggs treatment was the cause of this improvement, we believe a reasonable clinician would consider it likely that Riggs treatment played a significant role in reversing the downward trajectory of the lives of these patients, and in helping them recover from the brink of suicide.

Several psychotherapeutic approaches to treating suicidal borderline patients have been studied and found to be efficacious. The most widely known are Linehan's dialectical behavioral therapy (DBT; Linehan Armstrong, Suarez, Alman, & Heard,1991) and Kernberg's transference-focused psychotherapy (TFP; Clarkin, Levy, Lenzenweger, & Kernberg, 2007; Yeomans, Clarkin, & Kernberg, 2002). Here I am introducing an approach that many of us at Riggs use for establishing and maintaining a viable therapeutic alliance with highly comorbid suicidal patients with both mood and personality disorders. Faced with the challenge of treating these high-risk patients while a trainee at Riggs over 30 years ago, I became curious about defining what senior clinicians seemed to know that I did not, and so I began to observe their work to extract the principles they seemed to follow. I have been presenting workshops and courses on these principles in working with suicidal and self-destructive borderline patients for more than 20 years at annual meetings of the American Psychiatric Association and elsewhere, and aspects of the approach have been described in three publications (Plakun, 1993, 1994, 2001). In negotiation with staff at Riggs, I have come to call the approach Alliance-Based Intervention for Suicide, or ABIS. ABIS has similarities with, and differences from, DBT and TFP.

Although DBT is not a psychodynamic psychotherapy, but rather a cognitive–behavioral therapy that focuses on skills training to improve a patient's capacity to manage and contain affect states without self-destructive action, it shares with ABIS and TFP use of and attention to the therapeutic alliance in working with suicidal patients. TFP is a psychodynamic treatment approach, but it differs from ABIS in being an independent, stand-alone, manualized form of psychodynamic psychotherapy. TFP shares with ABIS and DBT careful attention to the establishment and maintenance of the therapeutic alliance as an important component of the treatment. However, TFP focuses primarily on the resolution and consolidation of identity diffusion in borderline patients through identification and interpretation of past conflicted object relationship dyads and their associated affects, and on interpretation of shifts in the nature of the operational object relationship dyad that emerges within the transference relationship. Like ABIS and DBT, in TFP suicide is addressed as a therapy-interfering behavior.

This convergence of points of view about treatment approaches to suicidal patients coming from three separate groups of clinicians with divergent theoretical orientations is unusual and has been noticed elsewhere in the field. Currently, the Group for the Advancement of Psychiatry (GAP) psychotherapy committee is undertaking an effort to explore what these approaches have in common and how they differ, in the hope of improving psychotherapeutic treatment of suicidal patients. Recently Weinberg et al. (2010) have reported on similarities and differences between approaches to suicide, including DBT, TFP, mentalization-based therapy (MBT), schema-focused therapy (SFT), and CBT. They report considerable convergence among the disparate points of view, including clarity of treatment framework, an agreed-upon strategy for suicide management, close attention to affect, a relatively active therapist, and an emphasis on exploratory and change-oriented interventions.

ALLIANCE-BASED INTERVENTION FOR SUICIDE

As noted, ABIS is quite intentionally not conceptualized as a separate, stand-alone treatment, but rather as an aspect of psychodynamic psychotherapy that focuses on establishing and maintaining a viable therapeutic alliance with suicidal patients so that the central interpretive work of psychodynamic psychotherapy can proceed. Unlike TFP and MBT, the other arguably psychodynamic therapies, ABIS is not manualized. Also unlike these other therapies, ABIS has not been subject to randomized efficacy trials. Other kinds of evidence suggesting the utility of ABIS have been described above.

One advantage of manualization is its potential to support adherence to a form of therapy among those trained in the use of the manual. With ABIS it is the treatment culture of Riggs, with its educational program, supervision, clinical case conferences, and staff discussions among a group of full-time doctoral-level staff therapists, rather than manualization, that help ensure a relatively uniform approach to treating suicidal patients. Another advantage is the ability manualization confers to carry out randomized trials of adherent treatments with demonstrated efficacy. This has been particularly valuable for such psychodynamic therapies as TFP and MBT, which often face a field with disbelief about its merits. Disadvantages of manualization include a potential loss of spontaneity and flexibility in engagement of the patient, problems demonstrating adherence even with the existence of a manual, potential exclusion of patients with comorbidity, and the frequent practice of defining the manualized treatment as a stand-alone therapy—that only a handful of people know how to carry out. This latter issue, in particular, poses a part-versus-whole problem for TFP and MBT that seems to exclude these stand-alone psychodynamic therapies from the rest of psychodynamic therapy, with its long and complex history of teaching and technique.

THE THERAPEUTIC ALLIANCE

Before examining how ABIS emphasizes the use of the therapeutic alliance in work with suicidal patients, it is worth reviewing the history and evolution of the concept of the therapeutic alliance and defining it for the current purpose. Foreshadowing the use of the term, Freud (1912/1975) takes on the problem of transference serving both as resistance and as assistance in "Dynamics of the Transference." He notes that the transference is composed of a range of elements, some of which are easily seen as related to the notion of resistance, whereas others are aligned with the patient's perseverance in the treatment. Here Freud makes reference to "unobjectionable aspects of the positive transference." Elaboration of the notion of the therapeutic alliance came from Sterba (1934), Zetzel (1956), Greenson (1965/1978), Shapiro, Shapiro, Zinner, and Berkowitz (1977), among others

Sterba (1934) suggested that analysis could proceed only when part of the patient's ego entered an alliance with the analyst in opposition to instinct and repression. Zetzel (1966) suggested the therapeutic alliance precedes analysis and is distinct from and in opposition to the transference neurosis. Greenson (1965) preferred the term *working alliance* and, joining Zetzel, saw it as separate from the transference neurosis. Extending Sterba's notions, Greenson viewed the working alliance as a rational alliance between the patient's reasonable ego and the analyst's analyzing ego. Implementation of Greenson's concept of the working alliance led him to alter his analytic technique to include explanations, discussions of real problems without searching for unconscious determinants, and other deviations from complete neutrality and a strictly interpretive stance. Greenson (1965) defines the working alliance as "the relatively non neurotic, rational rapport which the patient has with his analyst" (p. 157). Shapiro and his colleagues emphasize that the alliance is a mutual commitment between therapist and patient to a work task, including agreement to try to hold a recollection of the role of the therapist as potentially helpful even in the face of the development of regressive negative transferences. In Chapter 6 of this volume, Muller notes that the alliance as "pact" is an aspect of the Third. Here Muller makes a point similar to Shapiro's: that for the patient the allegiance sought in the alliance is not to the therapist but to therapeutic task to which they are both subservient.

Introduction of the concept of the therapeutic or working alliance, however, was not uniformly greeted with enthusiasm. Some, like Brenner (1979), saw the concept as neither valid nor useful and as essentially a component of the transference. Many others, though, such as Gutheil and Havens (1979), and Meissner (1992, 1999), have argued for the value of the concept. Gutheil and Havens (1979, p. 479) suggest that the therapeutic alliance involves the "therapeutic split in the ego which allows the analyst to work with the healthier elements in the patient against resistance and pathology."

Addressing the subject of the therapeutic alliance, Meissner (1992) argues that the therapeutic relationship consists of three concurrent, distinguishable, but inevitably overlapping components: the transference, the real relationship, and the therapeutic alliance. The notion of the transference as projection into the therapist of elements of past relationships is clear enough, and the real relationship involves components of the reality of the person of the analyst (e.g., gender, age, ethnic traits) and his or her character, and the similar distinctive reality elements of the person of the patient. Meissner sees these two aspects of the relationship as distinct from the third part of the therapeutic relationship: the therapeutic alliance. As Meissner notes (1992, p. 1068): "The establishment and consolidation of a secure and firm alliance becomes a necessary condition for the more regressive emergence of more powerful, meaningful, and even dangerous transference dimensions. In such cases the alliance offers a safe context within which intense, powerful, and frightening transference derivatives can be allowed access to consciousness and analytic processing."

Meissner (1992) lists components of the therapeutic alliance as including empathy, freedom, trust, autonomy, initiative, ethics, the therapeutic framework, and the concepts of responsibility and authority in both analyst and patient, including the creation of a situation in which the patient becomes an "egalitarian participant in the process of discovering and understanding" (p. 1078). In his 1999 paper on the subject, Meissner notes that the alliance is interactive, suggesting that the "interpersonal dimension of the alliance elevates negotiation . . . to a central position in this process, allowing for meaningful contributions by both participants leading toward establishing a shared consensual reality" (pp. 5–6). Meissner goes on to suggest that the alliance requires the analyst to "adopt a firm and consistent position vis-à-vis the patient, holding him consistently responsible for participation in the therapeutic process" (p. 6).

Meissner notes that in the treatment of sicker patients, such as Winnicott's false self patients, the setting plays a more significant role than in work with neurotic patients, where interpretive work is primary. With false self patients environmental holding (and the therapeutic alliance is part of environmental holding) increases in importance. It seems reasonable to assume that suicidal, highly comorbid, previously treatment-refractory patients with significant Axis II pathology resemble Winnicott's false self patients more than the neurotic patients treated in classical analysis. Yet, much of the psychoanalytic theory and technique described in the analytic literature was written by those treating healthier neurotic patients. It is thus no surprise that theory largely derived from the treatment of healthier neurotic patients emphasizes interpretation and the transference neurosis, with the importance of environmental holding, including the therapeutic alliance, deemphasized because it could be largely taken for granted in work with these patients.

With a more impaired patient it cannot necessarily be comfortably assumed, in the same way as with a patient with neurotic pathology, that the patient is held by a reliable agreement or alliance in the service of doing the work. This is especially true of patients with prominent action defenses, including those struggling with suicide. From the perspective of descriptive psychiatry, many of these patients are those with treatment-refractory disorders comorbid with personality disorders. These patients often present with difficulties abstaining from impulsive action because action is their principal means of communicating distress (Shapiro & Plakun, 2008). They often have difficulties with basic trust because of early experiences of deprivation, abuse, or neglect, and have considerable difficulty developing the kind of "unobjectionable positive transference" to which Freud made reference. For these patients, a focus on the therapeutic alliance, which can often be taken for granted with higher-functioning analysands, becomes central. Hence, explicit efforts to establish and maintain an alliance are a key first step in moving them toward the possibility of settling into psychodynamic treatment by first focusing on their commitment to the work of therapy (even during regressive negative transference storms), and, as a result, to survival as a condition of treatment.

> The therapeutic alliance is the intentionally and explicitly negotiated agreement between the patient and the therapist to collaborate in the treatment task, to which they are both committed.

For the current purpose, I propose to define the therapeutic alliance as the intentionally and explicitly negotiated agreement between the patient and the therapist to collaborate in the treatment task, to which they are both committed. This agreement includes the patient's recognition that the therapist is separate, potentially helpful, and also committed and subservient to the task of treatment even when he or she seems least so. The therapeutic alliance (1) is predicated on the notion of mutual but differentiated responsibility for the treatment, (2) is a necessary but not sufficient condition for the treatment to occur, and (3) is aligned with those aspects of the transference that offer assistance rather than resistance to the therapeutic task. However, varying with Meissner, I suggest that, unlike transference and the real relationship, which are inevitable aspects of the therapeutic relationship, the therapeutic alliance is co-created by therapist and patient, is part of the transference and part of the real relationship, but cannot and should not be assumed to exist unless it is specifically and explicitly (or perhaps implicitly with healthier patients, e.g., candidates in analytic training) negotiated. The therapeutic alliance brings together the three components of work with treatment-refractory patients that have been emphasized in this volume: the importance of relationships in therapy; the recognition of, and respect for, the authority (and, with it, the responsibility) of the patient; and the importance of attending to the meaning of human interactions.

> ABIS engages suicide not as a symptom but as an interpersonal event that has meaning in the relationship and is outside the terms of the alliance.

One implication of this definition of the therapeutic alliance in work with a suicidal patient is that the work cannot proceed from the perspective that it is the therapist's job to keep the patient alive, while the patient holds the wish to die and may put this wish into action at any time. Instead, the alliance is based on a notion that the patient's commitment to the work of therapy, as signified by agreement to the terms of the alliance that authorize the work, comes with an unavoidable condition that being in treatment requires being alive. Only the patient has the capacity to keep him- or herself alive. Negotiation of a therapeutic alliance based on this stance is central to ABIS. It engages suicide not as a symptom but as an interpersonal event that has meaning in the relationship. Seen through the lens of the real relationship, suicide is conceptualized as a decision to end the therapy insofar as it is inconsistent with the mutually negotiated but nevertheless required terms of the therapeutic alliance. Seen through the lens of the transference, suicide has a discoverable but unconscious or unstated transference-based reason for being chosen over the terms of the therapeutic alliance (which require a commitment to the work of therapy), and it is considered an aspect of the patient's negative transference. Put another way, although the therapeutic alliance may represent, as Freud hinted, the unobjectionable part of the positive transference, suicide is the most objectionable part of the negative transference. Engagement of suicide as an aspect of the negative transference offers a useful opportunity in work with suicidal patients.

APPLYING THE PRINCIPLES OF ABIS IN WORK WITH SUICIDAL AND SELF-DESTRUCTIVE PATIENTS

As noted in Chapter 1, from a psychodynamic perspective, symptoms, including suicide and self-destructive behavior, may be viewed as encoded, nonverbal communications that have meaning. The meaning may be unconscious or in the realm of an unthought known (Bollas, 1987) or may even be conscious to the patient, but communication of the meaning occurs through actions instead of through words. The task of psychodynamic therapists is, in effect, to break the code and to translate the meaning in suicidal and self-destructive behavior into words. This translation allows the patient to communicate pain, despair, and rage verbally rather than behaviorally, in action, and acknowledge, bear, and put them into perspective. However, it is a sine qua non of engaging with suicidal patients in psychodynamic psychotherapy that they must first be out of an acute suicidal crisis and able to function more or less adaptively between sessions so that therapeutic work can take place. Psychodynamic therapists also have an obligation to face the meanings and associated affects that underlie suicidal behavior as they emerge in the transference. This implies a willingness to face murderous rage since, from a psychodynamic perspective, whatever other meaning it may have, suicide is a murderous act.

The goal of the first phase of psychodynamic work with suicidal and self-destructive patients is helping them gain control of, and develop the capacity to delay acting on, suicidal and self-destructive impulses. The principles of ABIS may help psychodynamic therapists and their patients avoid a cycle of chronic crisis management so that the pair can settle into and do the work of psychodynamic psychotherapy. The principles of ABIS may help dynamic therapists establish and maintain a viable therapeutic alliance with suicidal and self-destructive borderline patients, with or without other comorbid disorders, while using the vicissitudes of the alliance to notice, engage, and put into words the interpersonal meaning of suicide. The principles depend on negotiation of a therapeutic alliance that shifts suicide from a symptom to an interpersonal communication between therapist and patient that can ultimately be brought under the patient's conscious control if the positive transference attachment between patient and therapist is strong enough. Although the principles of ABIS are extracted from work in the intensive treatment setting of the hospital-based residential continuum of care at Riggs, with four-times-weekly psychotherapy, they have also been used successfully in once-weekly outpatient therapy with suicidal and self-destructive patients. Though often beneficial, ABIS is not effective with all patients, and always requires also treating associated comorbid conditions such as substance use and mood disorders. It is, of course, often the case that comorbid disorders have already been treated by the time a patient comes to psychotherapy and that pharmacological options for mood disorders have been largely depleted. ABIS can give the therapist traction around the issue of suicide, but it does not relieve the therapist from anxiety and vigilance vis-à-vis the patient's suicide risk. Table 8.1 lists the principles of ABIS described below.

Differentiate Consulting from Therapy

As used here, *therapy* implies a commitment from both parties to work together over time, whereas *consultation* does not. The significance of this distinction may be illustrated by noting how patients are admitted to Riggs. Given that most patients who seek Riggs treatment have failed prior treatments and often struggle with suicide as an issue, and, given the open, unrestrictive, fully voluntary milieu of Riggs, patients can be admit-

Table 8.1. Principles of ABIS

In an Alliance Based Intervention for Suicide, treatment works best when therapists:

- Differentiate consulting from therapy.
- Differentiate lethal from nonlethal behaviors.
- Include the patient's responsibility to stay alive as part of the therapeutic alliance.
- Nonpunitively interpret the patient's aggression in considering ending therapy through suicide.
- Contain and metabolize the countertransference.
- Hold the patient responsible for preservation of the therapy.
- Engage affect.
- Search for the perceived injury from the therapist that may have precipitated suicidal thoughts or behavior.
- Provide an opportunity for repair.

---

ted only after an admission consultation that assesses risks and benefits of treatment—but that also does more. In the admission consultation patients are clinically assessed and educated about the nature of the treatment program *and* about the expectations of and their responsibilities in the clinical culture they *may* be invited to enter. The consultation includes an assessment of their ability to join a tentative dynamic formulation of their difficulties, use trial interpretations, think psychologically, and speak authentically about their experience. A central component of the consultation is careful engagement of the limits of the prospective patient's capacity to be responsible for his or her safety in an open setting based on the previous pattern of suicidal or other potentially therapy-interfering behavior. For example, given a previous pattern of impulsive overdoses without informing his or her therapist, as a condition of this treatment in this setting, can the individual take responsibility for turning to others for help before carrying out impulsive self-destructive behavior again? How authentically does a patient respond to framing his or her responsibility for safety in this way? Ultimately, a patient is admitted only if it is the judgment of the admissions officer that he or she is clinically appropriate, and that an adequate initial therapeutic alliance has been negotiated. This kind of engagement of the patient in a consultation is illustrated in the case of Joe in Chapter 4.

Hence, the admission consultation takes place in a different relationship to Riggs than does treatment at Riggs—that is, outside versus inside

Riggs. This differentiation of a consultation from therapy also makes sense in outpatient practice. There is a difference between agreeing to conduct ongoing therapy and agreeing to meet with a patient for one or more consultations to determine whether therapy is potentially workable and to make clear what the differentiated responsibilities of each participant are. Consultations are scheduled as is convenient for therapist and patient, but there is no assumption in a consultation session that another will necessarily be scheduled. If the pair decides to work together, there is a shift from consulting to therapy. In therapy, whatever the frequency negotiated, sessions are 45 or 50 minutes long and scheduled at regular, ongoing, and predictable times. Such regularity of sessions helps hold the patient in a way that sessions scheduled at each meeting cannot. This distinction between consultation and therapy is an essential principle of ABIS.

The Terms of the Therapeutic Alliance

When therapy is established, it is bound and limited by the terms of the therapeutic alliance, as described above. These terms include an agreement that discovering the meaning of behavior is the work of therapy. My own preference, whether or not suicide is an issue, is to let patients know that I ask them to do four things as part of their responsibility in our shared task: come on time, leave on time, pay the bill, and speak about whatever is on their mind while they are in the sessions. These are offered as my expectations, given what I understand to be their interest in doing the work of therapy, but, except for payment of the bill, are not treated as absolute requirements. Identifying these and certain other expectations described below creates an opportunity to become curious about the meaning of behaviors that may interfere with any of the expectations.

Differentiate Lethal from Nonlethal Behaviors

Differentiating potentially lethal from nonlethal self-destructive behaviors is a central principle of ABIS. When we embark on a consensual outpatient psychodynamic therapy of the sort described here, the patient is in charge of the decision to seek treatment, but we are in charge of setting its terms. It is a fundamental given that a patient must stay alive to benefit from treatment. A decision to end life is inevitably a decision to end treatment and is always a focus of treatment. Nonlethal self-destructive behaviors (e.g., superficial cutting) are not necessarily a focus of treatment unless the patient wants them to be or because of the consequences of such behaviors. Nonlethal self-destructive behavior is not prohibited in the way suicide is for this reason: The therapist will undoubtedly be interested in the meaning communicated by nonlethal self-destructive behavior, but these behaviors can be tolerated as they are explored and understood. Potentially lethal behaviors, including suicide attempts, but also such potentially lethal behaviors as life-threatening self-starvation in anorexia nervosa, are inevitably a focus of treatment because they risk the interruption of treatment and cannot be tolerated.

Nonlethal self-destructive behaviors may have numerous meanings, such as atonement for a sense of evil, replacing emotional pain with physical pain, finding one's skin when one feels without boundaries, or as a substitute for actual suicide. Such possible meanings can all be explored in the dynamic work. Failure to recognize that nonlethal self-destructive behaviors differ from potentially lethal behaviors can make treatment untenable, as illustrated in the following vignette.

A 29-year-old woman with borderline personality disorder, recurrent major depressive episodes, and posttraumatic stress disorder (PTSD) had a history of sexual abuse and a suicide plan to immolate herself outside the picture window of the home of her abuser. She often engaged in relatively superficial cutting that she explicitly used as an alternative to carrying out impulses to travel to her abuser's home to implement her plan for self-immolation. When she began psychodynamic psychotherapy, her therapist found the patient's superficial cutting intolerably anxiety provoking and made the prohibition of such superficial cutting a condition of the treatment. The therapist failed to recognize that the cutting was an explicit alternative to carrying out her suicide plan, and that it helped the patient contain herself and remain in therapy. Although the patient struggled to comply with her therapist's condition, she found herself overwhelmed and ended the treatment within a few months.

Include the Patient's Responsibility to Stay Alive as Part of the Therapeutic Alliance

When suicide has been an issue in the patient's history or is part of the clinical presentation of a patient seen in consultation for consideration for psychodynamic psychotherapy, ABIS calls for inclusion of the meaning and impact of suicidal behavior within the therapeutic alliance. A frank discussion of suicide and what it means to each party is an essential part of negotiating the therapeutic alliance with suicidal patients. Thus, as noted above, the terms of the therapeutic alliance include the patient's responsibility for staying alive.

Although it is reasonable to ask a patient to take responsibility for staying alive as a condition of therapy, this is by no means a simple request. Clarification of what steps the patient will take if he or she feels unable to keep the agreement is essential. Even with the best state-of-the-art communication technology allowing patients access to therapists, outpatient therapists cannot prevent a patient from committing suicide. A reasonable backup procedure, perhaps including relevant family members or use of the local crisis team, needs to be put in place so that a patient who feels unable to keep the terms of the alliance and stay alive until the next session has a plan for reaching a safe environment where he or she can be assessed, and, if necessary, hospitalized until the suicidal crisis passes. Some therapists prefer to be contacted before a patient implements such a backup procedure, but this varies from therapist to therapist. What is essential is that a patient understands what to do in the event that he or she feels unable to keep the commitment to stay alive in the service of allowing therapy to unfold.

Interpret Suicide as Aggression Directed at the Therapy
Establishing the patient's responsibility for keeping him- or herself alive is a necessary but not sufficient condition for doing the work. Thoughts of suicide will likely emerge and may be put into action. In ABIS the therapist conceives of the emergence of suicidal thoughts and feelings in the course of the therapy as representing thoughts and feelings about stepping outside the terms of the therapeutic alliance and ending the work. The therapist conceives of suicidal action in the same way. In either case, the therapist responds by offering a contextually appropriate, empathic, nonpunitive interpretation of the patient's aggression in considering ending therapy through suicide—or actually choosing to end it in the event of a suicide attempt. This follows naturally from the terms of the alliance that have transformed suicide into an interpersonal event that has meaning in the relationship. A suicide attempt or its threat inevitably raises the question of what is happening that leads to the choice of death over therapy, and this deserves exploration, too, as is described below.

In the treatment system at Riggs, therapists who do not take this kind of stance from their role as the individual therapist can count on colleagues to wonder why they don't and/or take the issue up with patients on the therapist's behalf, as noted by the following vignette.

A new Riggs staff member was treating a 25-year-old suicidal borderline woman who, during a visit home, began to implement a suicide attempt by carbon monoxide poisoning in the basement garage of her family's home, while her parents slept above her. The patient called Riggs nursing staff after initiating the attempt, but refused to turn off the car or awaken her parents, and put down the phone without hanging up so that they could not be called. Nursing staff contacted the local police, who brought the patient to an emergency room, where she was assessed medically, released, and then returned to Riggs. When the therapist suggested at a staff meeting that the best way to understand the patient's suicide attempt was as representing her longstanding experience of being misunderstood and emotionally abandoned by her parents, nursing staff members voiced their dismay. They were filled with feelings of anger and betrayal because of having been forced to manage a crisis by telephone from hundreds of miles away with a patient who offered little cooperation. Nursing staff felt betrayed by the patient irrespective of the nature of her relationship with her parents. Other therapists suggested that the therapist think about the choice the patient had made about their work in initiating a suicide attempt, suggesting that only by engaging the issue as having meaning for and between them in the "here and now," rather than in a "then and there" formulation related to early experience of her parents, was there any hope of helping the patient settle into viable treatment at Riggs. The patient was moved into a 2-week reevaluation phase at Riggs, which carries out many of the principles of ABIS (see below).

In a treatment system like that at Riggs, not only are difficult transferences and countertransferences dispersed around the institution in a way that makes treating difficult patients possible, it is also possible to disperse the responsibility for engaging patients around the principles of ABIS. This is difficult to replicate in individual outpatient psychotherapy, where a therapist is usually on his or her own in knowledgeably and fully taking up the stance associated with ABIS. However, seeking supervision or consultation in work with suicidal patients or developing a peer supervision group are useful opportunities to approximate what is available at Riggs, and works well in many instances.

Contain and Metabolize the Countertransference

When a patient threatens or attempts suicide, powerful countertransference feelings are evoked that may include dread, guilt, anxiety, and anger. These intense countertransference feelings are important to contain and "metabolize"—that is, to acknowledge, process, and put into perspective rather than respond to the patient out of the countertransference feelings. Failure to contain and metabolize these countertransferences leads to a high likelihood of entering an enactment (see Chapter 2). Enactments are, of course, inevitable therapeutic phenomena, but to be avoided rather than embraced when a therapist is filled up with the intensity of countertransference feelings evoked by fear of a patient's suicide.

Metabolizing the countertransference often requires consultation with colleagues or supervisors, and is one reason personal psychotherapy or psychoanalysis is important for therapists who intend to work with difficult patients. The outside perspective that colleagues offer provides a useful perspective from the "Third." Metabolism of the countertransference is more difficult and crucial when a patient has actually attempted suicide, but careful attention to this issue is essential when working with patients who experience an upsurge of suicidal ideation, even if no attempt is made.

Hold the Patient Responsible for Preservation of the Therapy

If the patient has experienced an upsurge of suicidal ideation in the sessions, ABIS suggests that it is essential to explore the origin of these feelings. If a patient has attempted suicide, the therapist's first obligation is to respond as efficiently and compassionately as possible to help save the patient's life. In this instance the priority of intervening to save life supersedes efforts to understand what happened. However, once a patient is stabilized after an attempt, and countertransference feelings have been contained and metabolized, it is appropriate to interpret, in an empathic and nonpunitive way, the patient's aggression in the decision to end the therapy by acting outside the terms of the therapeutic alliance. This includes noting that preservation of the therapy may be possible, but a large measure of the responsibility for that preservation belongs to the patient. Scheduled therapy sessions end because the patient who has attempted suicide has chosen to end therapy by breaching the terms of the agreement that allowed therapy to proceed. On the other hand, the therapist remains willing to meet with the patient in the "consulting" role to discover what led the patient to choose to end the therapeutic work. Such consulting may require one or more sessions, but is time-limited and distinct from the previous therapy relationship. Patients may react to this stance by feeling abandoned, but it is not too difficult to make clear that the patient has exercised a choice, through action, to end therapy, given the terms of the therapeutic alliance.

At Riggs a patient who has unsuccessfully attempted suicide may be readmitted after medical stabilization if he or she is safe enough to return to the open setting. In such cases the patient enters a 2-week reevaluation phase. This time-limited reevaluation phase is comparable to "consulting" rather than resumption of therapy, as it is not clear treatment will continue after the 2 weeks. During this phase the patient meets not only with the therapist, but also with nursing staff, the treatment team, and the patient community for a series of often difficult but important discussions that operationalize ABIS principles and that give the patient the opportunity to take in the impact of his or her behavior on others with whom he or she is engaged. Family meetings and a psychotherapy consultation may also be part of the engagement during the reevaluation phase. At the conclusion of the reevaluation ("consulting") phase the data are reviewed at a staff conference and decisions are made about continuing the patient's treatment at Riggs—and, if Riggs treatment is to continue, whether to resume therapy with the previous therapist or reassign the case to another therapist. In individual outpatient psychotherapy a comparable model can be utilized, with a period of consultation during which the possibility of resuming therapy is explored and a decision made.

Engage Affect

Whether a patient has exhibited an increase in suicidal ideation or ended the therapy by making a suicide attempt, discovery of what led to these changes is facilitated by a genuine discussion that engages affect. Therapist and patient are at risk of retreating from honest engagement with each other when suicide emerges as an issue. Psychiatrist therapists are at particular risk of retreating into the medical model, seeing the patient's underlying mood disorder as worse and considering which medication to add or change, but it is not so much molecules as direct and authentic human engagement that can unearth what happened on an affective level. Superficial or textbook explanations (for example, that the increase in suicidal ideation was because a therapist was going on vacation or because the patient's depression got worse) often avoid engagement of affect. What is called for is a genuine effort to sort out the reason for the sudden emergence of murderous rage in the form of thoughts of suicide, and the sudden shift of the therapy from a side-by-side collaboration to a toe-to-toe battle to the death.

Search for the Therapist's Role in the Emergence of Suicide

This principle is perhaps the most important. It involves a search for the perceived injury from the therapist that may have precipitated suicidal thoughts or behavior. Here the therapist, not just the patient, is held potentially accountable for what has happened in the therapy and to the alliance. Cooperman (1983) has suggested that disruptions, like suicide attempts, may follow empathic failures or narcissistic injuries unwittingly perpetrated by therapists. If the therapist raises this question in an affectively engaged, genuine discussion, and from an empathic stance, something will often emerge that reveals how the therapist has enraged, humiliated, or otherwise injured the patient and triggered increased suicidal ideation or a suicide attempt. In Chapter 6 Muller notes that such actions by the therapist may have collapsed the Third. Failure to take seriously a patient's distress, distraction from a listening stance, or a tone or remark experienced as condescending may be perceived by the patient as a painful abandonment, empathic failure, or narcissistic injury that led to the wish (or decision to act) to get even with the therapist by killing the therapist's patient and destroying the therapy.

This is a difficult but rewarding part of work with suicidal patients, with great potential for learning by both therapist and patient, and with great potential for deepening the intimacy of the work. It is the place where enactments are sometimes detected, analyzed, and utilized in ways that reveal previously unknown material. To carry out this kind of exploration the therapist must genuinely grasp his or her importance to the patient and be willing to look at his or her own fallibility. This kind of exploration often leads to an "Aha!" moment, when the patient's suicidal wish or action suddenly has an understandable context that may make resumption of therapy possible.

It is appropriate to apologize for injuring a patient if we have erred. Apology is far more useful than defensively refusing to accept responsibility for the error, as if only patients make mistakes. However, therapists are also well advised to avoid premature apology. Patients deserve opportunities to express directly to us their hurt, anger, or sense of being abandoned, while we listen and take it in. An apology includes a culturally bound implicit and difficult-to-refuse request for forgiveness. We do not want to be forgiven before patients have been able to vent feelings, and we don't want to apologize if we have not erred, though we may want to empathize with our patient's experience.

Provide an Opportunity for Repair

This final principle is applied when a patient has taken a step toward implementing a suicide plan, as in the purchase of a rope for hanging or stockpiling of pills, or has attempted suicide and survived—in which latter case the therapy ends and a consultation phase begins. When means of suicide have been procured, adequate repair may involve giving to the therapist, or otherwise getting rid of, the means for suicide. When a suicide attempt has occurred, the provision of an opportunity for repair requires that the therapist consider whether it is genuinely possible to move beyond any lingering sense of injury, mistrust, and betrayal evoked by a suicide attempt. In many instances exploration of the negative transference meaning of a suicide attempt allows therapist and patient to learn something new. If the capacity to trust and the credibility of the participants have not been too severely damaged, it may be possible to repair the therapeutic alliance, end the phase of consulting, and resume therapy.

A patient's apology may be less important than an indication of new awareness of the meaning behind suicide, new and deeper recognition that the meaning includes a choice to end therapy, and renewed determination by the patient to keep to the terms of the alliance by using words rather than action when angered or hurt by the therapist. Meanwhile, the therapist must assess his or her capacity to move beyond any lingering countertransference hurt, anger, or mistrust for therapy to resume, as noted above.

In the treatment program at Riggs the possibility of reparation includes not only attention to injuries that may have affected the relationship between therapist and patient, but also how the relationship with nursing staff and the rest of the treatment team, as well as other patients, may have been damaged, and whether these can be engaged and repaired. In the application of ABIS in a treatment system like Riggs, considerable attention is paid to staff discussion and consultation to help maximize the chance of dealing with countertransference injuries that may have been experienced by specific clinicians or disciplines on or off the treatment team. However, it is not always possible to reach a place where continuing the treatment makes sense. There is no point in continuing treatment with a patient if a therapist or the nursing staff or even the patient community cannot relinquish a sense of betrayal or injury after a patient's suicide attempt. There is also no point in continuing psychodynamic therapy with a patient who seems unable to join the terms of the therapeutic alliance, so referral to an alternate form of treatment may make sense.

COMMENTS ON THE CASE OF JOE

In Chapter 4 on working with negative transference, I describe the case of Joe, a divorced father of three in his 40s with a treatment-refractory mood disorder, borderline personality disorder, and relentless suicidality. Although the case of Joe was offered to illustrate the importance of working with the negative transference in such patients, it also illustrates clinical implementation of the principles of ABIS. For example, the case initially unfolds with a clear distinction between a consultation phase and a therapy phase, and there is an implicit distinction between potentially lethal and nonlethal behavior in the case. The description of the preadmission consultation illustrates elements of negotiating a therapeutic alliance that assign responsibility to the patient for remaining alive as a condition of therapy.

The case description also illustrates the therapist's use of principles of ABIS when Joe threatened suicide a couple of weeks after admission, including viewing the upsurge of suicidal thinking as a unilateral revision of the therapeutic alliance they had negotiated in good faith. The therapist holds Joe to the terms of the alliance and nonpunitively but firmly interprets Joe's aggression in the unilateral revision of the terms of their alliance, while holding Joe responsible for the preservation of the therapy by returning to the mutually negotiated terms of the therapeutic alliance. Here and elsewhere in the case, the therapist contains and metabolizes a range of countertransference responses to Joe, as the therapist struggles with and eventually uses his countertransference responses to the emergence in action of Joe's negative transference.

Engagement of affect is illustrated in several places in the case, as when the therapist refuses to accept Joe's first apology for bringing anger into the session instead of some "fake, candy coated niceness." The creation of a space in which Joe's rage could be engaged and contained made it possible for him to bring into the work his fantasies of murder–suicide involving his children and his wishes to defeat all treaters.

Although not explicit in the original description of the case of Joe, the response to Joe's dangerous driving incident illustrates how a perceived injury by the therapist precipitated Joe's flirtation with implementing thoughts of murder–suicide that were kept out of the sessions. After the driving incident, when the therapist wondered how he might have played a role in Joe's flirtation with death, Joe reported he had felt injured by what he experienced as his therapist's distressed and judgmental tone when thoughts of murdering his children and then committing suicide first arose. This experience of the therapist led to deepening discussions of their relationship. Joe felt he had to keep these thoughts secret lest he lose the therapist. Further, Joe feared that the therapist could not tolerate Joe's dependency in the face of murderous wishes toward his own children, and would end their work through the therapist's own unilateral revision of the terms of the therapeutic alliance. Based on subtle responses in the therapist, and the institution's requirement that his close call while driving be reported to child welfare authorities, Joe feared the therapist was as intolerant of his dependency as Joe was terrified of it. Over time, Joe realized that what he experienced as the therapist's distressed and judgmental tone reflected his own distress and guilt about harboring such thoughts.

The provision of an opportunity for repair is also illustrated in the story of Joe's flirtation with carrying out a murder–suicide plan while driving with his children. Here the therapist accepted Joe's second and more genuine apology for keeping such important material secret. With his apology, Joe took fuller responsibility for his wishes to defeat the therapist, and made it clear that he was ready to try to work with more honesty and openness. Subsequently the work unfolded more productively.

CONCLUSION

The principles of ABIS are designed to help therapists establish and maintain a viable therapeutic alliance with suicidal patients so that the interpretive work of psychodynamic therapy can proceed. The principles of ABIS emphasize the patient's authority and responsibility and make suicide an interpersonal event between therapist and patient that can be explored through the vicissitudes of their relationship. Suicide is not viewed as simply a symptom of a treatment-refractory illness, but as an aspect of their relationship and of their mutual commitment to the terms of the therapeutic alliance. From the perspective of transference, suicide is viewed as a manifestation of negative transference that is to be understood, contained, and engaged, especially inasmuch as it is likely to be associated with a corresponding negative countertransference that can be hard to endure.

The principles are easily misunderstood by patients or even some clinicians, who may understand the therapist's use of the ABIS principles to be saying, "If you attempt suicide, I will quit as your therapist." In fact, the stance is closer to, "If you attempt suicide, it is inevitably a choice to end our important work. What is going on between us that makes you want to end our work? How have I pushed you to that choice?"

ABIS is intimately connected with the core themes of this volume. It is based on the central importance of recognizing the authority of the patient; it depends on the establishment of a significant relationship between therapist and patient; and it holds the elucidation and exploration of meaning to be central to therapeutic work with suicidal patients. ABIS will not work with all patients, but it offers a powerful intervention for many. Patients are engaged in a way that links the vicissitudes of suicidal ideation and behavior to the transference relationship, particularly the negative transference, and to the terms of the therapeutic alliance. Until suicide recedes as an issue, other interpretive work is not the principal focus of therapy. Before exploring how patients' life histories, conflicts, and unconscious fantasies may lie beneath their symptoms and distress, they must first be able to stay alive to come to sessions. ABIS can increase the likelihood of that outcome.

REFERENCES

Bollas, C. (1987). *The shadow of the object: Psychoanalysis of the unthought known.* London: Free Association Books.

Brenner, C. (1979). Working alliance, therapeutic alliance and transference. *Journal of the American Psychoanalytic Association, 27S,* 137–157.

Chemtob, C.M., Bauer, G.B., Hamada, R.S., Pelowski, S.R., & Muraoka, M.Y. (1989). Patient suicide: Occupational hazard for psychologists and psychiatrists. *Professional Psychology: Research and Practice, 20,* 294–300.

Clarkin, J.F., Levy, K.N., Lenzenweger, M.F., & Kernberg O.F. (2007). Evaluating three treatments for borderline personality disorder: A multi-wave study. *American Journal of Psychiatry, 164,* 922–928.

Cooperman, M. (1983). Some observations regarding psychoanalytic psychotherapy in a hospital setting. *The Psychiatric Hospital, 14*(1), 21–28.

Freud, S. (1975). The dynamics of transference. In J. Strachey (Ed. & Trans.), *The standard edition of the complete psychological works of Sigmund Freud* (Vol. 12, pp. 97–120). London: Hogarth Press. (Original work published 1912)

Greenson, R.R. (1978). The working alliance and the transference neurosis. In R.R. Greenson (Ed.), *Explorations in psychoanalysis* (pp. 199–224). New York: International Universities Press. (Original work published 1965)

Gutheil, T.G., & Havens, L.L. (1979). The therapeutic alliance: Contemporary meanings and confusions. *International Journal of Psychoanalysis, 6,* 467–481.

Hendin, H., Haas, A.P., Maltsberger, J.T., Szanto, K., & Rabinowicz, H. (2004). Factors contributing to therapists' distress after the suicide of a patient. *American Journal of Psychiatry, 161,* 1442–1446.

Linehan, M.M., Armstrong, H.E., Suarez, A., Alman, D., & Heard, H.L.(1991). Cognitive–behavioral treatment of chronically parasuicidal borderline patients. *Archives of General Psychiatry, 48,* 1060–1064.

Meissner, W.W. (1992). The concept of the therapeutic alliance. *Journal of the American Psychoanalytic Association, 40,* 1059–1087.

Meissner, W.W. (1999). Notes on the therapeutic role of the alliance. *Psychoanalytic Review, 86,* 1–33.

Neves, S.N., Malloy-Diniz, L.F., & Correa, H. (2009). Suicidal behavior in bipolar disorder: What is the influence of psychiatric comorbidities? *Journal of Clinical Psychiatry, 70*(1), 13–18.

Perry, J.C., Fowler, J.C., Bailey, A., Clemence, A.J., Plakun, E.M., Zheutlin, B., et al. (2009). Improvement and recovery from suicidal and self-destructive phenomena in treatment-refractory disorders. *Journal of Nervous and Mental Disease, 197*(1), 28–34.

Plakun, E.M. (1993). Principles in the psychotherapy of the self-destructive borderline patient. In A. Tasman & W. Sledge (Eds.), *Clinical challenges in psychiatry* (pp. 129–155). Washington, DC: American Psychiatric Association.

Plakun, E.M. (1994). Principles in the psychotherapy of self-destructive borderline patients. *Journal of Psychotherapy Practice and Research, 3,* 138–148.

Plakun, E.M. (2001). Making the alliance and taking the transference in work with suicidal borderline patients. *Journal of Psychotherapy Practice and Research, 10*(4), 269–276.

Plakun, E.M., & Tillman, J.G. (2005). Responding to the impact of suicide on clinicians. *Directions in Psychiatry, 25,* 301–309.

Shapiro, E.R., & Plakun, E.M. (2008). Residential psychotherapeutic treatment: An intensive psychodynamic approach for patients with treatment-resistant disorders. In S.S. Sharfstein, F.B. Dickerson, & J.M. Oldham

(Eds.), *Textbook of hospital psychiatry* (pp. 285–297). Washington, DC: American Psychiatric Association.

Shapiro, E.R., Shapiro, R.L., Zinner, J., & Berkowitz, D.A. (1977). The borderline ego and the working alliance: Indications for family and individual treatment in adolescence. *International Journal of Psychoanalysis, 58,* 77–87.

Simon, R. (2004). *Assessing and managing suicide risk: Guidelines for clinically based risk management.* Washington, DC: American Psychiatric Association.

Sterba, R. (1934). The fate of the ego in psychoanalytic therapy. *International Journal of Psychoanalysis, 15,* 117–126.

Tillman, J.G. (2006). When a patient commits suicide: An empirical study of psychoanalytic clinicians. *International Journal of Psychoanalysis. 87,* 159–177.

Weinberg, I., Ronningstam, E., Goldblatt, M.J., Schechter, M., Wheelis, J., & Maltsberger, J.T. (2010). Strategies in treatment of suicidality: Identification of common and treatment-specific interventions in empirically supported treatment manuals. *Journal of Clinical Psychiatry, 71*(6), 699–706.

Yeomans, F.E., Clarkin, J.F., & Kernberg, O.F. (2002). *A primer of transference-focused psychotherapy for the borderline patient.* Northvale, NJ: Jason Aronson.

Zetzel, E. R. (1956). The concept of transference. In E.R. Zetzel (Ed.), *The capacity for emotional growth: Theoretical and clinical contributions to psychoanalysis 1943–1969* (pp. 168–181). New York: International Universities Press.

Zetzel, E. R. (1966). The analytic situation. In R. E. Litman (Ed.), *Psychoanalysis in the Americas* (pp. 86–106). New York: International Universities Press.

Chapter 9
The Boundaries Are Shifting

Renegotiating the Therapeutic Frame

Edward R. Shapiro, MD

Psychodynamic treatment is under siege. Shifting societal values and increasing economic pressures are shaking the structures of our work. In this chapter, I examine this crisis by looking at the phenomenology and current treatment of personality disorders, a central element in treatment resistance. Using personality disorder as a lens, I consider the impact of current pressures on therapists' ability to establish a reliable framework for dynamic treatment. Such a framework has always included the interplay of interpretation and management (Baranger & Baranger, 1966; Langs, 1976; Milner, 1957). The increasing intrusion of third parties into the treatment setting, however, requires us to reconsider the relationship between these two methods of intervention.

Establishing the framework for an interpretive treatment requires competent management. Once patient and therapist agree on a framework, interpretation can become the principal vehicle for analytic work. With the increased power of third-party payers, however, establishing the frame has been disrupted by difficulties negotiating payment, frequency of appointments, and duration of treatment. Providing a setting for interpretation is yielding to a form of business and behavioral management that primarily attends to resources and symptoms (de Nobel, 1989; Halpert, 1972). This dramatic change has altered the ways in which patients can engage in deepening therapeutic work. For patients with financial resources, traditional psychoanalysis remains available and will continue to provide us with rich ideas about human psychopathology and development. The challenge that faces us is how to apply these ideas with integrity for patients in treatment settings affected by new forms of resource management.

PERSONALITY DISORDER

A personality disorder is an adaptation an individual makes to an aberrant interpersonal environment, usually the environment of a family (Shapiro, Zinner, Shapiro, & Berkowitz,1975). Families create a shared human context to meet the needs of individuals within them. In families whose members have personality disorders, individuals often form rigid defenses against recognizing limitations in themselves, in others, and in available resources (Shapiro, 1982b). These defenses protect them from feelings of helplessness, anxiety, rage, and grief. The price of this protection is the development of rigid or aberrant interpersonal and family boundaries (Shapiro, 1982a; Shapiro et al., 1975). Children's adaptation of their personality structures to fit their experience of these boundaries—no matter how traumatic—is functional. It helps with their emotional survival and supports parents' engagement in some kind of caretaking roles. Adaptation to a constricted family environment does not, however, help develop the child's long-term capacity to grapple flexibly and creatively with the ever-changing reality outside the family.

The world does not conform to the individual's needs. In response, the so-called personality-disordered person displays what the *Diagnostic and Statistical Manual of Mental Disorders–IV* (DSM-IV; American Psychiatric Association, 1994, p. 633) calls "an enduring pattern of inner experience and behavior that deviates markedly from the expectations of the individual's culture." This pattern represents an effort by the individual to change the world into a familiar place (Shapiro & Carr, 1991). Limitations in the world—impassible boundaries marked by insufficient resources or conflicting needs—can cause the character-disordered individual to become symptomatic. For example, obsessive patients faced with time limitations may become anxious, and narcissistic patients confronting the unavailability of significant people may withdraw or become angry. Clearly defined task and role boundaries in therapy—which help articulate experience so that patients can fully acknowledge it—may allow for a different outcome. These boundaries slow the interactions so that the obsessive can notice how his or her efforts to control contribute to his or her anxiety. The narcissist can recognize his or her need for the other's attention. For patients, experiencing and studying transactions across these therapeutic boundaries offers an opportunity for learning (Bion, 1962/1977). Patients begin to recognize their desperate efforts to change the outside world to fit their needs. With this recognition, they have a chance to gain perspective on their childhood and current maladaptive style and notice that situations in the world require negotiation.

Mental health professionals are in a comparable position. We have grown up in a professional "family" to which we have adapted. Generations of thinkers in dynamic psychiatry have taught us to offer our patients a particular therapeutic setting in the hospital or in the therapeutic dyad. This included time for an externalization of aspects of the patient's personality within the transference. Seeing these externalizations provided an opportunity for the patient to gain perspective on what he or she was trying to repeat or reconfigure. Our increasingly focused interpretive efforts and therapeutic zeal allowed us, with our patients, to extend treatments. Although the individual session was determined by the beginning and end of the hour, psychotherapy itself was without time boundaries. For some, therapy became a way of life, lasting more than a decade. Deep became deeper, with formulations and case reports emerging in the psychoanalytic literature about the recovery and fruitful analysis of infantile, preverbal experience. Because our focus was relentlessly inward, we were more likely to overlook the impact of a decade-long intensive therapeutic relationship on our lives and families and those of our patients. For example, to my knowledge, there has been no study of the incidence of therapist or patient divorce following extended psychodynamic work. We decreased our attention to outer world boundaries—initially noted with the establishment of the frame—in exchange for an extended focus on interpretation.

The outer world has now intruded (Shapiro, 2001). For most patients in psychoanalysis, psychotherapy, or hospital care, we can no longer provide this traditional setting. Like our character-disordered patients, we, too, are now facing unanticipated boundaries and limits in the outer world. Psychodynamic therapists had found it difficult to incorporate resource management functions into their settings because of their involvement in the therapeutic process. Insurance companies and managed care organizations have now taken authority for these functions. As Plaut (1990, p. 310) noted, "that part of common reality which we shut out for the sake of the necessary seclusiveness . . . has a way of reasserting itself." It does not look like we can change this world back into a familiar place. Our difficulty in acknowledging and integrating aspects of the altered external context into our treatment framework may even repeat boundary disturbances characteristic of our patients' families. To maintain our integrity and keep our therapeutic enterprise grounded in reality, we must reexamine the basics of our treatment setting in this new context.

THE FRAMEWORK

Over the years, psychoanalysts have learned to define and manage a therapeutic framework within which a deepening treatment can take place (Baranger & Baranger, 1966; Langs 1973, 1976; Milner, 1957; Raney, 1982). Milner (1957) noted that the frame has a crucial boundary function, in that it "marks off an area within which what is perceived has to be taken symbolically, while what is outside the frame is taken literally" (p. 158). It is our responsibility to manage this framework, which includes confidentiality and role boundaries, time, place, setting, financial arrangements, and vacations. We structure these arrangements in the outer world of our contractual negotiation with another adult, who agrees to take up the patient role. We do all of this both to take care of ourselves and to support an interpretive treatment task.

The framework thus has footholds in reality and in the therapeutic dyad. For example, we set our fees according to pressures in our outer world, in response to the market and our patients' resources. Fees, vacations, the management of missed sessions—all of the framework issues—are the context within which our patients make sense of us. These structures, therefore, link the developing transference to external world pressures on both patient and analyst. If the patient's spouse and child require particular vacation times that do not coincide with the therapist's vacation, it raises a framework issue. When the therapist requires the patient to pay for sessions missed during the patient's vacation, it affects the patient's family relations. If the therapist does not charge, the patient's vacation affects the therapist's income and, indirectly, his or her family. Every aspect of framework negotiation is deeply embedded in the inner and outer worlds of both participants.

When patient and therapist negotiate a clearly structured framework, they respectfully address this complexity and provide a safe, predictable, transitional space for therapeutic work. With this security, an individual can take up the patient role and risk a symbolic regression in which an interpretable transference to the therapist can evolve. Though the management structures of the framework quickly enter the patient's inner world of private meaning (Dimen, 1994; Raney, 1982; Rudominer, 1984) and what Ogden (1994) calls "the third of the analyst–patient intersubjectivity," the therapist is responsible for establishing them. The way in which the therapist manages these issues is a reflection of how he or she manages the boundary between his or her inner and outer worlds. It therefore provides information to patients about the therapist's character (Langs, 1976). The patient's interpretation of the therapist's management is a reflection of the patient's inner world. We meet our patients at this intimate management boundary to engage in the task of interpretive treatment.

The management of the framework and its incorporation into an interpretable transference illuminate the necessary integration in dynamic treatment of management and interpretation. There can be no interpretation without competent management and no useful management without interpretation. When linked to the shared task of understanding, the two methods—understood psychodynamically—provide tools for examining the boundary between the patient's inner and outer worlds.

Interpretation and management are two tasks of a therapist. Treatments work best when the therapist recognizes their interdependence.

For neurotic patients, the framework is largely a silent aspect of the work. These patients have internalized a stable psychic structure. Patients with personality disorders, especially those who become treatment resistant, in contrast, crash against boundaries. Many enter the hospital because of their inability to manage a secure framework for their outside lives. Quite often, it is within and around the framework of treatment that these patients enact their psychopathology. These interactions impinge on therapists at our management boundary, evoking countertransference reactions and framework errors. The study of these mutual enactments has deepened our learning about the fine distinctions between transference and countertransference (see Chapter 2). In such treatments, our authority for the framework, our ability to manage it, and our commitment to holding the treatment task as primary become crucial.

MANAGEMENT AND INTERPRETATION

Advanced technology has contributed to an increasingly interdependent world. We are more aware both of our needs for others and our limited resources. Institutions that society has counted on to manage dependency—the family, religion, education, health care—have become less dependable (Shapiro, 2001). These changes make growing up in this society more difficult and have escalated demands for mental health care. In response, the field has grown enormously. Now that its required costs have threatened to exceed limited resources, its variously trained practitioners have reacted to the pressures with both disarray and rigidity.

The therapeutic pair is deeply embedded in a world where there is less time available for sustained intimacy. An intensive, intimate relationship makes powerful demands on both participants. Pressure builds to meet dependency needs instead of interpreting them. We can see the disarray in the increasing number of therapists who have lost their capacity to manage themselves in role. One reaction is for therapists to surrender their management capacities in exchange for a quasi-delusional intimacy manifest in sexual involvement. Alternatively, for some, time boundaries can become irrelevant with the therapeutic grandiosity of an endless treatment.

Another response to the intensity of the work and the limited resources is to develop a defensive, rigid, hypermanagement style. Questioning the dangers of interpretive intimacy, many mental health practitioners are turning to the use of prescribed and highly organized management interventions without interpretation. For many practitioners untrained in dynamic thinking, this mode of intervention serves as an adaptive defense against powerful feelings—the patients' and their own—that they can neither tolerate nor understand. However, such prioritization and monitoring of the patient's behavior transform the semipermeable learning boundaries between therapist and patient into impermeable barriers and risk depleting the treatment of meaning.

In each instance, one aspect of the work is lost: management or interpretation. In each, we move away from the combined interventions that allow for containment and exploration of the patient's inner world. We substitute either the delusion of "oneness" or the safety of arbitrary and rigid management. We fuse with our patients, or we direct them. Both responses are defensive substitutes for the risky possibility of learning with them in a transitional space that allows for both empathy and interpretation (Brickman, 1993). Both groups engage in an irrational split where projections and counterprojections flourish. The heartless fiscal manager is no less a projected stereotype than the greedy, self-indulgent clinician.

In the face of this anxiety and splitting, extraordinary changes have taken place. Business people run psychiatric hospitals and have developed new approaches to manage money and to attempt to ensure institutional survival. Clinical thinking no longer guides institutional life. Even more disturbing is the way that manic defenses have replaced terrified withdrawal. The soberest clinicians are now touting the effectiveness of 7-day treatments for patients with lifelong personality disorders. Treatment-resistant patients are seen only through the lens of biology and the medical model, and are left in a passive and dependent position in terms of their authority for treatment and negotiation about its continuation or ending. To a certain extent this change represents a course correction from our past avoidance of external reality. However, there is real danger that the power of a genuinely negotiated interpretive understanding of people's lives will be lost irrevocably in the service of managerial efficiency.

At a symposium at the 1994 annual meeting of the American Psychiatric Association, I discussed several papers on the treatment of personality disorder in the managed care era, which had only recently begun. What was true then, remains true now. The papers inevitably focused on short-term interventions into lifelong disorders and offered a range of approaches in response to the current pressures in the field to manage symptoms without interpretation.

One group of authors represented the managers. They discussed the need to focus behavioral and educative interventions in a brief period. One (Silk, 1994) described how his staff works effectively with hospitalized borderline patients in 7–14 days. The staff advises patients in advance about the time limits and encourages them to have modest goals. Staggered by the rapid turnover and severe patient pathology, staff members benefit from having clearly defined offerings; group and educational sessions help patients by structuring their brief time in the hospital. Patients agree to work on cognitive–behavioral learning, which bolsters their defenses against the feelings of abandonment that lead to their intolerable actions. Silk suggested that a regularly interrupted but essentially long-term relationship with the institution allows patients gradually to recognize and face these feelings. The task of hospitalization is to educate patients about their illness and teach them to manage their symptoms.

There is no time for interpretation, and no secure relationship within which one can interpret. Silk does not comment on the possible social implications of setting up a covert managerial system of chronic care. Nor does he consider the possible enactment of a potentially interpretable dynamic of sustained dependency, not unlike that of interminable dynamic treatment.

Another author (Falcon, 1994) assessed this strategy by pooling statistics from a Blue Cross/Blue Shield utilization review. Intensive management of mental illness (through constricting hospital stays and duration of treatment) appeared to save a great deal of money. However, when he examined the total expenditures, he found that the costs remained the same, before and after managed care. What had shifted was the accounting of these costs from the psychiatric column to the medical. Patients with mental illness who received no definitive treatment ended up in emergency rooms and internists' offices with behavioral and physical manifestations. Management without interpretation seemed to lead to cost shifting without cost saving.

Glen Gabbard (1994) spoke in defense of the work of the interpreter. He noted that the artificial limits imposed by rigid resource management caused damage to patients working in an interpretive frame. In his studies, borderline patients begin to allow the development of a negative transference at approximately the 30th session. This is a customary limit of outpatient resources. Arbitrary interruption at this point was particularly traumatic, as patients regularly experienced it as confirmation of their negative transference, which made it impossible to interpret. Gabbard focused on the need for continuity in the therapeutic relationship, suggesting that a primary task of treatment is to help patients develop a sense of self-continuity over time. Speaking to the necessity for extended treatment, he portrayed resource managers as unwittingly attacking and endangering patients' treatment. He did not comment on the possibility of integrating the external limits into the therapist's framework.

The differences between managers and interpreters are evocative. Interpreters imply that resource management is destructive and argue for long-term treatment. Their therapeutic neutrality gives patients room to take charge of their lives. It may not, however, sufficiently attend to the covert gratifications of interminable treatment for both participants. The passionate argument of interpreters—which gives management little significance—makes it increasingly unlikely that third-party payers will continue to finance this approach.

Managers offer patients coping strategies, frequent short-term admissions, and cognitive schema. Interpretations are irrelevant. Managers use less expensive staff, place patients in groups to study behavior, and prescribe a combination of medication and education. They move people along. Patients treated this way may not take charge of their illness. They remain in passive roles in their lives, as in their treatments, and may end up receiving nonpsychiatric care that is just as expensive as definitive psychological treatment.

Such management interventions have unexpected side effects for patients with personality disorders and those with treatment-resistant disorders whose authority has been eclipsed in previous treatment efforts. Many of these patients use externalizing defenses, blaming others for what happens to them. In intensive treatment, these patients reveal that behind the externalization lies punitive unconscious self-criticism (Kris, 1990), a phenomenon that leads to their self-destructive behavior. In a treatment environment where managerial experts judge and correct their behavior, show them their vulnerabilities, and teach them "more adaptive" ways to live, these patients readily mobilize this self-criticism. They can interpret a managerial approach as confirmation of their incompetence. In addition, many of these patients have grown up in families where parents believe they know what is going on in the child's mind. They *tell* the child the way to live rather than helping him or her discover his or her own way. This "pathological certainty" (Shapiro, 1982a) contributes to the despairing sense many of these patients have that their ideas, their motivations, and their efforts to understand are of no interest and no value. Managerial therapists may unwittingly contribute to an unproductive repetition of this experience.

Interpreters also run into problems. Gabbard (1991) noted how patient and therapist can join to idealize interpretation and exclude and stereotype the financial manager. This response repeats a different familial pattern, in which one parent forms an exclusive dyad with the child, stereotyping and excluding the other parent. The use of the child as an ally interferes with learning and excludes the third party necessary for grappling with reality. Collusive pairing between therapist and patient in an endless treatment is problematic; it can conceal a shared hatred of limitations, a fantasy of endless resources, and a delusional dyadic structure. Bion (1961) described the shared irrationality inherent in any "pairing" disconnected from the larger group's task. The notion of an isolated dyad, however, is an illusion. The therapeutic pair has always been embedded in a larger context: the community, the profession, the managed care networks, the mental institution. Though we do not always pay attention to this context, there is inevitably a "third" that keeps the pair grounded in reality.

There is increasing interest within the analytic literature in the notion of "the third." Abelin (1971) wrote about early triangulation and the function of the father for both mother and child in protecting the pair from being overwhelmed with symbiosis. Lacan (1975/1988) developed the idea of the symbolic third ("le nom du pere") as a function that grounds the individual in a larger context. Brickman (1993) described interpretation as a third factor facilitating separation from therapeutic symbiosis, and Ogden (1994) described "the third" factor of the analyst–patient intersubjectivity. In Chapter 6 Muller further elaborates the notion of the third.

Though the issues differ, these notions are applicable to the external third of the managed care reviewer and insurance company. In the childhood triad, the father shares the same task as the mother–infant dyad: facilitating the child's development. The payer's task, however, is different from that of the therapy pair: financial management, not treatment. But these latter two tasks are linked: Both financial management and treatment require attention to the reality of limitations.

Inevitably, the patient brings external parties into the relationship and incorporates them into the interpretive space. This is a familiar phenomenon of psychodynamic work (Schafer, 1985). It is not just the patient, however, who introduces third-party resource managers. These agencies bring pressures to bear on both members of the dyad in ways that affect the therapist's capacity to focus on the patient's experience. The therapist must come to terms with them to undertake the work and to clarify what "the work" can be, given the limitations.

Focusing on the dyad, Freud once referred to the patient's family as "an external resistance to treatment" (Freud, 1917/1966). Some have argued (e.g., Langs, 1973; Raney, 1982) that managed care providers constitute such a powerful external resistance that interpretive treatment is impossible. Others disagree (de Nobel, 1989; Rudominer, 1984). No matter the source, patients struggle with these external third parties over available resources and interpret that struggle according to their own psychopathology. Therapists can use these struggles as a part of the treatment, if they can find a way to take in the external limitations as an aspect of their treatment frame.

Patients with personality disorders chronically repeat problematic be-

havior. These repetitions, however, are more than self-destructive enactments—they are also desperate efforts to learn something new, to gain
perspective on an unconscious process. When the patient's experience is
not conscious and is enacted through dangerous behavior, a safe space
within a secure frame is essential. A secure framework represents a negotiated reality that incorporates the limitation of resources. For many
patients, third-party managers represent an aspect of that reality. If the
therapist can incorporate this external factor into the framework, he or
she can help the patient understand the transference meaning of these
limitations and how such meaning has governed behavior in the past or
governs it in the present.

AN INSTITUTIONAL MODEL

The Austen Riggs Center has developed a management structure called
the Resource Management Committee that brings together financial people and clinicians to address the financial framework for treatment. Limitation of resources is viewed here as both reality and metaphor. Staff,
family, insurer, and patients all share the reality: They must recognize and
manage it. The metaphor requires discovery and interpretation. Our effort has been to bring the patient and family into the financial discussions
between the hospital and the external third party. This allows them to
examine their assumptions regarding the need for treatment and the limitations of resources. The process eventually authorizes the patient to
speak and act as the critical agent of change. Inevitably, the patient's reactions to limitations reflect a character-driven response to frustration and
illuminate repetitive dynamic themes. Excluding patients from this experience or confusing them by discounting or devaluing the financial managers deprives them of an opportunity for speaking as well as learning,
and leaves them in a passive and dependent position that is not in the
service of taking up their agency in life. This is an especially important issue with treatment-refractory patients who have comorbid personality
disorders.

> Financial limitations are both a reality and a metaphor for other limi-
> tations in a patient's life. Including patients in discussions of the cost
> of treatment, the reality issues, and the metaphorical meaning allows
> them to rage, grieve, and mobilize their agency in the service of tak-
> ing charge of their lives.

Plakun (1996) described how a patient's mother continually rescued him—both emotionally and financially—from taking charge of his life. She repeatedly bailed him out when he overextended himself. In the hospital, when the insurance coverage was about to end, the patient's behavior worsened. He requested a rate reduction from the hospital to stay longer. The financial officer was inclined to agree. In the clinical–financial discussion, the clinical staff recognized and interpreted to the patient the repetition of his family dynamic, with the hospital in the role of mother. He saw how he was enacting a lifelong pattern of inviting his mother's overprotective response. He began to see his pattern of blaming his mother for her overprotectiveness while demanding through regression that she continue to meet his needs. The discussion led to a decision by the patient to step down to a less expensive program. He obtained a job to support the program and negotiated a small fee reduction from the hospital and a contribution from his mother. Through the staff's integration of management and interpretation, the patient could begin to take charge of the conflict.

With the help of this interdisciplinary Resource Management Committee, we invite patients to take responsibility for making moves to less expensive settings in our system. Facing their own financial limitations, they initiate requests for transition rather than allowing others to move them. Stimulated by pressures from insurance companies, managed care firms, or families, our patients frequently resist assuming authority for these moves. The clinical staff works with them toward articulating their resistance within the developing transference. Feelings of abandonment, neglect, and abuse regularly recur. The therapist, with the help of the institution, attempts to mediate these pressures and feelings with the patient, sustaining the reality limitation and placing the feelings within an interpretive context. Grief often results. With this working link between clinical and financial thinking, patient, family, and staff have an opportunity to learn from their shared irrationality about limits. In this setting, the negotiated management of limitations becomes the framework for interpretation.

It is possible in a short period, even with disturbed patients, to develop collaborative dynamic interpretation of these reactions. The therapist must, however, incorporate the reality of limitations into his or her framework and interpret within that space. When therapist and patient develop a shared recognition that resources are limited, the patient often directs rage at the therapist as representative of that reality. The rage is an opportunity to engage an aspect of the negative transference (see Chapter 4 on this topic). Working through this rage leads to grief, mourning, and a genuinely intimate engagement around treatment and its limitations.

For example, an adopted patient had lost his biological father at an early age and did not get along with his stepfather, who had legally adopted him after marrying his mother. Throughout his life this patient was physically abused by his stepfather when he could not perform adequately. Unable to provide help or recognize his stepson's need for him, the older man would strike him. This patient gradually developed a characterologic adaptation to challenges, oscillating between helpless vulnerability with wishes for idealized rescue and aggressive grandiosity. The vulnerability reflected his need for a loving father; the grandiosity, his angry effort to manage everything himself. When faced with a task, he thus unconsciously evoked his relationship with his stepfather. He needed help in seeing the pattern, tolerating the experience, and putting it in perspective so that he could increase his choices (Semrad, 1969). This patient was overwhelmed by his fear of his wish to rely on a man. Without containment and interpretation, he could not allow himself to recognize and identify with a man's strength, vulnerability, and competence to become his own man. He needed help to separate from his past.

This patient was hospitalized because of a decompensation after initiating a lawsuit when he was fired from his job. Enacting his defensive character solution, he did not hire a lawyer to represent him. He grandiosely took up his own defense and ended up feeling battered by the complexities of the case. In the hospital, he wanted the institution to take his side in court. A success would provide the resources for the long-term treatment he needed. As it stood, he had resources only for short-term treatment. The repetition was familiar. The patient wanted the therapist (as the idealized father) magically to help him get the resources he needed for a better developmental solution. Any failure to respond meant abandonment. When the therapist noted that they only had a short time to work together, it provided a reality boundary. With this, the patient could experience and begin to interpret his negative transference. He saw the therapist as a bad father who was "knocking him down" without helping him develop his "inadequate resources." With the recognition of a familiar rage, he could begin to see his terror of turning himself over to his therapist for what the therapist had realistically available—treatment, not legal advice. This recognition freed him sufficiently to allow the therapist to define with him an achievable goal. In a brief stay, this patient learned enough about his terror of relying on a man so that he could dare to hire an effective male lawyer to represent him.

DISCUSSION

A familiar and painful life experience for patients with personality disorders, particularly those who become treatment resistant, is the lack of resources in their families and their lives to ease their emotional development. They have shaped their characters to deny this fact. Managed care—as metaphor—represents this experience. In establishing a treatment setting in which patients can address these issues, therapists must face the changes in our world caused by the limitations of resources. Third-party reviewers—no matter how untrained or clumsy—are the representatives of that reality. We must integrate their perspectives into our own framework to provide a safe transitional space in which the patient can risk an interpretable transference.

These third parties—whether insurance companies or families—often do not make their limitations clear. In such cases, they represent not a well-delineated reality, but an uncertain, chaotic, and unresponsive resource. This, too, is the way of the world, but its impact on dynamic treatment can be devastating. Patient and clinician feel they have no boundaries, no security, no resting place. Clinicians can respond to this relentless ambiguity as an attack on their efforts to provide a safe space for treatment. A defensive response, however, interferes with the possibility of providing either management or interpretation for the patient. Both patient and clinician become incompetent and despairing. This was the experience for one patient, who wrote:

> I'm confused about every thing. Should I stay or should I go? I'm so ambivalent and apathetic, it's making any decision impossible. It was my assumption that I'd come to the hospital, cut to the chase, as it were, and concentrate on intensive therapy. But the insurance company has made that quite impossible. I don't have a clue when they'll say, "You're out of here," so I had a mindset to go home this week because I thought they'd kick me out. Talk about undermining any work to be done. So now that I'm in this mindset, I want to go home. It has become more appealing the more I've thought about it. That's tough though, because the stuff makes me feel so bad, and I sure don't want to go to school with all this dredged-up

shit making me feel bad. . . . The insurance company is also making me feel really uprooted here and since I know I'm going home before school anyway, I might feel more settled by moving home. I've been living on the edge for more or less 8 years, so I personally don't see the difference where I am. Home, school, hospital. Now it's all the same. Because I couldn't get what I wanted out of hospital, and that was my last resource. So I'll just have to keep doing what I've been doing.

Even in these cases, however, the therapist can manage a dynamic intervention if he or she holds to her interpretive task. The recognition that treatment-resistant patients with personality disorders regularly use aspects of the frame for enacting a repetitive theme is central. With our help, they can use this experience to discover their metaphor. The patient does not initially experience his or her behavior as either repetition or metaphor. Grasping the metaphor, however, is itself a shift toward recognizing and stopping the repetition. For this patient, her suicidal depression and isolation stemmed from the disruption of her family in early adolescence. During this period, her family was unpredictable and chaotic, intermittently absent, and confusing. She had to take charge of her life alone, with resulting despair. In the face of the managed care response, this patient could see how she chose a familiar interpretation for a more complex reality. The third-party reviewer was, like her parents, confused, uncertain, and not attending to her needs. However, the therapist, who had incorporated this reality, was available to her to make sense of this, both as reality and as transference. Choosing the familiar and devastating chaos as the reason for her despair was this patient's repetition. The overwhelming repetition of childhood confusion did not allow her to discover her adult perspective and resources. With a stable focus on the interpretive task within this framework, she could recognize this and choose from more complex options.

The title of this chapter is "The Boundaries Are Shifting: Renegotiating the Therapeutic Frame." I suspect that this apparent shift in framework boundaries and our pressure to redefine and renegotiate them are both reality and illusion. The confusion derives from our anxious uncertainty about the future and our reluctance to see how we have contributed to the development of systems of external management. As Muller (1996) has noted: "If the contemporary rush toward the dyad in our theories has served to eclipse the place we give the Third, one possible outcome is to leave the field vacant for an unwelcome intruder. The place of the third . . . has been seized by the managed care effort; the managers now structure the dyadic process from first phase to last, determine its semiotic conditions, influence what is to be said or not said, dictate what shall be taken as meaningful and what shall be desired as an outcome . . ." (p. 72). I suggest that if we hold to the essence of our frame, we have a chance to ride out this storm. We can continue to provide our patients with definable structures for interpreting their lives if we can help them manage sufficient resources for even the beginnings of an interpretive space. Then, we may rediscover how competent management and reliably negotiated interpretation are inextricably linked in the provision of dynamic treatment.

REFERENCES

Abelin, E. L. (1971). The role of the father in separation–individuation. In J. McDevitt & C. Settlage (Eds.), *Separation-individuation: Essays in honor of Margaret Mahler* (pp. 229–252). New York: International Universities Press.

Baranger, M., & Baranger, W. (1966). Insight in the analytic situation. In R. Litman (Ed.), *Psychoanalysis in the Americas* (pp. 56–72). New York: International Universities Press.

Bion, W. R. (1961). *Experiences in groups*. London: Tavistock.

Bion, W.R. (1977). Learning from experience. In *Seven servants* (pp. 1–111). New York: Aronson. (Original work published 1962)

Brickman, H. R. (1993). Between the devil and the deep blue sea: The dyad and the triad in psychoanalytic thought. *International Journal of Psychoanalysis, 74*, 905–915.

de Nobel, L. (1989). When it is not the patient who pays. *Psychoanalytic Psychotherapy, 4*, 1–12.

Dimen, M. (1994). "Money, love and hate: Contradiction and paradox in psychoanalysis. *Psychoanalytic Dialogues, 4*, 69–100.

Falcon, S. (1994, May). *Finances and insurance*. Paper presented at the annual meeting of the American Psychiatric Association, Philadelphia.

Freud, S. (1966). *Introductory lectures on psychoanalysis*. In J. Strachey (Ed. & Trans.), *The standard edition of the complete psychological works of Sigmund Freud* (Vol. 16, 448–463). London: Hogarth Press. (Original work published 1917)

Gabbard, G. (1991). A psychodynamic perspective on the clinical impact of insurance review. *American Journal of Psychiatry, 148*, 318–323.

Gabbard, G. (1994, May). *Character disorder in the managed care era.* Paper presented at the annual meeting of the American Psychiatric Association, Philadelphia.

Halpert, E. (1972). The effect of insurance on psychoanalytic treatment. *Journal of the American Psychoanalytic Association, 20,* 122–133.

Kris, A. (1990). Helping patients by analysing self-criticism. *Journal of the American Psychoanalytic Association, 38,* 605–636.

Lacan, J. (1988). *The seminar: Book I.* Cambridge: Cambridge University Press. (Original Published in 1975)

Langs, R. (1973). *The technique of psychoanalytic psychotherapy.* New York: Jason Aronson.

Langs, R. (1976). *The bipersonal field.* New York: Jason Aronson.

Milner, M. (1957). *On not Being able to paint.* New York: International Universities Press.

Muller, J. (1996). *Beyond the psychoanalytic dyad.* New York: Routledge

Ogden, T. H. (1994). The analytical third: Working with intersubjective clinical facts. *International Journal of Psycho-analysis, 75,* 3–20.

Plakun, E.M. (1996). Economic grand rounds: Treatment of personality disorders in an era of resource limitation. *Psychiatric Services, 47,* 128–130.

Plaut, A. (1990). The presence of the third: Intrusive factors in analysis. *Journal of Analytical Psychology, 35,* 301–315.

Raney, J. O. (1982). The payment of fees for psychotherapy. *International Journal of Psychoanalytic Psychotherapy, 9,* 147–181.

Rudominer, H. S. (1984). Peer review, third party payment, and the analytic situation: A case report. *Journal of the American Psychoanalytic Association, 32,* 773–795.

Schafer, R. (1985). The interpretation of psychic reality, developmental influences, and unconscious communication. *Journal of the American Psychoanalytic Association, 33,* 537–554.

Semrad, E. (1969). *Teaching psychotherapy of psychotic patients.* New York: Grune & Stratton.

Shapiro, E. R. (1982a). On curiosity: Intrapsychic and interpersonal boundary formation in family life. *International Journal of Family Psychiatry, 3,* 69–89.

Shapiro, E. R. (1982b). The holding environment and family therapy with acting out adolescents. *International Journal of Psychoanalytic Psychotherapy, 9,* 209–226.

Shapiro, E.R. (2001). The effect of social changes on the doctor-patient relationship. *Organisational and Social Dynamics, 2,* 227–237.

Shapiro, E. R., & Carr, A.W. (1991). *Lost in familiar places: Creating new connections between the individual and society.* New Haven, CT & London: Yale University Press.

Shapiro, E. R., Zinner, J., Shapiro, R.L., & Berkowitz, D.A. (1975). The influence of family experience on borderline personality development. *International Review of Psychoanalysis, 2,* 399–411.

Silk, K. (1994, May). *Short-term hospitalization.* Paper presented at the annual meeting of the American Psychiatric Association, Philadelphia, PA.

Chapter 10

Integrative Psychodynamic Treatment of Psychotic Disorders

Jane G. Tillman, PhD

Psychotic-spectrum disorders present major challenges to patients, families, and clinicians. Medications have succeeded in providing many patients with relief from the positive symptoms of the disorder, such as delusions, hallucinations, or mania, and atypical antipsychotics may even help some negative symptoms. But even when symptom suppression has been achieved, clinicians, patients, and their families are left to try to put together the pieces of a life devastated by serious mental illness. The person suffering from the aftereffects of a psychotic episode still has a life to live while coping with these effects and the meaning of his or her symptoms. Often, because of the severity of the trouble, the relapsing and remitting course of the disorder, the limitations of medications, and the upheaval in interpersonal, occupational, and social functioning, these patients become among those considered "treatment resistant."

Psychoanalytic or psychodynamic psychotherapy as a treatment modality for psychotic-spectrum disorders remains a source of controversy, both within biological psychiatry and the field of psychoanalysis. The American Psychiatric Association Practice Guideline for the Treatment of Patients with Schizophrenia (2004), which recognizes that fully a third of patients with schizophrenia fail to respond adequately to antipsychotic medication, endorses cognitive–behavioral therapy (CBT) for these patients but not psychodynamic psychotherapy. In the field of psychoanalysis, most training programs have removed courses on the treatment of psychotic disorders from their curricula (Gottdiener, 2006), finding that these patients present too great a challenge for insight-oriented analytic work. The dualism between biology and psychology is often magnified when approaching the treatment of psychotic disorders. How one thinks about the etiology of psychotic disorders often determines the treatment modality. In the current zeitgeist of biological psychiatry, psychological factors that may either mitigate or promote symptom expression are often overlooked, and psychotherapy, if prescribed at all, is subordinated to the biological perspective.

At the Austen Riggs Center 10–15% of our patients struggle with psychotic disorders, many of whom have become treatment resistant over time. Given the current preeminence of biological treatments in training and practice, often these patients are essentially psychotherapy naïve at the time of their admission, having tried numerous medications but having had relatively little sustained intensive psychotherapy or other psychosocial interventions. Our treatment model at Riggs closely parallels the "need-adapted treatment" described by Finnish researcher Yrjö Alanen, a treatment tailored to the specific needs of the individual with schizophrenia, using psychodynamic psychotherapy, family systems work, medication, and community support (Alanen, 1994a, 1994b, 1997a, 1997b; Alanen, Lehtinen, Räkköläineen, & Aaltonen, 1991). Practicing in the complex system of the Austen Riggs Center presents an opportunity to authentically integrate biological perspectives, sociocultural factors, individual dynamics, and family systems psychodynamic processes.

This chapter first reviews the history of the dualism between the biological and psychological theories of psychotic disorders. After surveying contemporary research related to the etiology and treatment of psychotic-spectrum disorders, I then describe the integrative approach used at Riggs to treat these patients. The usefulness of psychodynamic psychotherapy, when embedded in a larger context of a therapeutic community for psychosocial learning (see Chapter 11), a psychodynamic psychopharmacology approach to prescribing (see Chapter 3), and family treatment (see Chapter 12), is examined. All of these psychotherapeutic approaches are grounded in Muller's sophisticated concept of the Third as a structuring function and external referent for staff and patients in our work together. I advocate for a *both–and* approach to the treatment of psychotic disorders rather than the historical and now contemporary *either–or* approach regarding biological and psychological therapies. Finally, I present case material illustrating the comprehensive approach to the treatment of a patient with a psychotic disorder within the open setting of the Austen Riggs Center.

HISTORY

Biological theories about the cause of mental illness have their roots in ancient traditions. Hippocrates offered a theory of four humours to account for changes in personality or the presence of illness in his patients. When the four humours of black bile, yellow bile, phlegm, and blood were out of balance, patients might present as depressed, melancholic, hot tempered, amorous, or unemotional. Such theories of "chemical imbalance" have remained popular since that time. With the neoclassical revival in 18th-century Europe, ancient theories led to such treatments as applying leeches or blood letting by other means to try to rid the body of toxins or excesses. The film *The Madness of King George* (1994) has a dramatic scene of cupping the back of the king—or applying heated glass bowls to the skin of the back like suction cups—in an effort to treat his severe mental illness, now thought to be a manifestation of acute intermittent porphyria.

Moral therapies for psychiatric disturbance became popular in the late 18th century as well, after thinkers such as Kant popularized the notion of individual rights and responsibilities, and Rousseau offered the notion of the social contract as an ordering principle for balancing the conflict between the individual and society. Such theories are still evident in contemporary therapeutic community practices. As a result of the work of these early thinkers, moral therapy for mental illness became more common.

In 1882 the German physician Robert Koch reported the discovery of mycobacterium tuberculosis, providing a biological marker for one of the most feared diseases of that time. Infected people could now be identified, isolated, and treated with rest cures and other medically directed but morally tinged therapies. Great enthusiasm surfaced for finding a bacteriological basis for many human illnesses within the medical community. Psychiatry, a newly formed medical specialty at the close of the 19th century, also aspired to identify the biological/bacteriological basis for mental illness.

The rift between biological and psychological theories and treatments deepened throughout the 20th century. Andrew Scull (2005) gives a harrowing account of the supposedly scientific zeal of Henry Cotton, MD, the superintendent of the Trenton State Hospital from 1910 to 1933. Enthused by Koch's discoveries related to tuberculosis, Cotton surmised that the "functional psychoses" were caused by "focal sepsis" that was bacteriological in origin and could be treated surgically. He spent his tenure at the Trenton State Hospital attempting to cure the psychoses by extracting the teeth, colons, uteri, gallbladders, and other organs of his patients, many of whom died in this pursuit. The data Cotton collected and reported in journals and at professional meetings were later found by a young psychiatrist, Phyllis Greenacre, to have been fabricated and misinterpreted (Scull, 2005). Scull reports that Greenacre's description of Cotton's scientific misconduct was suppressed by Adolf Meyer, and Cotton was never held accountable for the enormous harm he caused to thousands of psychiatric patients entrusted to his care.

If Cotton's story is one of the most gruesome, it is certainly not the only example of some overzealous but misguided physicians injuring or maiming their patients in an effort to cure psychotic disorders. Insulin coma, deep hypothermia, lobotomies pioneered by Egaz Moniz and Walter Freeman, Metrazol-induced seizures, and other somatic therapies were applied in a variety of situations, often without informed consent. Psychologically traumatized World War I soldiers were subjected to severe electrical shocks of the pharynx, forehead, and other parts of the body in an attempt to cure them of "malingering" by a 1927 Nobel Prize winner in medicine, Julius Wagner von Jauregg, a contemporary and, at times, an antagonist of Freud in Vienna.

Contemporaneous with the focus on drastic somatic and surgical therapies for psychotic disorders, Ernst Simmel, a young psychiatrist in the Prussian army during World War I, petitioned the government to create a psychoanalytic hospital for the treatment of the war neuroses. Although this did not happen immediately, by 1927, with the help of his colleagues at the Berlin Polyclinic, the Berlin Psychoanalytic Society, and the endorsement and help of Sigmund Freud, Simmel opened the first psychoanalytic hospital, the Schloss Tegel sanitarium, which functioned from 1927 until 1931. The patient population of this hospital included severe alcoholics and patients with character disorders, and likely higher-functioning psychotic patients. Extending psychoanalytic treatment to a hospitalized population of seriously disturbed individuals introduced the element of group phenomena. This approach gradually evolved elsewhere over the next several decades into the development of therapeutic communities and milieu treatment as adjunctive to the psychoanalytic task.

Drs. Karl and Will Menninger visited Simmel in the 1930s, seeking his consultation about their pioneering psychiatric hospital in Topeka, Kansas. Trained as psychoanalysts, they sought to develop a hospital based on psychoanalytic principles, but with greater flexibility to allow for the treatment of psychotic patients. Here, classical psychoanalytic technique was modified based on the assessment of the patient's capacity to work in such a treatment modality.

Parallel to the ongoing developments occurring in biological psychiatry, progressive adaptations of technique were occurring in psychoanalytic circles that allowed this method of treatment to be extended to a more troubled population. With the end of World War II the need for psychiatric services for returning veterans was apparent. In this context, the Menningers founded the Menninger School of Psychiatry in a partnership with the Veteran's Administration Hospital in Topeka. One Menninger Clinic psychoanalyst, Robert Knight, MD, left Topeka in 1947 to become the medical director of the Austen Riggs Center in Stockbridge, MA, bringing with him such luminaries as Roy Schafer, Margaret Brenman-Gibson, David Rapaport, Merton Gill, and Alan Wheelis. Knight's interest in articulating a theory and treatment for borderline conditions led him to contribute to the discussions of the time about the widening scope of psychoanalysis.

With the well-documented disasters of biological psychiatry (El-Hai, 2005; Scull, 2005) becoming apparent by the late 1940s, psychoanalysis stepped in, developing hegemony in American academic psychiatry and hospital treatment. Theories about the etiology and treatment of schizophrenia were developed, but were difficult to test empirically. Clinicians from the interpersonal tradition of psychoanalysis, led by Harry Stack Sullivan, Clara Thompson, and Frieda Fromm-Reichmann, began treating patients with schizophrenia at the Chestnut Lodge Hospital in Maryland using primarily psychoanalytic psychotherapy. In a 1948 paper, Fromm-Reichmann posited that a potential contributor to the development of schizophrenia could be traced to the "schizophrenogenic mother." This theory was an attempt to locate the etiology of the psychoses in the earliest relationships. Although these theorists were often accurate in many of their observations about schizophrenic social and family dynamics, terms such as "schizophrenogenic mother" or "refrigerator mother" (in the case of autism) have a tone of mother blaming, to which there has been an understandable backlash, and also proved difficult to validate with empirical research findings. When Otto Will became the medical director of the Austen Riggs Center in the late 1960s, he brought from Chestnut

Lodge a psychoanalytic theory and technique for treating patients with schizophrenia that had been practiced there for several decades, and was informed by the theories of early developmental trauma and/or neglect.

The role of the mother as a contributor to the development of severe psychopathology enjoyed a dubious psychoanalytic career from the 1940s until the mid-1970s (Neill, 1990; Willick, 2001). The mother as a protective agent facilitating the infant and child's development was more central to the work of Winnicott and provided a counterbalance within psychoanalytic thinking. Like biological psychiatry, developments and advances in psychoanalysis were often accompanied by authoritarian statements about cause and cure that went beyond the bounds of good practice. Although many in the psychoanalytic community resisted the use of medication in treating their patients, over time it became apparent that for many patients, combined treatment was superior to either medication alone or psychotherapy alone. There were notable exceptions, where psychodynamic psychotherapy alone produced symptom remission and therapeutic gain (Gottdiener, 2006), which should not be of great surprise to clinicians who have worked psychotherapeutically with patients in the psychotic spectrum who have recovered.

The hegemony of psychoanalysis in the United States "led to a significant de-emphasis on diagnosis and nosology . . . and a de-emphasis on careful observation of signs and symptoms" (Andreasen, 2007, p. 110). Without such scientific means, the systematic classification and study of the psychotic disorders were impossible. The response of general psychiatrists was to develop a more careful descriptive taxonomy of psychiatric illness in the *Diagnostic and Statistical Manual of Mental Disorders* (DSM). By 1980, with the publication of DSM-III, field trials of the nosology were included to demonstrate diagnostic reliability and to facilitate psychiatric research about the validity of the categories of psychotic and other disorders described and their longitudinal course and outcome (McGlashan, 1983; Plakun, Burkhardt, & Muller, 1985). American psychoanalysis resisted such schematization and did not work to join the conversation early on. However, in 2006 psychoanalytic researchers and clinicians introduced the *Psychodynamic Diagnostic Manual* (2006), attempting to articulate in a systematic way theory-based psychoanalytic diagnosis. Unfortunately, the lack of field trials demonstrating reliability and validity of categories limits the potential utility and acceptance of such a manual within descriptive psychiatry.

By the late 20th century psychoanalysis was largely purged from academic medicine, and many of the long-term hospitals providing private treatment based on a psychoanalytic model had closed (Plakun, 2006). McWilliams (2000) observes that psychoanalysis has had a steady hand in its own demise through arrogance and refusal to engage in outcomes research verifying the efficacy of psychoanalytic treatment for both neurotic and psychotic disorders.

Psychoanalytic psychotherapy and intensive treatment are time-consuming and expensive. Biological psychiatry came into ascendancy with advances in the field of psychopharmacology—producing medications with a demonstrated positive effect in treating such active symptoms of psychosis as hallucinations, delusions, and mania, and reducing the time and cost to treat psychotic patients in the acute phase of illness. The psychotherapeutic relationship between the patient and the therapist is now often relegated to merely supportive or educational status, and medication has become the great hope for many patients, families, and doctors. Enthusiasm for scientific psychiatry was ascendant in the 1970s and continues to shape treatment guidelines in contemporary psychiatry. General psychiatry recognized the necessity of scientific research far earlier than did psychoanalytic clinicians. The field of psychoanalytic research may be characterized as idea-rich but also as methodology and resource poor (Reiss, 2008). This bleak picture has begun to change in the past several years.

Recent studies of psychodynamic psychotherapy outcomes using sophisticated meta-analytic techniques demonstrate the effectiveness of psychodynamic treatments (Leichsenring, Rabung, & Leibing, 2004; Leichsenring, 2005; Leichsenring & Rabung; 2008). Milrod et al. (2007) demonstrated in a randomized controlled trial that short-term psychodynamic psychotherapy is an effective treatment for panic disorder. Shedler (2010) reviewed eight quantitative studies of psychodynamic psychotherapy using meta-analytic procedures showing that psychodynamic psychotherapy is an effective treatment for many patients. He also observed the irrational basis for the popular perception that psychodynamic approaches lack empirical support, which may "reflect selective dissemination of research findings" (p. 98). With these exciting new developments in psychoanalytic research, it is now well demonstrated that psychodynamic psychotherapy is a sound treatment for many patients, although outcome studies linked to various diagnostic groups continue to be needed, particularly in the treatment of psychotic spectrum disorders. The conclusion of many in the scientific community that psychodynamic treatments lack an evidence base is no longer consistent with empirical evidence supporting psychodynamic psychotherapies.

CONTEMPORARY RESEARCH ON PSYCHOTIC DISORDERS

Contemporary research on psychotic disorders must confront the reality that the psychotic spectrum disorders present with widely disparate symptom pictures implying different etiologies, longitudinal course, variable responses to different treatment methods, and differing prognoses. In the next section, theories about the etiology of psychotic spectrum disorders are reviewed along with controversies in treatment approaches.

Etiology

Schizophrenia research is difficult because the disorder may not be a single entity, but rather an umbrella term for a heterogeneous set of symptoms with a range of etiological factors. Biological researchers are now pursuing in great detail the neurobiology of psychotic-spectrum disorders. For the past 50 years, a focus on the dopamine system has been a mainstay of neurobiological research in psychotic disorders. In any contemporary psychiatric journal one is likely to see articles related to the component symptoms of psychotic disorders full of the names of complicated chemicals and enzyme systems. These articles are the foundation of current psychiatric bench research and clinical trials.

Other studies look at structural and functional neurobiology, neurodevelopment, and genetic components of schizophrenia. Genetic research aims to identify heritable conditions that may render a person vulnerable to developing schizophrenia. In their well-known review of adoption and twin studies, Gottesman and Shields (1976) noted that in monozygotic twins, the concordance rate for schizophrenia was between 35 and 58%, compared with dizygotic twins, where the rate was 9–26%. This research suggests that it is possible for an individual to carry the same genes as someone who develops schizophrenia without ever developing the illness, suggesting that genes play a significant but not exclusive role in the pathogenesis of schizophrenia.

In a long-term follow-up study of Finnish adoptees, researchers compared the offspring of schizophrenic mothers who were subsequently adopted, to adoptees without a genetic risk for schizophrenia (Tienari et al., 2004). The adoptive families were rated for levels of function or dysfunction. In the high-genetic-risk group there was a significant association between family dysfunction and the adoptee being diagnosed with a schizophrenia-spectrum disorder. The demonstration of this gene–environment interaction led the authors of this study to conclude that neither high-genetic-risk nor dysfunctional family environment *alone* account for the development of schizophrenia-spectrum illness. Findings of a clear interaction effect support a stress–diathesis model of psychopathology.

Williamson (2007) notes: "The last two decades have been marked by a concerted search for the gene or genes which would account for schizophrenia. It has become increasingly obvious to many investigators in the field that these genes are not going to be found. Schizophrenia is not likely a simple genetic disorder nor is it likely accounted for by a few major genes" (p. 953). Researchers, however, are making progress in understanding the genetics of the cognitive components associated with schizophrenia, identifying intermediate phenotypes of heritable traits. The genetics of specific measurable cognitive functions are an important advance, but extrapolating to a diagnostic category via genetic evidence is unlikely (Goldberg & Weinberger, 2004; Tan, Callicott, & Weinberger, 2008). Overall, the evidence suggests around 50% of the variance in etiology of schizophrenia is attributable to environmental factors rather than to genetics, including such environmental factors as individual dynamics, family environment, migratory status, trauma, and environmental chemical influences. This kind of epigenetic exploration of gene–environment interactions is the likely focus of future research into the etiology of schizophrenia.

Research about the role of the environment in schizophrenia is less well known than biological research. In his review of the psychiatric literature, Jarvis (2007) concluded that there is a dearth of research related to the role of psychosocial factors in the etiology of psychotic disorders in North American journals. This regional disinterest notwithstanding, Jarvis notes that our European colleagues are leading the way in psychosocial research about the etiology and treatment of psychotic disorders.

Trauma is once again being investigated for the role it may play in the development of schizophrenia. British researchers Shevlin, Houston, Dorahy, and Adamson (2008) conducted a study to estimate the effect of cumulative trauma on the development of schizophrenia. Using two large community samples (one from the United States and one from the United Kingdom), they concluded that experiencing two or more types of trauma significantly predicted psychosis in a dose–response relationship.

The trauma of childhood molestation and physical abuse, along with serious injury, assault, and violence in the home, were significantly associated with an increased incidence of schizophrenia. Morgan and Fisher (2007) reviewed the question of whether childhood trauma is a factor in the later development of psychotic disorders. Although they noted many conceptual and methodological problems with the existing research, they also acknowledged that "a small number of recent population-based studies provide more robust evidence of an association, and there are now plausible biological mechanisms linking childhood trauma and psychosis" (p. 3). Such research may confirm the clinical experience of psychodynamic clinicians, who observe a relationship between childhood trauma and the treatment-resistant symptoms of seriously disturbed patients.

Psychosocial adversity associated with migration is also associated with the development of schizophrenia (Cantor-Graae & Pedersen, 2007; Cantor-Graae & Selten, 2005). Research implicates migration as a significant risk factor for schizophrenia, where "high incidence rates for schizophrenia have been found for persons of Surinamese, Dutch Antillean, and Moroccan background in the Netherlands . . . and an increased risk for developing schizophrenia has recently been found for all migrants in Denmark, particularly those from Australia, Africa, and Greenland" (Cantor-Graae & Selten, 2005, p. 12). Both first- and second-generation migrants are more vulnerable to psychotic disorders, suggesting an intergenerational transmission of trauma or sociocultural dislocation. Hypotheses surrounding the idea of "social defeat" and the discrimination that many black-skinned migrants face have been offered as causal pathways to the higher incidence of schizophrenia in this population. Here, empirical research validates psychoanalytic theorists positing a social link in the development of psychotic disorders (Davoine & Gaudilliere, 2004).

Treatment Approaches

A current trend in psychiatry, as in the rest of medicine, is toward the development of practice guidelines promoting "evidence-based medicine." Of course, what constitutes evidence is an area of dispute. Much money and energy have been spent researching brief psychotherapeutic and psychopharmacological treatments for various disorders, whereas psychoanalysis and dynamic therapies are late to the table in this arena, are rarely funded by NIMH and other large granting agencies, and have not produced a robust body of quantitative outcome research literature.

An important study in this regard is the NIMH-funded Schizophrenia

Patient Outcomes Research Team (PORT), which was charged with developing and implementing evidence-based treatment recommendations for schizophrenia. These findings greatly influenced the development of the American Psychiatric Association Practice Guideline for the Treatment of Patients with Schizophrenia (American Psychiatric Association, 2004). The PORT study utilized a comprehensive review of the treatment outcomes research literature to craft guidelines for the treatment of schizophrenia based on the efficacy of various treatment approaches (Lehman, Steinwachs, et al., 1998). Criteria levels for evidence were established: Level A was characterized by "good research-based evidence, with some expert opinion, to support the recommendation"; level B evidence was characterized by "fair research-based evidence, with substantial expert opinion"; and level C as "recommendation based primarily on expert opinion, with minimal research-based evidence, but significant clinical experience" (p. 2). Psychodynamic therapies did not fare well in this methodology, understandably relegated to level C criteria at best.

The PORT study made 30 recommendations for the treatment of schizophrenia. The first 21 of these recommendations addressed pharmacotherapy and ECT. Recommendation 22 states: "Individual and group psychotherapies adhering to a psychodynamic model (defined as therapies that use interpretation of unconscious material and focus on transference and regression) should *not* be used in the treatment of persons with schizophrenia" (Lehman, Steinwachs, et al., 1998, p. 7). Recommendation 23 was in favor of "individual and group therapies employing well-specified combinations of support, education, and behavioral and cognitive skills training approaches designed to address the specific deficits of persons with schizophrenia" (p. 8). Other recommendations include family treatments, but specifically avoiding those "based on the premise that family dysfunction is the etiology of the patient's schizophrenic disorder" (p. 8). The final recommendations address the need for vocational support, "assertive case management," and "assertive community treatment" to prevent rehospitalization. Interestingly, the Finnish Turku project noted earlier (Alanen, 1991), demonstrating the efficacy of "need-adapted treatment" for schizophrenia, was not included in the PORT bibliography and does not appear to have been considered in formulating the treatment guidelines.

As you might imagine, there was a vigorous response to the PORT recommendations from psychodynamic clinicians experienced in providing effective treatment to patients with schizophrenia. At the second annual meeting of the U.S. chapter of the International Society for the Psychological Treatments of the Schizophrenias (ISPS) and other psychoses in October 2000, psychodynamic clinicians and the authors of the 1998 PORT study came together for an interdisciplinary discussion.

The *Journal of the Academy of Psychoanalysis and Dynamic Psychiatry* published the proceedings of that meeting along with other papers to address the short shrift the PORT study gave to psychodynamic psychotherapy and family treatment (Gottdiener & Haslam, 2003; Karon, 2003; Larsen, 2003; Margison, 2003; Silver & Larsen, 2003; Ver Eecke, 2003). Ver Eecke (2003) directly addressed recommendation 22 of the PORT study stating that psychodynamic psychotherapy for schizophrenia was contraindicated, and recommendation 26, discouraging addressing family dysfunction and its role in schizophrenia. Using empirical studies, Ver Eecke (2003) showed evidence for the usefulness of both insight-oriented treatments and those addressing family conflict and dysfunction. Other authors addressed the controversies of evidence-based medicine (Margison, 2003), a critique of the methodology of the PORT study (Gottdiener & Haslam, 2003), and the importance of psychotherapy in the treatment of schizophrenia (Karon, 2003). In response to these conversations, in the 2003 revisions to the PORT guidelines, Lehman and his colleagues retracted their prohibition against psychodynamic psychotherapy for schizophrenia stating:

> In the updated PORT recommendations, the old recommendations that warned against certain treatments, including psychoanalysis and family therapy based upon theories of family causation, have been eliminated. This revision is not because the evidence regarding these treatments has changed but rather because we made a strategic decision not to list the many treatments that have been applied historically to treating persons with schizophrenia but have now been shown to be ineffective. . . . Reductionistic treatment plans that use only pharmacotherapy, or any other single modality, are inadequate from an evidence-based perspective. (Lehman et al., 2004, p. 206)

Although the massive effort by the journal was effective in removing the prohibitions against psychodynamic psychotherapy and psychodynamic family therapy, the revised statement leads the reader to assume that psychodynamic treatment is among those "historical" treatments that have been "shown to be ineffective." This familiar error in logic perpetuates the problem of bias against psychodynamic approaches, equating the lack of evidence of efficacy with evidence of lack of efficacy. It is quite clear now that it is incumbent upon the psychoanalytic and psychodynamic communities to continue to produce evidence of positive treatment outcomes that meet the standard of rigorous research methodology in our respective disciplines.

Researchers sophisticated in psychodynamic treatment are responding to the challenge. Gottdiener (2006) reviewed the meta-analytic research on individual psychodynamic psychotherapy in the treatment of schizophrenia, concluding: "Individual psychodynamic psychotherapy for schizophrenia was associated with significant improvements when used with medication and even when used without medication" (p. 586). He also noted that there were fewer than 30 studies of psychodynamic psychotherapy for people with schizophrenia, encouraging researchers to develop randomized controlled trial (RCT) studies to study the efficacy of this treatment approach. The positive contribution of the PORT study in advocating for a biopsychosocial approach to the treatment of schizophrenia, and of Gottdiener's (2006) review of the meta-analytic literature supporting psychodynamic psychotherapy as a treatment modality, are a guide and an endorsement of the comprehensive treatment approach used at the Austen Riggs Center.

INTEGRATED TREATMENT

Treatment of psychotic-spectrum disorders has been carried out at the Austen Riggs Center since the late 1940s. Over time the treatment model has evolved into an integrated interdisciplinary approach to our patients. Our treatment may be favorably compared to the work of Alanen (1991, 1994a, 1994b, 1997a, 1997b) and his Finnish colleagues in Turku, who have conducted and researched what they term "need-adapted treatment." The main principles of "need-adapted treatment" are:

> 1) a basic psychotherapeutic attitude, 2) development of hospital wards into psychotherapeutic communities, 3) development of family therapy and other family-centered activities, 4) development of individual therapeutic relationships, 5) appropriate use of pharmacotherapy as a mode of treatment supporting psychotherapy, and 6) active participation of all

professional groups in the therapeutic work. (Alanen, 1997a,
p. 141)

In the Turku project long-term individual psychodynamic psychotherapy
with schizophrenic patients was associated with a significant reduction in
the days of acute hospital treatment needed over the course of 5 years
(Alanen, 1997a, p. 147).

Other chapters have addressed the various modalities and intricacies
of psychodynamic therapy and residential treatment with patients who
are often considered to be "treatment resistant." Riggs aims to integrate
"best practices" in the treatment of psychotic disorders through an interdisciplinary treatment team seeking to bring multiple perspectives and
understandings to the task of treatment. Throughout the integrative treatment effort at Riggs there is attention to three crucial factors: (1) respect
for the patient's authority in the treatment, viewing him or her as an active and responsible agent, including selection of only those patients with
psychotic disorders for whom this is a reasonable assumption; (2) attention to the importance of evolving and ongoing relationships as a central
component of treatment; and (3) a commitment to the uncovering of the
meaning of symptoms and of treatment resistance itself.

Meeting twice each week, the treatment team is headed by a team
leader and consists of psychotherapists, social workers with family therapy
credentials, psychopharmacologists, nurses, substance abuse counselors,
and representatives from the Therapeutic Community Program (see Chapter 13; Shapiro & Plakun, 2008). The psychotherapist is in charge of holding all aspects of the patient's care in mind and offering a dynamic
formulation to the team to help make sense of our work together. The
treatment plan often includes psychodynamic psychopharmacology, as
described in Chapter 3, where meaning effects of medication are articulated. The importance of the therapeutic community as a locus for social
engagement, feedback about behavior, personal responsibility, and patient
authority is intensively applied in an effort to help patients discover their
competence and to encourage independent functioning and adaptation to
the demands of independent living. This facet of the treatment program
meets the intent of the PORT recommendations for vocational rehabilita-
tion as patients pursue various work and leadership opportunities within
the treatment program.

Since nearly half the patients diagnosed with schizophrenia will have a
comorbid substance use disorder (American Psychiatric Association, 2004),

our treatment approach provides both individual and group substance abuse counseling with a substance abuse staff member on each treatment team. Finally, understanding the family system of the patient and the interaction effects of the patient with schizophrenia and the family system are an important component of the treatment team formulation (see Chapter 12).

Conflicts within the field get played out within the team dynamics, as do conflicts between the patient and the family. When all goes well, the team can get hold of the various conflicts and work to be a representative of a coherent Third to the treatment dyads. Obviously, this does not always go smoothly. Treating these patients over a long period of time through intense engagement produces powerful staff disagreements, anger, withdrawal, splitting, and other strains staff must contend with and understand in order to work effectively with our patients and their families. These strains are multiplied by our pursuit of psychodynamic treatment in a larger professional culture that often does not recognize the efficacy of an intensive approach that goes beyond the intent to manage and control patients' symptoms to invite patient authority in a collaborative treatment effort. Staff members carry the tension within themselves and within the group as we pursue a complex way of working with disturbed and disturbing patients and their families.

Principles of Riggs treatment of patients with psychotic disorders, comparable to "need-adapted" treatment, suggest that patients with psychotic disorders do best when:

- Treaters work from a basic psychodynamic perspective focusing on finding the meaning of symptoms.
- Individual intensive psychodynamic psychotherapy is part of treatment.
- Patients participate in a therapeutic community program that respects the authority of patients and examines interactions.
- Family work is part of treatment.
- Pharmacotherapy is used to minimize positive and negative symptoms and to support psychotherapy.
- Substance use disorder treatment is used to support abstinence.
- There is active participation of all professional disciplines in the therapeutic work, which is integrated in treatment teams.

In the following section I provide a clinical report illustrating the complex psychodynamic dilemmas encountered when treating psychotic-spectrum disorders. The patient presented with intermittent-mood incongruent psychotic episodes that could be clearly linked to developmental transitions in his life, demonstrating a stress–diathesis dynamic. Other likely contributing factors to developing a psychotic disorder included a family history of severe mental illness and his father's immigration to this country as a young man. The patient had a history of good interepisode recovery and was able to work with the treatment team and in his psychotherapy to develop a more complex understanding of how his conflicts and defenses were manifest in his psychotic episodes.

CLINICAL ILLUSTRATION

Mark was a married man in his 30s at the time of his admission to Riggs. He experienced his first psychotic episode after leaving home to attend college in a different area of the country. While there he experienced the traumatic death of a peer in a freak accident in the dormitory. Mark unraveled within weeks of this death and remained in bed for a week—mute, staring with his mouth open, as if catatonic except for making odd gestures with his hands. His roommate called his family, who came to the school and had Mark hospitalized. At the moment of separation from his family in the emergency room he became violent, assaulting staff, eventually winding up in four-point restraints and sedated. Mark remained delusional and paranoid during most of his several-week hospitalization, was diagnosed with a psychotic disorder, and was treated with an antipsychotic and a mood stabilizer. Returning home to live with his parents, Mark completed his degree in engineering at a nearby college.

The family history indicated that Mark's father immigrated to the United States from Belgium at age 25. Mark stated that although he had felt close to his father, there had also been a deep mystery about him because he had never talked about his childhood in Belgium or his family history. Mark's mother's family included the patient's great-grandfather, who was described as a "failed genius," living out his last years psychotic and in a state hospital. Two cousins on the maternal side had mental illness: one a schizoaffective disorder and one a bipolar disorder. Mark had three older siblings, one of whom carried a diagnosis of bipolar disorder.

Mark worked successfully as an engineer after college in a relatively low-stress business. He was not in psychotherapy, but continued to take antidepressants. His father became ill several years later and died of cancer. Mark was with the family for this important event, describing his father's condition at the end of his life as "gruesome." Several months later Mark had a second psychotic episode during which he tried to kill himself with carbon monoxide poisoning, but narrowly survived. He had delusions that he was riddled with cancer, that he was losing his vision, and that he was never going to be able to succeed in the world, maintaining a persistent fantasy that he was now a lost boy. Once again he recovered with the re-introduction of antipsychotic medication and supportive, once-weekly psychotherapy lasting 18 months. Mark married a woman and started his own surveying company, achieving financial independence from his family and developing a solid client base. He and his wife both described the early years of the marriage, before the birth of their first child, as "wonderful."

Upon the birth of his first child Mark once again fell apart. His wife was in a motor vehicle accident 2 weeks after the birth of their daughter and almost bled to death from injuries. Mark was tormented and could not bear the idea of the close call with death his wife had endured so shortly after giving birth. During her convalescence and the period of maternal preoccupation with their new child, he felt he had lost his wife as his own primary maternal support. Mark attempted suicide in his despair, but was discharged from the emergency room once stabilized following this attempt. At home he became progressively prone to rageful behavior and then regressed to the point of experiencing himself as an infant, insisting on maternal care from his wife. Mark feared that if left alone, he would either kill his daughter or himself. He was unable to work and imagined that he had a brain tumor or some other lethal illness that would kill him. After 6 weeks of progressive deterioration, including delusions, regressed behavior, and "rage attacks" in which he feared both destroying others and being destroyed by them, his physician placed Mark on two antipsychotics, a mood stabilizer, an antidepressant, and a benzodiazepine that seemed to abate his positive symptoms of affective dysregulation and paranoia. However, negative psychotic symptoms emerged, with Mark showing little interest in his daughter, his wife, or independent adult functioning. After another 8 months of unremitting lethargy and negative psychotic symptoms treated with various medication trials, his outpatient psychiatrist recommended ECT, which terrified Mark. He refused this recommendation, but after several more weeks his wife gave him an ultimatum: He could agree to ECT or seek long-term residential treatment. Reluctantly, Mark agreed to come to the Austen Riggs Center.

At the time of admission to Riggs Mark had negative psychotic symptoms, with marked psychomotor slowing, thought blocking, and a flat affect, as well as appearing overmedicated. He did not have prominent positive symptoms, although delusions and confusion were noted in the months prior to admission. Mark complained of being confused and disoriented. Psychological testing and the clinical history were consistent with the diagnosis of a psychotic illness, most likely a schizoaffective disorder. Interestingly, he was eager to engage in four-times-weekly psychodynamic therapy, felt deeply understood, and rapidly developed an idealizing transference. In an early session, out of a thick mental haze and with great effort, Mark spontaneously reported an early memory of being 4 years old in nursery school, where he developed such a yearning to be home with his mother that he left the school, running down the sidewalk in the snow, until a motorist stopped to pick him up and returned him to the school. He said he had felt in an absolute panic about separation from his family and that this feeling of panic about abandonment often led him to feel he was losing his mind and falling into a million little pieces that could never be retrieved.

In the context of the stable holding environment of the milieu, nursing support, and psychotherapy, Mark began to articulate his catastrophic fears about the end of the world, and how these underlying fears became exacerbated with the birth of his daughter. Gradually he was able to think about the dynamic conflicts underlying his acute and recurrent decompensations: his fear of annihilation; conflicts surrounding his hostile dependence on his mother and on his wife, and how coercive he could become if he felt dropped by them; his deep attachment to his father, who he felt had sustained him through a painfully shy and awkward childhood; his cherished position as the youngest child in his family, that he was angry about losing by growing up; and his lifelong difficulty meeting developmental milestones without major psychic disruption. Mark observed that he had never been able to construct a "big picture" narrative of his experience.

Family meetings with his wife and toddler daughter also became an important part of the treatment. His wife expressed her annoyance that Mark had abandoned his business while insisting that she go back to work full time to financially support the family. Mark had competitive and aggressive longings to be the center of his wife's world, insisting that she provide equally intensive care for their daughter and for him. His wife was able to confront Mark about his "rages" soon after the birth of their daughter, and about how frightened she had become of him. The couple worked hard to reconcile the events of the past 18 months and to come to some understanding about each of their family-of-origin dynamics that played out in the marriage. Contrary to the PORT recommendations, examining the intergenerational family dynamics of both members of the couple gave them both a greater appreciation for the conflicts each brought to the marriage, how these had been unconsciously lived out within the marriage, and how they contributed to the angry impasse they experienced with Mark's most recent decompensation.

Mark arrived at Riggs on lithium carbonate 1,200 mg/day, risperidone 4 mg/day, aripiprazole 30 mg/day, venlafaxine 150 mg/day, and clonazepam up to 6 mg/day (as needed). His psychopharmacologist worked with Mark to understand how he might be using such a medication regimen to dull his mind and his experience. Mark agreed but felt that all the medication was an effort to "keep the peace" at home by avoiding intense affective states he could neither understand nor contain. He was also desperately averse to the recommendation of his outpatient psychiatrist for ECT and hoped that if he took enough medication, he could live out his days in a stupor without further confrontation. Over time his medication regimen changed: The risperidone was eliminated, the clonazepam was decreased to 3 mg/day in 1 mg prn doses, and lithium carbonate was decreased to 900 mg/day. After consultation by a team of psychopharmacologists, methylphenidate 20 mg daily was added. The venlafaxine remained at 150 mg/day, and the aripiprazole at 30 mg/day. As with most of our patients, one aim of this patient's psychopharmacological treatment was to allow him to engage as productively as possible in therapy and the milieu, preserving a space for affective expression that was not suppressed by medication. Often, achieving this balanced effect involves addressing the patient's defensive overuse of medication to avoid painful, but manageable, affective states, as Mintz and Belnap note in Chapter 3.

Within the transference, Mark found the focused attention of his psychotherapist intensely gratifying and took the stance of an overly solicitous and compliant patient. Although a therapeutic regression within the transference is the expectable course of an intensive psychodynamic treatment, a paradox in Mark's case was his defensive use of the gratifying aspects of the therapeutic situation to reconstitute higher ego functioning within several months. In some respects he was eager to please the therapist to show her what a "good boy" he was, evoking his therapist's concern that this behavior was a flight into health—an issue that was engaged in the therapy in some depth.

Slowly, Mark grieved the losses in his life incurred through normal developmental milestones and separations, and also the deeply traumatic losses he had experienced. Feelings of being inferior to his own idealized father surfaced. He shamefully admitted that he felt he could never be as competent a father to his daughter as his own father had been to him. Mark used the shelter of the hospital and the support of the positive transference to begin the grieving process. He grieved more fully his experience of having nearly lost his wife in the car accident, and his anger that, though she survived this medical crisis, he again lost her through her necessary interest in and care of their infant daughter. Mark felt his mind was coming apart as he watched the maternal care he was accustomed to receiving being redirected toward his young daughter. His guilt about his murderous aggression toward his family and toward himself was gradually articulated. He came to understand the way his wish for maternal care and his delusional insistence on being the true infant in the household were defensive solutions to his dread of being the large and potentially aggressive man he might be.

While at Riggs, Mark worked with our woodworking instructor to construct a toy chest for his daughter. He used the freedom of the open setting to find ways of being alone and on his own for periods of time, developing an enjoyment of quiet time spent in the greenhouse. In these endeavors Mark regained a sense of mastery and also took small steps toward claiming himself as the father of his child and as a competent member of the adult community.

Mark left Riggs after 5 months to begin four-times-weekly psychodynamic treatment with a therapist in his hometown. At a 2-year follow-up he was reported to be doing well, having restarted his business and rebuilding his clientele. There had been no further psychotic episodes, and he remained stable on his medication regimen and in his psychotherapy. Continuing couples therapy helped repair the damage he had done to his marriage, while allowing the couple also to work out their parenting conflicts and improve their communication skills.

DISCUSSION

Working in a psychoanalytically oriented hospital with profoundly ill individuals, many of whom arrive at Riggs following the failure of all of the various treatments general psychiatry has to offer, presents unique challenges. Mark's prior treatments had consisted of multiple hospitalizations, multiple drug trials, and 18 months of once-weekly supportive therapy focused on symptom management and the development of coping skills. Following the failure of these standard interventions, Mark might be thought of as "treatment resistant." Coming to Riggs offered a treatment that allowed him, for the first time, to think about his developmental history and his family history. Over time he was able to construct a coherent meaning for his symptoms and to appreciate, with great sadness, the pain he had endured with each and every separation in his life, beginning in early childhood. Instead of a person with a catalogue of psychiatric symptoms to be managed exclusively through concrete, "evidence-based" interventions, Mark gradually became a man with a life narrative upon which he could reflect. This process was ego-strengthening for Mark who, once given the opportunity, had an excellent ability to begin to "connect the dots" of his life.

In many ways, Mark's story is a hopeful one. Some patients with psychotic disorders are not candidates for an open setting or for the assumption that they can be considered competent adults. Many of our patients with psychotic disorders do not possess such ready ability for engagement or insight. Mark's clear awareness of his own interpersonal hunger place him at the upper end of the psychotic spectrum. Other patients at Riggs suffer from more difficult psychotic disorders. They do not always have a history of occupational success, meaningful sustained relationships, or cognitive capacities for insight into their illness and its antecedents. The treatment of these more profoundly ill patients requires time and patience, while utilizing all the humane modalities we can bring to bear.

The despair of both the patient and family are prominent in situations where the pathology and course of the illness are not quickly responsive to treatment. Sometimes the focus of treatment in psychotic disorders is helping a patient and family come to grips with rage and grief related to profound limitations and deficits in a patient, while helping a family accept the child they have rather than the one they might wish for. Nevertheless, there are clear instances where even the most seriously disturbed individual, out of the mainstream of life and functioning marginally for years, can gradually achieve independent functioning with intensive treatment, including a resource-rich environment of community engagement, vocational opportunity, an expectation of personal responsibility, and a respectful stance that each person has his or her own story to tell about the meaning of his or her life both before and after the psychotic disorder emerged. It is this latter opportunity that is often lost in our contemporary culture; a careful psychotherapeutic treatment that invites the patient to bring his or her deepest concerns, hate, love, and confusion into a relationship where steadfast curiosity keeps the possibility of new discovery and change open for the patient. In this model the therapist engages the patient in an interest in the internal world while keeping an attentive eye on the task of ego adaptation to the demands of reality from the external world. The use of such a model for treating patients with psychotic spectrum disorders is not limited to facilities like Riggs, but can also be replicated in outpatient and other settings.

Whereas the PORT recommendations about treatment seem piecemeal and additive in nature, the treatment at Riggs seeks to apply "best practices" in an integrative, need-adapted fashion. Our aim is to help our patients develop the capacity for a well-lived life as full citizens of the community with the attendant rights and responsibilities of such citizenship. Given the dreadful history of the inhumane and misguided treatment of people with psychotic disorders, our first priority is to do no harm, respecting the vast complexity of mind, culture, and biology in our approach without becoming narrow or reductionistic in our thinking or our treatment. Patients with complex difficulties who have struggled in outpatient psychotherapy or in a fragmented system of care may benefit from pursuing more intensive treatment in a system that strives to provide a multidisciplinary and integrative approach to treatment. Communication among mental health professionals working with such patients is a crucial element of treatment in order for the treatment to cohere and have the best chance of success.

When faced with the choice of ECT or residential treatment, Mark was able to use his own authority to opt for treatment in the open setting and the responsibilities that choice entailed. He was interested in and able to use psychodynamic therapy to enlarge his understanding of the timing and the meaning of his most recent psychotic episode, and he was able to link his previous episodes to periods of stress around developmental transitions. He was able to use the network of supportive relationships available to him to create a safe-enough environment to do this work. Finally, Mark was devoted to working to preserve his marriage and to develop his paternal relationship with his young daughter. He was able to use all aspects of the Riggs approach and the open setting to begin developing his capacity for psychological insight and a return to family and occupational functioning.

REFERENCES

Alanen, Y.O. (1994a). An attempt to integrate the individual-psychological and interactional concepts of the origins of schizophrenia. *British Journal of Psychiatry, 164*(Suppl.), 56–61.

Alanen, Y.O. (1994b). Introduction. *British Journal of Psychiatry, 164*(Suppl.), 7–8.

Alanen, Y.O. (1997a). *Schizophrenia: Its origins and need-adapted treatment.* London: Karnac Books.

Alanen, Y.O. (1997b). Vulnerability to schizophrenia and psychotherapeutic treatment of schizophrenic patients: Toward an integrated view. *Psychiatry, 60,* 142–157.

Alanen, Y.O., Lehtinen, K., Räkköläineen, V., & Aaltonen, J. (1991). Need-adapted treatment of schizophrenic patients: Experiences and result of the Turku project. *Acta Psychiatrica Scandinavica, 83,* 363–382.

American Psychiatric Association. (2004). *Practice guideline for the treatment of patients with schizophrenia* (2nd ed.). Washington, DC: American Psychiatric Association.

Andreasen, N.C. (2007). DSM and the death of phenomenology in America: An example of unintended consequences. *Schizophrenia Bulletin, 33,* 108–112.

Cantor-Graae, E., & Pedersen, C.B. (2007). Risk of schizophrenia in second-generation immigrants: A Danish population-based cohort study. *Psychological Medicine, 37,* 485–494.

Cantor-Graae, E., & Selten, J.P. (2005). Schizophrenia and migration: A meta-analysis and review. *American Journal of Psychiatry, 162,* 12–24.

Davoine, F., & Gaudilliere, J.M. (2004). *History beyond trauma: Whereof one cannot speak, thereof one cannot stay silent.* New York: Other Press.

El-Hai, J. (2005). *The lobotomist: A maverick medical genius and his tragic quest to rid the world of mental illness.* Hoboken, NJ: Wiley.

Fromm-Reichmann, F. (1948). Notes on the development of treatment of schizophrenics by psychoanalytic psychotherapy. *Psychiatry, 11,* 263–273.

Goldberg, T.E., & Weinberger, D.R. (2004). Genes and the parsing of cognitive processes. *Trends in Cognitive Sciences, 8,* 325–335.

Gottdiener, W.H. (2006). Individual psychodynamic psychotherapy of schizophrenia: Empirical evidence for the practicing clinician. *Psychoanalytic Psychology*, *23*, 583–589.

Gottdiener, W.H., & Haslam, N. (2003). A critique of the methods and conclusions in the Patient Outcome Research Team (PORT) report on psychological treatments for schizophrenia. *Journal of the American Academy of Psychoanalysis and Dynamic Psychiatry*, *31*, 191–208.

Gottesman, I., & Shields, J. (1976). A critical review of recent adoption, twin and family studies of schizophrenia: Behavioural genetics perspectives. *Schizophrenia Bulletin*, *2*, 360–401.

Jarvis, G. E. (2007). The social causes of psychosis in North American psychiatry: A review of a disappearing literature. *Canadian Journal of Psychiatry*, *52*, 287–294.

Karon, B.K. (2003). The tragedy of schizophrenia without psychotherapy. *Journal of the American Academy of Psychoanalysis and Dynamic Psychiatry*, *31*, 89–118.

Leichsenring, F, Rabung, S, & Leibing, E. (2004). The efficacy of short-term psychodynamic psychotherapy in specific psychiatric disorders: A meta analysis. *Archives of General Psychiatry*, *61*, 1208–1216.

Leichsenring, F. (2005). Are psychodynamic and psychoanalytic therapies effective?: A review of empirical data. *International Journal of Psychoanalysis*. *86*, 841–868.

Leichsenring, R. & Rabung, S. (2008). Effectiveness of long-term psychodynamic psychotherapy. *Journal of the American Medical Association*, *300*(13), 1551–1565.

Lehman, A.F., Kreyenbuhl, J., Buchanan, R.W., Dickerson, F.B., Dixon, L.B., Goldberg, R., et al. (2004). The schizophrenia Patient Outcomes Research Team (PORT): Updated treatment recommendations 2003. *Schizophrenia Bulletin*, *30*, 193–217.

Lehman, A.F., Steinwachs, D.M., & the Co-Investigators of the PORT project (1998). At issue: Translating research into practice: The schizophrenia Patient Outcomes Research Team (PORT) treatment recommendations. *Schizophrenia Bulletin*, *24*, 1–10.

Margison, F. (2003). Evidence-based medicine in the treatment of schizophrenia. *Journal of the American Academy of Psychoanalysis and Dynamic Psychiatry*, *31*, 177–190.

McGlashan, T.H. (1983). The borderline syndrome. *Archives of General Psychiatry*, *40*, 1311–1323.

McWilliams, N. (2000). On teaching psychoanalysis in anti-analytic times: A polemic. *American Journal of Psychoanalysis*, *60*, 371–390.

Milrod, B., Leon, A., Busch, F., Rudden, M., Schwalberg, M., Clarkin, J., et al. (2007). A randomized controlled clinical trial of psychoanalytic psychotherapy for panic disorder. *The American Journal of Psychiatry, 164* (2), 265–272.

Morgan, C., & Fisher, H. (2007). Environmental factors in schizophrenia: Childhood trauma—a critical review. *Schizophrenia Bulletin, 33,* 3–10.

Neill, J. (1990). Whatever became of the schizophrenogenic mother? *American Journal of Psychotherapy, 44,* 499–507.

Plakun, E.M. (2006). Finding psychodynamic psychiatry's lost generation. *Journal of the American Academy of Psychoanalysis and Dynamic Psychiatry, 34*(1), 135–150.

Plakun, E.M., Burkhardt, P.E., & Muller, J.P. (1985). 14-year follow-up of borderline and schizotypal personality disorders. *Comprehensive Psychiatry, 26,* 448–455.

(2006). Psychodynamic diagnostic manual (PDM). Silver Spring, MD: Alliance of Psychoanalytic Organizations. Retrieved from PsycINFO database.

Scull, A. (2005). *Madhouse: A tragic tale of megalomania and modern medicine.* New Haven: Yale University Press.

Shapiro, E.R., & Plakun, E.M. (2008). Residential psychotherapeutic treatment: An intensive psychodynamic approach for patients with treatment-resistant disorders. In S. Sharfstein (Ed.), *The textbook of hospital psychiatry* (pp. 285–297). Washington, DC: American Psychiatric Association.

Shedler, J. (2010). The efficacy of psychodynamic psychotherapy. *American Psychologist, 65*(2), 98-109.

Shevlin, M., Houston, J.E., Dorahy, M.J., & Adamson, G. (2008). Cumulative traumas and psychosis: An analysis of the National Comorbidity Survey and the British Psychiatric Morbidity Survey. *Schizophrenia Bulletin, 34,* 193–199.

Silver, A.-L., & Larsen, T. (2003). Frontline: The schizophrenic person and the benefits of the psychotherapies—seeking a PORT in the storm. *Journal of the American Academy of Psychoanalysis and Dynamic Psychiatry, 31,* 1–10.

Tan, H.Y., Callicott, J.H., & Weinberger, D.R. (2008). Intermediate phenotypes in schizophrenia genetics redux: Is it a no brainer? *Molecular Psychiatry, 13U,* 233–238.

Tienari, P., Wynne, L.C., Sorri, A., Lahti, I., Läsky, K., Moring, J., et al.

(2004). Genotype–environment interaction in schizophrenia spectrum disorder: Long-term follow-up study of Finnish adoptees. *British Journal of Psychiatry, 184,* 216–222.

Ver Eecke, W. (2003). The role of psychoanalytic theory and practice in understanding and treating schizophrenia: A rejoinder to the PORT report's condemnation of psychoanalysis. *Journal of the American Academy of Psychoanalysis and Dynamic Psychiatry, 31,* 11–29.

Williamson, P. (2007). The final common pathway of schizophrenia. *Schizophrenia Bulletin, 33,* 953–954.

Willick, M.S. (2001). Psychoanalysis and schizophrenia: A cautionary tale. *Journal of the American Psychoanalytic Association, 49,* 27–56.

———◄◆◆◆►———

Chapter 11
Silencing the Messenger

The Social Dynamics of Treatment Resistance

Donna Elmendorf, PhD, and Margaret Parish, PhD

"People are only ever as mad . . . as other people are deaf. . . ."
—A. Phillips (1996, p. 34)

The life stories of those who come to be known as treatment resistant are often difficult to speak and to hear. They are painful stories, often suppressed or silenced through generations that may reflect family conflict, betrayal, and shame. Affected by the pressures of others, these individuals may have given up the possibility that anyone can hear, understand, or help them. Consequently, they often tell their stories to others in condensed and displaced forms, through acts of self-destruction, defiance, attack, perversion, flight, and withdrawal. In turn, such acts, because they are threatening, bewildering, and offensive, are often met not with attempts to understand but instead with desperate efforts to control. "Treatment-resistant" people—the carriers of these stories—may come to be seen as if their only identity is their disturbance, exacerbating an existing sense of alienation and objectification.

Social dynamics play an important role in psychological disturbance. Patients engage in entrenched symptomatic behavior when social forces act to silence more direct or authentic communication. Treatment resistance often responds to "social" engagement in a milieu that appreciates and addresses these social elements.

In a psychiatric context, treatment-resistant patients are those who, despite repeated medical, psychopharmacological, psychotherapeutic, cognitive, and behavioral interventions, remain unable to manage disturbed and disturbing emotional states and behavior, to function adaptively, or to lead satisfying lives. As earlier chapters in this volume have suggested, for such people in individual psychotherapy, escalating negative transference and countertransference feelings can become intolerable, leading to problematic enactments and therapeutic impasse. Hospitalization often occurs when disturbances that cannot be sufficiently understood and translated in the dyadic context of the therapy are dispersed into the patient's other relationships and expressed in actions that create significant alarm. Many view hospitalization as a way to control or sequester the disturbance; indeed, hospitalization is often endorsed or funded only in cases of "danger to self or others," with the implication that confinement is the best way to manage that danger.

In fact, such a strategy may perpetuate the problem by encouraging passivity and compliance that, paradoxically, foster "treatment resistance" in cases where "resistance to treatment may be the only way left for a patient to exercise authority" (see Chapter 1). Put differently, when treatment is framed around securing compliance, treatment resistance may be a sign that the patient still holds hope, albeit unconscious hope, that his or her story may yet be spoken and heard. Within this frame of reference treatment resistance represents the unconscious refusal to join a community that will not acknowledge meaning that may be threatening. Hospitalization or other extended treatment in an open setting, within a therapeutic community, although rare in the current climate of short-term stays, is valuable not only because such treatment discourages passivity, but because much psychological disturbance is essentially social and can only be ameliorated through social solutions. "Treatment resistance" may be a result of the failure of those in charge of "treatment" to recognize the social dimensions of the problems being treated.

The approach to treatment that has evolved at Riggs rests on the belief that human relationships are a central agent of change, that disturbed and disturbing behaviors are an attempt to communicate meaning, and that change is facilitated by the recognition and support of patients' authority for their treatment and their lives. The multidisciplinary treatment approach we have found effective provides numerous differentiated relationships that support patients' efforts to translate their disturbing actions into meaningful language and that recognize their strengths and competence, not just their "patienthood."

Other chapters describe theory and technique in individual psycho-therapy and link it to the notion of the Third. At Riggs, the therapeutic community is in some ways the most concrete representative of the Third, providing a social environment within which everyone participates (even if via an apparent refusal, as in the case of a patient who shuts him- or herself alone in his or her room), within which patients and staff join in articulating shared social standards, and within which the tasks and roles of the dyadic relationships (therapist–patient, psychopharmacologist–patient, therapist–psychopharmacologist, patient–patient, etc.) are de-fined. In this chapter we describe the values and assumptions of this kind of therapeutic community and offer two case examples of work with chronically disturbing people. While most clinicians work with patients without the benefits of an organized therapeutic community, all treat-ment takes place in some social environment. Our approach highlights the potential interpersonal meaning of symptomatic action and illustrates the importance of keeping in mind the impact of social context on human functioning and development.

PATIENT AUTHORITY AND COMPETENCE

From the perspective of the therapeutic community, treatment resistance reveals as much about the context as about the individual. Interpersonal settings that are based on control, coercion, reward, and punishment rein-force compliance and work against the discovery of meaning and the emergence of a "true self" (Winnicott, 1960). When patients begin to tell their stories through action, or in other condensed or displaced form, such settings are "deaf" (Phillips, 1996, p. 34). Therapeutic communities, begin-ning with the Northfield experiments in the United Kingdom in the 1940s (Main, 1989b), existed in various forms in psychiatric inpatient programs throughout the second half of the 20th century.

For over 50 years, the therapeutic community at the Austen Riggs Center has been unusual for existing in an open (i.e., unlocked) setting, focusing on the development of a noncoercive partnership between pa-tients and staff aimed at mutual problem solving, and at creating an envi-ronment that supports satisfying living and effective treatment (Belnap, Iscan, & Plakun, 2004; Shapiro & Plakun, 2008; Stern, Fromm, & Sack-steder, 1986; Talbot & Miller 1966; White, Talbot, & Miller, 1964). No matter how disturbed, all people have strengths and competencies, and all people benefit from having some ability to influence their surround. We invite patients to work collaboratively with us around running the milieu, and, in fact, the center. We ask for their input as we administer our programs, reflect on our functioning, and look to the future. Through a system of patient government, patients run a daily community meeting; plan and carry out group leisure time activities; reach out to members who are isolated, alienated, or alienating; help orient and welcome new patients; and recognize and celebrate such milestones as birthdays, moves to a new program within Riggs, and discharges. The life-affirming benefits of these real contributions and the invitation to join with the staff as citizens in a shared community act in opposition to the regressive pull of the patient role (Jones, 1953; Kennard, 1998; Talbot & Miller, 1966). As Muller (1992, p. 4) states, we actually work to "undermine the patient's compliance as the most subversive aspect of their pathology."

> Interpersonal treatment contexts—for example, family therapy, individual therapy and psychopharmacology, inpatient, partial hospital, or residential treatment settings—that are based on control, coercion, reward, and punishment reinforce compliance and work against the discovery of meaning, thereby contributing to treatment resistance.

The mobilization of the citizen role begins during the admission process, when, as part of negotiating the initial therapeutic alliance, we make clear to patients that the price of joining our community includes each patient's agreement to take responsibility for his or her safety and that of other community members. Patients agree to work collaboratively with staff to preserve the environment for their and others' treatment. This agreement is essential to treatment in any open setting, in which people are not locked up or otherwise physically controlled, but instead participate in a culture that depends on shared agreement about what behavior is acceptable and on shared efforts to understand and speak about the meanings of behavior. There are only a few "rules," which, if broken, will end treatment. From the beginning we enlist the Third as "pact," as Muller describes in Chapter 6, as the chosen social container, rather than a locked building and a system of privileges, prescribed behaviors, or forced participation.

THE TRANSLATION OF IRRATIONAL ACTION
IN THE SOCIAL CONTEXT

As citizens of this kind of therapeutic community, patients are responsible for their actions and are welcome to participate in creating social structures in the milieu; they may be called upon, like citizens of a country, to represent others through explicit roles. Representation can also happen unconsciously, when a person is mobilized to express something otherwise unspoken on behalf of a community, a family, or the larger society. Side by side with the affirmation of patients' capacities to create a working community in partnership with the staff is the recognition that those disturbing behaviors that led to hospitalization will inevitably emerge in action in the community. This setting allows these behaviors and their impact to be brought into the individual dynamic therapy, where there is an effort to decode the meaning embedded in actions, and to enable the individual to find expression in language instead of behavior. Beyond the individual work, though, the therapeutic community enables us to see more clearly the context in which action happens. We see action not only in relation to a therapist, but also in relation to other people and to groups of people. The therapeutic community, like any community, provides a wealth of opportunities for projection, for reworking old problems, and for encountering new ones. Individuals may use the group as an arena in which to relive the sometimes unspeakable and as yet unspoken experiences they bring from their families, in a way that allows interpersonal and intrapsychic dynamics to be more fully seen, grasped, and reworked. Reflecting on these experiences, that is, on the interpersonal motivations for, and effects of, patients' choices and behaviors, is a powerful tool for learning.

The community, however, is much more than a stage for reliving old experiences and reflecting on them; it is also an evolving social system in its own right, in which resistance, irrationality, and pressure to silence threatening ideas all emerge. From this perspective, what might look on the surface like "acting out" is actually an enactment (akin to enactment in individual psychotherapy) co-created by the patient and the group, with meaning for both. The existence of irrationality in staff behavior and in organizational structures in psychiatric hospitals is well documented (Menzies, 1960; Shapiro & Carr, 1987). Psychodynamic therapy, aimed at self-understanding, has a foundation in the Socratic declaration that "the unexamined life is not worth living." In an effort to counter potentially destructive trends in the therapeutic community and to maximize the benefit of the therapeutic milieu, we take "examined living" into the social realm. All community members—staff and patients alike—are encouraged to be open to observations about one another and about the system as a whole. Understanding previously obscured meanings of enactments can then contribute to individual, community, and organizational learning and development. Ideally, this practice of collaborative "examined living" not only enhances the treatment of the individual patient, but also fosters the development of a better functioning organization by containing, through reflection and translation, what was previously extruded.

Insofar as intrapsychic, interpersonal, and organizational experience are separable, the domain of psychotherapy is the intrapsychic and the (dyadic) interpersonal, while the domain of the therapeutic community is the (multi-person) interpersonal and the organizational. Patients are free to bring their inner lives into the community dialogue, but ideally it is the interpersonal and organizational aspects that are worked with publicly. We encourage patients to take their learning from the community back into their individual psychotherapy for an exploration of intrapsychic determinants and implications. Conversely, individual learning in the psychotherapy allows patients to gain a clearer view of their maladaptive and self-defeating interpersonal relationships, and supports experimentation with new ways of being in the community.

Just as the individual may act in and on the group to communicate, the group may also, wittingly or unwittingly, enlist the individual for its own purposes. A group can find expression through the action of one of its members, for example, by pressuring that person to behave in ways that unconsciously serve others (Main, 1989a). It is not only individual struggles that are communicated behaviorally; when enlisted to act as representatives of groups, individuals also reveal unspoken feelings of others as well as their own. For example, an outspoken person might be subtly encouraged to argue on behalf of more timid or less expressive people who share the same opinions. Or a person might be encouraged to remain in a sick role, so that others can be particularly strong and helpful while still vicariously satisfying their own need to be cared for. Both these scenarios are relatively common in a psychiatric hospital, and, of course, not only among the patients.

Staff members, like patients, are both subjects and objects in this examined living process, since staff, too, enact conflicts and at times respond irrationally. With regard to the staff, what is up for public scrutiny are staff behaviors, including speech, that emerge in the implementation of staff roles and in the representation of institutional stances and decisions. The openness of staff to examination is an essential element in therapeutic community life because it affirms that we are learning about and from *human* dynamics that apply to all, not only about psychopathology that exists solely in patients. Because many "treatment-resistant" patients have been "filled" with what was unbearable in their families (see Chapter 5, this volume; Shapiro & Carr, 1987), they are often particularly vulnerable to the inevitable projections from others, including staff. The invitation to reflect on staff actions helps to create a context in which staff irrationality can be identified and translated, thereby supporting patients' development—first, by not asking them to manage that which is not theirs; second, by modeling a willingness to consider unconscious meanings; and third, by using staff countertransference as a window into unconscious family dynamics (Shapiro & Carr, 1987). In addition, as staff members notice their projections, they can try to make sense of how such projections may relate to problematic dynamics of the larger organization. Once these dynamics are seen, they can be addressed in the service of the development of the institution. These approaches to identifying barriers to organizational development and attending to the reality of imperfection in the institution or therapist, as well as in the patient, are, of course, relevant to a wide range of treatment settings, not only those with therapeutic communities. For example, a patient may experience an outpatient clinic's billing or scheduling error in ways that recall early experiences of neglect or abandonment which they can better understand through reflection in their outpatient psychotherapy at the clinic, while the experience may at the same time highlight systemic problems in the clinic's procedures for billing or scheduling.

While staff enactments may lead staff members to reflect on the personal aspects of their involvement—that is, their own conflicts, anxieties, and defenses (and such reflection undoubtedly enables staff members to think more clearly in their role)—the details of these reflections are relevant to the community work only insofar as they are linked to the staff role and to patient or institutional learning (Shapiro & Carr, 1991). This distinction is not always self-evident, and making it requires considerable self-awareness on the part of staff. The work of maintaining an internal boundary between public and private is part of the strain of working in a therapeutic community in which unconscious life is taken seriously.

COMPETENCE AND IRRATIONALITY: AN ESSENTIAL DIALECTIC

Significant learning takes place at the intersection of a respect for patient competence and responsibility, on the one hand, and an acknowledgment of the meaning embedded in seemingly destructive acts, on the other. To expect our patients to engage only in competent functioning could easily be experienced as an invitation to adopt a compliant false self. Yet, to assume that psychiatric patients are incapable of mobilizing strengths and competence would be an invitation to a malignant regression or to unrealistic dependency on the experience or expertise of the staff. Patients and staff sometimes worry that any attempt to understand the meaning of a destructive action is an attempt to relieve the individual of responsibility. On the other hand, patients sometimes too quickly claim responsibility or try to change their behavior as a way to end a discussion before uncovering psychologically threatening meaning. The space created by respecting patients' competence, while also noticing their unconscious enactment of "that which cannot yet be spoken," holds enormous potential for working with treatment-resistant patients.

In a therapeutic community of the sort we are describing, there is a need for a subsystem of patient government that creates a space for review and reflection on the meaning of behavior when someone acts disruptively or otherwise raises concern in others. Within the open setting of Riggs, this group is known as the "Task Group," and it is comprised of an elected patient chairperson, patient representatives, and staff consultants. We use the Riggs name for this group in what follows, but it should be clear that the name is far less important than the function such a group serves within any open and noncoercive community of examined living. If the therapeutic community, as a whole, embodies the Third as a social and ideological context for treatment, the Task Group is its most concentrated representative. Sometimes the group mediates a destructive dyadic encounter (e.g., challenging a retreat into a sexual pair that separates a couple from others, or hearing the various conflicts that can arise among people who live together). Often mistaken by newcomers as a punitive quasi-court of law, the Task Group does hold in mind the impartial standards governing action in the community, but in doing so it strives to become an "ideal listener" that can understand the principles at stake for the individuals involved. The group works to understand the implicit meaning of disturbing action and to affirm the value of relationship. And it is perhaps the clearest possible example of the mobilization of patient authority in the service of treatment as well as living together amicably.

In practice, this kind of group works in a range of ways, offering observations and perspectives about how members view or feel affected by the person and the problem presented. Task Group members try to understand what led to the disturbing behavior and to help the person to establish or repair relationships with other community members. This often begins with the Task Group members themselves finding their own connection to the person being seen, either by empathizing with what led to the action or by speaking directly about the specific ways the person's behavior has affected them. They work toward understanding the individual's role in the community and the potential function for the community of this disturbing action. When it is successful, this process fosters the cohesion and functioning of the therapeutic community by encouraging alienated and destructive individuals to rejoin their peers' efforts to maintain community standards. The Task Group follows its meeting with an individual of concern by giving an account of the discussion at the larger community meeting, providing an opportunity for broader discussion with more community members.

The authority for running the Task Group and community meetings rests with the patients. In addition to sharing and expressing their own stake in the community's social standards, staff consultants listen for what the group members might be expressing, through words and actions, outside their conscious awareness. Often the interaction between the patient and the Task Group in some way replicates the original problem—for example, a person whose behavior has been irritating will irritate the group; one who has been isolated or alienated will be difficult for the group to reach, and so on. The staff pays attention to how the here-and-now process of the group might illuminate various relationships—between the individual patient and his or her peers, including the Task Group itself; between the Task Group and the larger patient community; between the patients and the staff. Staff members pay attention to the associative links in the discussions, attempting to hear implicit communications. If these can be made explicit, and other group members can begin to speak for themselves, the unconscious pressures on an individual to act on behalf of the group can be eased. Ideally this process enables individuals to feel freer to behave in less stereotyped ways and contributes to the development of the community.

CASE ILLUSTRATIONS

We offer two case examples to illustrate how the engagement of both individual responsibility *and* unconscious meanings helps create a reasonably safe and sane environment that fosters learning and development for individuals and the organization as a whole. As we have indicated, treatment-resistant patients often carry silenced messages for others, most often their families, who are "deaf" to them because of their own conflicts. Cultivating a community "ear" creates the possibility that the painful messages can be heard, contained, and applied to individual and group learning. The examples illustrate the ways in which society (in this case, patients and staff) may contribute to "treatment resistance." Both examples involve patients who broke a simple rule against smoking inside the center's buildings, a rule required by the center's own accrediting body, the Joint Commission. Since staying accredited and preserving the buildings, staff, and patients for the treatment task are imperative to the center's staff and board of trustees, repeated violation of the prohibition against smoking in the center's buildings is one of the short list of actions that can lead to a patient's discharge from the program. On closer examination, though, in neither of the cases offered was breaking the rule a simple matter. In the first example, uncovering the seemingly unbearable interpersonal meanings of this apparently solitary act allowed for reflection on repetitive family dynamics as they were played out in the community, for this patient as well as for others. In the second example, an individual is unconsciously enlisted to illuminate a dynamic between patients and staff and an underlying organizational problem.

Leslie

Leslie was a mother of four referred to the center with a treatment-refractory major depressive disorder, a personality disorder, an abiding wish to die, and a history of multiple suicide attempts. She was referred for admission in the context of her husband's leaving their marriage. At the preadmission consultation, she became mute and, at one point, fled the consulting room as if to underscore her investment in silence. Ultimately, she negotiated her way in by speaking for her interest in treatment and her willingness to take responsibility for her safety in the open setting. Through her treatment it emerged that rage at her husband's abandonment and her subsequent withdrawal from her children had filled her with unbearable guilt. This dynamic could neither be acknowledged by her nor spoken of within the family, both because of the fragility in the system created by her husband's absence and her anxiety about further hurting her children. These feelings, unbearable both for Leslie and her family, led her into a treatment-resistant, suicidal depression and withdrawal from others.

Leslie arrived at a time when the patient community was struggling with tensions between older patients and those in their early 20s and late teens. Early in her stay Leslie revealed enormous anxiety about being a member of the community, describing herself as either a withdrawn, silent, "nonperson" or as a "controlling, demanding leader who will be hated," leaving her with powerful feelings of self-repudiation. She commented that in the past she had seen herself as "totally capable" and that now she felt "completely useless." In her first community meeting she established herself both as a maternal presence and as a competent citizen, worrying that the recent acting out of two younger patients in the local community might have compromised their safety and reflected badly on the institution.

During a particularly difficult time in her treatment, Leslie broke the rule against smoking in Riggs buildings and began to smoke in her room. In addition to an administrative warning about the consequences if she continued to smoke in the building, she was referred to the Task Group. Prior to Leslie's arrival at the Task Group meeting, members spoke about her as a hostile, abrasive "bitch." Not surprisingly, given this view of her, Leslie was guarded and hesitant when she entered the meeting. She made several sarcastic comments, and then said her smoking in her room was self-defeating, self-abusive, and a sign that she felt depressed and defeated. Members pressed her beyond this pathology-oriented, isolated stance and spoke with her about how her behavior affected them. When a patient commented that Leslie had hurt her with one of her snide comments, Leslie began to cry. She described herself as feeling like a frightened animal that lashes out when it feels cornered.

Leslie apparently felt cornered in the Task Group meeting, reporting later to a staff member that she had felt misunderstood and "slammed." She decided to write a "rebuttal" letter, outlining how the Task Group had misunderstood her. At the beginning of the community meeting, when the Task Group chair was about to give her report on Leslie's meeting with the Task Group, Leslie interrupted and began to read her "rebuttal." Immediately a member of the Task Group asked her not to read the letter, but to try to listen to the report. Leslie continued reading, though, criticizing the Task Group members for their harshness and stating that she would not smoke in her room anymore, and that she saw no reason to continue the discussion. In her defensive stance, she saw the Task Group only as interested in enforcing behavioral guidelines and not the potential meaning of behavior. Similarly, in their initially harsh response to her, the Task Group members were caught in a critical enactment that obscured meaning. Provoked by her dangerous (and unconsciously rageful) behavior, the group had unwittingly taken up the role of Leslie's harsh self-criticism, leaving her to struggle against false compliance.

Fortunately, a member of the community responded to Leslie's attempt to stop the discussion by remembering that Leslie had said that she retreated to her room to smoke to escape from feeling she was a mother who was abandoning her children. With this comment Leslie began to cry, stating that she was trying to protect people from her self-loathing about what she saw as her failed motherhood. Several community members joined this comment, stating they thought this was the heart of the matter. They cited their own despair about themselves as failed siblings, parents, and children, and their wish to withdraw because of the guilt and humiliation associated with these feelings. Leslie then acknowledged that she felt she could not be around the younger patients because of her assumption that they would be horrified by the fact that she had left her children at home while she sought treatment. The smoking area in the backyard was the place that many of the younger patients congregated, and Leslie acknowledged that she had not wanted to "inflict" herself on them. With this comment, the recent rift in the community between older and younger patients, which had been interpreted as a result of the loudness of younger patients and the somberness of older patients, was recast. The rift could now be seen by all as a difficulty treating one another with respect because of painful feelings about family roles and intergenerational conflict. Toward the end of the meeting one of the younger patients told Leslie that she really wanted to hear about Leslie's dilemmas as a mother. A follow-up discussion was scheduled for the next community meeting, with a range of patients noting the difficulty reaching out across the age divide because of painful family experience.

The turning point in this follow-up meeting seemed to come when Leslie asked why she should try to keep understanding her smoking in her room since she had taken responsibility for it and would not do it again. The response back to her was, in essence—*you should do it because there is meaning in your behavior for you and for us, and if we don't figure it out, we will all be deprived.*

Staff difficulty in getting to this understanding sooner may have been linked to similar generational issues in the staff group. The staff group was in the midst of a transition authorizing younger staff to take up some of the roles formerly held by older staff, with attendant feelings of anxiety, loss, and competition. Further, two female staff leaders of the community privately recognized their own defensiveness around the "abandoning mother" dynamic; one was working in the community while her young child was at home with a caretaker and the other was the mother of a seriously ill adult child.

Leslie did stop smoking in her room and began to tolerate talking about her experience of herself as a mother in a range of groups in the community. She felt more at ease smoking in the designated smoking area in the backyard with the younger patients. Eventually she even ran for and was elected to be the chair of the Task Group. Other community members continued to speak more openly about their feelings about themselves as family members. There was dawning recognition that they had much to offer each other in learning about family roles and experience, particularly in speaking across the generational divide. Two weeks later, when patients were asked to express interest in what topic-focused groups they would like to see offered for the next rotation, a large number requested a parent–child group. This was the first time this group was offered. Part of its explicit task was for those who saw themselves primarily as parents to learn from those who saw themselves primarily as children, and vice versa.

Alice

Alice was a woman in her 20s with a personality disorder, a treatment-refractory mood disorder, and a substantial history of substance abuse. Previous treatment efforts had failed to alter her downhill slide. Alice's behavior was always on the edge of the law; she often ragefully and provocatively injured herself and challenged authority figures to step in and take over. After an extended period of treatment at Riggs, and in the middle of a very cold winter, Alice took to smoking in the attic of the wood frame building in which she lived, a residential program a block from the main hospital campus. After the housekeeping staff found her ashtray in the attic, Alice chose to refer herself to the Task Group rather than be referred by a staff member. In an unusually conscientious manner she attempted to offer a frame for the discussion, expressing curiosity about her motives (hiding from feelings, delving into something dangerous) and concern about her effect on her housemates and the rest of the community. Alice was thinking about her motivations on an individual level and in the context of her personal history; she was thinking about how she affects those around her. But she wasn't thinking about how those around her have affected her, how they might have contributed to her action, how they might wish to act through her or to pressure her to act on their behalf.

The Task Group members tend to think similarly; in fact, they can be quite resistant to considering their own participation in—their own responsibility for—another person's action. To the extent that community members enlist Alice to express parts of themselves that they are motivated to disown, they will understandably resist re-owning those parts and actively work to keep Alice in the role she has assumed on their behalf. Insofar as Alice's personal characteristics lend her to this sort of use by a group, it will be hard for her to extricate herself from this role.

This is why staff consultants attend to aspects of the *process* that illuminate the group's involvement. In this case right from the beginning of the patients' discussions of Alice's self-referral to the Task Group, several people questioned whether this rule breaking ought to be dealt with entirely by the center's administrative staff rather than the Task Group. Given that the group often deals with patients involved in rule infractions, their hesitation about doing so on this occasion was noteworthy and alerted us to the possibility of a brewing patient–staff conflict. It was as if the patient group were saying, "This shouldn't involve us. It is between Alice and the administration." Ultimately, however, the group decided that Alice's pattern of rule breaking might be a way of communicating some other problem, and was therefore worthy of their consideration.

Members of the Task Group often feel torn between dual tasks, on the one hand wishing to be helpful to the individual, whose behavior often expresses felt estrangement from others, and on the other hand feeling responsible for upholding community standards by stopping the troubling behavior. At this particular time they were feeling unhappy about being seen by the wider community as judgmental or punitive, and were tending to adopt a "helping" attitude. Staff, too, regularly feels pulled in similar directions. In consulting to the group's process, staff members listen for the implicit and unspoken in the interest of understanding, but as community members, staff members have an interest in upholding certain standards of behavior, which includes holding individuals accountable for their actions. And, of course, staff can be invested, unconsciously, in maintaining behavior that obscures painful or conflicted staff dynamics.

The first part of the Task Group meeting focused on some of Alice's personal concerns. As her self-referral implied, she was quite open to examining her own motivations and hearing what others had to say. She spoke primarily about a pattern in her actions—she felt lonely, and this led her to seek connections with others in self-destructive and rule-breaking activities. Alice said she was not inclined to break rules for the sake of it, but she did feel she was very susceptible to group influence and peer pressure. She also noted her difficulty asking for help when distressed, and thought that perhaps leaving the ashtray behind might have been an unintentional appeal for attention.

Struck by the helpful, therapy-session feel of this group meeting, the staff consultant asked whether any of the Task Group members cared whether people smoked in the attic of the building. Some said they did. One person said she wished Alice didn't smoke at all, because of the health hazard. Others recalled that this particular building had been damaged by a fire in the distant past.

Almost as an aside, Alice then mentioned that she had informally polled the other residents of the house about the smoking. No one had seemed to care about it, which made Alice feel less guilty. One of her housemates, present in the Task Group, acknowledged that he had said the smoking was no big deal, though he hadn't intended by that to grant permission. But by giving at least tacit consent, all the building's residents were in some way joining in smoking in the attic. The consultant to the Task Group wondered whether this apparent disregard of the rules of Riggs was expressing something on behalf of the larger patient community, something about the current state of their relationship to staff.

Task Group members, interested in these ideas, raised them for the community to consider when they delivered their report in the next day's community meeting. To what extent were people looking to others to sanction destructive behavior? What do people do when they are on the receiving end of such a request? Were patients more or less intentionally colluding in breaking rules identified as belonging to the staff? Perhaps because of the high value placed in this community on personal responsibility, the patient leader's report emphasized the origin of the action in the individual, Alice, who had sought tacit support from the members of the group. It is worth taking this a step further, though. At times, members of a group may have an unconscious, subtle, but nonetheless active role in encouraging destructive, defiant, or problematic behavior in order to encourage the expression of something in which many people have an interest but for which none have yet found words.

It happened that in this same community meeting another patient had earlier raised an apparently unrelated issue about this same residential program. It was scheduled for renovation, and during the renovation, the current residents would be relocated to two separate houses in town. The patient wondered if this was deterring people from applying to the program, which was currently nearly empty. She wondered how people were feeling about the plan to renovate some of the Riggs properties and expand the census. No one had a word to say in response to her questions, but they stayed in the consultant's mind as she listened to the Task Group's report. The consultant silently wondered whether, in addition to her own motivations, Alice might also unconsciously be expressing, on behalf of others, anger toward staff about the disruptive renovation plans? The Task Group's frequent references to the previous fire in the building may itself have expressed a fantasy of retaliation, as if to say, "If you disrupt our home, we will burn down the building!" This fantasy wasn't "heard" until the Task Group's work with Alice was reviewed in the community meeting.

Several staff members in the community meeting began to raise the possibility that all the patients in the residential program might have been involved in the rule breaking as an attempt to express anger about the recent disruptions to their living space. Perhaps Alice was lending herself to use by the group to express this without her—or their—conscious intent. Alice was open to this exploration. In addition to her habit of feeling drawn by others into self-destructive actions, she recognized that in her family of origin she had become familiar with the role of being the one to express or cause trouble on behalf of others. Though Alice was interested in looking at the participation of others in what she had done, the other members of the community meeting preferred to focus on Alice, and remained reluctant to explore the meaning of their own involvement in breaking Riggs rules. As she continued to talk with such openness and in such detail about herself, Alice was in that moment enacting the very issue she was commenting on—that is, she was preventing the others from considering their own part in the situation. The staff consultant's comment to this effect elicited a burst of anger from another resident of the building in which Alice resided, who exclaimed, "You are dividing the group!" Ostensibly he was referring to the suggestion that if Alice weren't so active, others might find their own place in the conflict, a suggestion that threatened a relatively comfortable established social order in which patients were more or less united. However, his choice of words was striking, given that Riggs's plan was to relocate the residents of the program to two separate houses in town during the renovation process—literally, to divide the group.

Once these concerns had been spoken, it was possible to have a freer, fuller discussion of the various reactions to the plans for renovating the building. But the process was not just a matter of increased awareness of individual or group dynamics; it also translated back into action that helped the community function better. Staff, now alerted to previously hidden reactions of the patients, were more sensitized to patients' needs and responded by soliciting their active involvement in managing the upcoming transitions in the program.

Of course, the community's use of Alice in this instance is only one part of the story; Alice was also using them for reasons of her own. Through this process she had the opportunity to reflect on her own vulnerability to destructive enactment of her rage at self-preoccupied authority figures. We have highlighted the pressure originating in the group because it is less readily seen, particularly in a community in which personal responsibility is so highly valued and so essential. This brings us to a paradox. Some might worry that saying that the group is responsible for Alice's actions risks absolving Alice of things for which she *is* responsible—in other words, it gives her an excuse to blame her own actions on others. This is always possible, but arguably people are better able to take responsibility for themselves (and move from being "treatment resistant") when their capacity to do so is not undermined by interpersonal and group dynamics that burden them with responsibility for what is not theirs.

DISCUSSION AND CONCLUSIONS

One of the most striking elements of the stories of Leslie and Alice is that both women were all too willing to offer intrapsychic interpretations of their behavior. These interpretations, if accepted by the group, would have located the disturbance in the particular individuals, shielding the community and organization from acknowledging their own participation. In essence, the symptoms, if not translated, could have stood as these patients' sacrifice to preserve a fragile social order in which "good" mothering is both reduced and stereotyped, and which denied the negative implications of organizational change that Alice's actions helped illuminate. Instead, because the group worked toward a more complex set of translations of their actions, both the individuals and the social system could be better understood. In the case of Leslie, her isolation had preserved the stereotypes that "bad" mothers leave their children and "bad" patients break rules. The community's capacity to hear her more complicated, painful story led to a treatment-enhancing deepening of her relationships and to a previously feared intergenerational discussion that benefited many.

In the second case, Alice came to better understand that she, self-destructively, recreated her involvement with self-preoccupied authority, while the administration learned that there were negative effects of institutional development on individual patients that must be acknowledged and addressed. The experience of having their barely spoken voices heard and attended to in a larger community of people that took some responsibility for the interaction, was an important element in the treatments of both Leslie and Alice, helping them each to find words for what was previously wordless experience, to join them to a more benign community of fellow human beings, and slowly to diminish the frequency and intensity of their destructive actions.

Effective engagement of treatment-resistant patients is supported by therapeutic milieus that:

- Support patient competence and authority.
- Hold patients responsible for their problematic behavior.
- Work to translate the interpersonal meaning of that behavior.
- Foster understanding of the ways patients unconsciously live out the past in the present.
- Address irrational group processes that interfere with competent functioning.

We regard the therapeutic community less as "treatment" itself and more as the context in which treatment happens, thus supporting the broader psychotherapeutic endeavor to translate symptoms into language. For the treatment-resistant patient, such a context may be essential, because a lone therapist often finds the symptomatic actions too threatening to tolerate and too bewildering to understand. When a patient in outpatient treatment acts in dangerous ways and the patient–therapist pair are unable to understand what is driving the action in a way that leads to deescalation, the pair is likely in need of a broader context such as consultation, family involvement, residential treatment, or even hospitalization. Such interventions are often most helpful when they include an attempt to understand the experiences in the psychotherapy that the patient and therapist have been unable to comprehend or to bear alone. Without the acknowledgment and support of a community of people who can empathically identify with and share responsibility for their troubles, patients like Leslie and Alice often continue shouldering their burdens alone, while expressing them only in symptoms and disturbances. It is no wonder that such patients "resist" or fail to respond to treatment, when treatment tries to eliminate the disturbances without understanding their source and their social context.

Families, groups, and societies can all be invested in silencing information and ideas that are too controversial, too painful, or too threatening to the status quo. Patients identified as treatment resistant often carry this information tacitly and contort themselves through symptomatic behaviors and speech so as to stay loyal to the pact of silence. While protecting some homeostasis, the silence not only takes its toll on the individual who "knows" that which cannot be spoken, but the silence also deprives the social surround of potentially useful learning. When the meaning of seemingly treatment-resistant behavior is faced, an individual may feel relief from the burden of the role of bearing the unbearable. By finding words for that which has been wordless and unspoken, the community can begin to incorporate meaning that was previously split out and carried by antisocial or self-destructive action, allowing for the emergence of a more complex and more containing social structure. This process is always constrained by the inevitable limitations of the particular individuals and groups; it is always a work in progress. But without respect for the competent voice of the patient, and for the meaning of seemingly regressive action, and without the recognition that irrationality also exists in the social surround, "disturbance" may be mistakenly cast as an intrapsychic or biological phenomenon in treatment-resistant patients.

Patient government can enhance patient responsibility and competence when it enlists patients in upholding behavioral standards and invites staff and patients to collaborate in *decoding* the social (interpersonal, group, and institutional) meaning embedded in problematic behavior.

This decoding of meaning:

- Relieves individuals of the burden of collective projections, freeing them to speak rather than act.
- Increases individual self-understanding by noticing characteristic ways an individual uses, and is used by, a group.
- Fosters the development of the milieu and the organization by addressing unconscious group dynamics that block learning.

REFERENCES

Belnap, B.A., Iscan, C., & Plakun, E.M. (2004). Residential treatment of personality disorders: The containing function. In J.J. Magnavita (Ed.), *Handbook of personality disorders: Theory and practice* (pp. 379–397). New York: Wiley.

Jones, M. (1953). *The therapeutic community*. New York: Basic Books.

Kennard, D. (1998). *An introduction to therapeutic communities*. London: Jessica Kingsley.

Main, T. (1989a). Some psychodynamics of large groups. In J. Johns (Ed.), *The ailment and other psychoanalytic essays* (pp. 100–122). London: Free Association Books.

Main, T. (1989b). The concept of the therapeutic community: Variations and vicissitudes. In J. Johns (Ed.), *The ailment and other psychoanalytic essays* (pp. 123–141). London: Free Association Books.

Menzies, I. (1960). A case study in the functioning of social systems as a defense against anxiety. *Human Relations, 13,* 95–121.

Muller, J. (1992). *Reflections on the open setting*. Unpublished manuscript.

Phillips, A. (1996). *Terrors and experts*. Cambridge, MA: Harvard University Press.

Shapiro, E.R., & Carr, A.W. (1987). Disguised countertransference in institutions. *Psychiatry, 50,* 72–82.

Shapiro, E.R., & Carr, A.W. (1991). *Lost in familiar places: Creating new connections between the individual and society*. New Haven, CT: Yale University Press.

Shapiro, E.R., & Plakun, E.M. (2008). Residential psychotherapeutic treatment: An intensive psychodynamic approach for patients with treatment-resistant disorders. In S. Sharfstein, F.B. Dickerson, & J.M. Oldham (Eds.), *Textbook of hospital psychiatry* (pp. 285–297). Washington, DC: American Psychiatric Association. Stern, D.A., Fromm, M.G., & Sacksteder, J.L. (1986). From coercion to collaboration: Two weeks in the life of a therapeutic community. *Psychiatry, 49,* 18–32.

Talbot, E., & Miller, S. (1966). The struggle to create a sane society in the psychiatric hospital. *Psychiatry, 29,* 165–171.

White, R., Talbot, E., & Miller, S. (1964). A psychoanalytic therapeutic community. *Current Psychiatric Therapies, 25,* 199-212.

Winnicott, D. W. (1960). Ego distortion in terms of true and false self. In *The maturational processes and the facilitating environment* (pp. 140–152). New York: International Universities Press.

Chapter 12

Working with Family Resistance to Treatment

Ave Schwartz, LICSW

Earlier chapters have made reference to the emergence of family system dynamics within the psychotherapy, the psychopharmacology, the logical structures of the treatment process, and patients' participation in their social world. Inherent in these discussions of family dynamics is the concept that the family functions as a system. The family is more than a collection of its members, more than the primary developmental context for the identified patient; it is a system that functions as a complex psychosocial entity with its own adaptive and developmental characteristics. As the family system engages with new contexts, it responds in characteristic ways. When a family member is hospitalized the entire family responds, not only to the identified patient, but also to the treatment context as a whole. In the context of residential and hospital treatment, the family may respond with resistance to the treatment process. In those cases when family system issues contribute significantly to treatment resistance in the identified patient, family therapy may be an effective clinical modality. This chapter focuses on the use of family therapy to work with family resistance to treatment. Specifically, it discusses the application of psychodynamic and systems thinking in working with families to establish a working alliance between the family, patient, and clinicians in the early phases of treatment.

It is a common experience for individual therapists to work with adult patients who may have considerable ability, but have not successfully achieved the developmental milestone of separation from their family of origin. In many of these cases adult patients are dependent on their families to pay for the treatment. Often these patients are seen to be in a hostile–dependent relationship with the family. In these cases the patient may present as "stuck" or treatment resistant—unable to take even small steps toward autonomy and preoccupied by both conscious and unconscious assumptions, fantasies, and conflicts that directly impede his or her development. These unconscious dynamics can interfere with the patient's development of a sense of his or her own authority and agency in the treatment context and in the world. The patient often expresses these unconscious dynamics in actions rather than words, with subsequent acting-out behaviors contributing to a presentation as treatment resistant.

It is also often observed in these cases that the family may, out of its frustration and fear about the patient's treatment resistance, become intrusive or overinvolved in the treatment, even to the point of ending it by withdrawing financial support. Alternatively, the patient may experience having been "forced" into treatment by the family, who subsequently disengages, leaving the patient alone with the individual therapist who is supposed to "fix" the patient. Both of these scenarios can lead to the patient's acting out of feelings and conflicts in a manner that appears treatment resistant. This chapter attempts to understand these experiences by conceptualizing the individual patient in the context of the family system. Specifically, it explores how all members of the family system may share common defenses that can manifest as treatment resistance. It is therefore important to recognize that the term *family* always includes the identified individual patient. A case example illustrates how working with the family system in a way that develops a relationship over time, recognizes individual authority (including the patient's), and finds and interprets the meaning of shared family defenses can help the family, including the patient, move out of a stuck and treatment-resistant position.

A word about the practical application of what follows. Riggs provides treatment in a therapeutic milieu that incorporates multiple disciplines and differentiated forms of treatment within a reflective, integrated, and collaborative model. The reality for most clinicians is that multifaceted and therapeutically integrated mental health treatment is not easily available. My hope is that the conceptual model for family work described below can be adapted to clinic environments, group practices, and other contexts where outpatient, inpatient, residential, or other treatment is provided by several collaborating clinicians.

> When a patient is treatment resistant it makes sense to look beyond the patient to the family system and the way the patient may be locked into a pathological role.

THINKING SYSTEMICALLY

The term *system* is pervasive in the postindustrial world. There are many different kinds of systems: social, mechanical, economic, biological, computational, political, philosophical—the list is virtually endless. Whether simple or complex, all systems must be understood from more than one point of view or frame of reference because systems are not uniform in their internal composition and structure. Systems are not reducible to their composite elements.

There are two key questions to consider when thinking about the family as a system: What is a system? How is the family a system? A system is defined as interacting or interrelated elements that, when taken together, form a whole whose properties cannot be found in the constituent elements. This central aspect of all systems is often expressed by the conceptual phrase: "The whole is greater than the sum of the parts." The family can be understood as a human system comprised of interacting individuals who recognize each other as related and who participate in an evolving network of relationships throughout the life cycle.

Understanding the family as a system requires the integration of information derived from multiple frames of reference. These frames of reference include the developmental and intrapsychic dynamics of each individual member, the particular contexts and life histories of family members, the patterns and processes of interaction between family members, the group dynamics of the individual members acting as a family, and the family as an evolving psychosocial entity with its own history and legacy—a legacy embedded in an even larger set of cultural–historical contexts. To think about a family systemically is to think from any and all these points of view in both analytic and synthetic modes.

At Riggs the patient is primarily understood in psychodynamic and psychosocial frames of reference, some of which have been described in earlier chapters. I have already outlined how the family may be understood as a system. For the purpose of this discussion the "treatment" is a complex system made up of, but not limited to, the clinicians; the clinicians' roles as defined by their tasks; the training, expertise, and experience of the clinicians that comprise the treatment team; the milieu; the institutional structure within which the treatment takes place; professional ethics and standards of care; and the larger context of psychiatric treatment in the society as a whole. Although all these elements are intrinsic to the treatment as a system, for the purpose of this chapter the "treatment system" is understood as a subset of the total treatment system: the patient, the family, and the clinicians providing direct patient care. The "clinicians" are the individual therapist and the family therapist. When there is a family meeting, these two clinicians act as a family's co-therapists to facilitate the process. The co-therapists serve to integrate the family context with the individual treatment process.

WHEN FAMILY SYSTEMS GET INTO TROUBLE

One way to think about a family system is in terms of the family tasks. Primary tasks of the family system are to provide for the care of children and other members; to provide for the reciprocal, but not necessarily symmetrical, satisfaction of needs; to enable its members to experience a bond of affection; to support them in negotiating the developmental extremes of dependency and autonomy; to help them develop an identity that enables them to both belong to and be individuated from the group; to assist them in accepting and understanding the reality and function of limits in life; to help them learn about and adapt to the changing demands of different stages of life; to prepare them for meaningful and purposive activity in the world; and to foster the capacity for creativity and satisfaction. In short, the overall task of the family is to provide the conditions in which family members can grow and develop throughout the family life cycle (Ackerman, 1966). Families that are functioning well succeed to some "good-enough" degree at most of these tasks. Family systems that are not functioning well, which are in trouble, display clear difficulty in achieving even minimal success at many of these tasks (Ackerman, 1966).

> The family is a system with the task of providing the conditions in which all family members can grow and develop throughout the family life cycle.

Psychological defenses are intrinsic to the psychodynamics of all family systems. Families of all types typically use a variety of defenses to manage the experiences of conflict, loss, ego-dystonic affect, and anxiety. In good-enough family systems these defenses do not chronically interfere with reality testing. They allow for adaptive processes of reflection, recognition, and reparation within and between family members. In good-enough family systems, defenses do not interfere with the development of rich, complicated, and integrated senses of self and other. They help manage anxiety, affect, and conflict, but not at the expense of relationship.

However, in family systems that are in trouble, defenses often function rigidly and nonadaptively. They impair reality testing and distort perceptions of self and other. The dynamics of these defensive processes have been explored in a number of key papers that focus on the mechanics of projective identification and splitting within families (Shapiro, 1978, 1982; Shapiro et al., 1977; Zinner & Shapiro, 1972). Several concepts developed in this body of work are of particular importance for this discussion. One is the use of projective identification as a defense that reduces family relationships to a repetitive dance of denial, aversion, unconscious identification, and reciprocal "pathological certainty" (Shapiro & Carr, 1991) about the motivations, thoughts, and feelings of other family members. The second concept, derived from the study of projective identification, is the development of complementary "defensive delineations" that reduce the experience of self and other to conflicted stereotyped representations. These fixed stereotyped perceptions impair reality testing by denying the presence of data in the family system that might otherwise contradict the distorted perceptions. Defensive delineations are the mechanisms by which some family members, over time, can acquire distorted attributes of being "healthy" or "ill" or even "treatment resistant."

Defensive delineations contribute to a common result: They keep family members locked into rigid patterns of perception, interaction, and mutual reaction that define the baseline state of the family system's dynamics. A family in this state has great difficulty integrating new information about itself and its members. It can neither maintain an adaptive position in the face of changing life circumstances nor achieve its developmental tasks. Over time, the family becomes "stuck" in the repetitions of its fixed and complementary patterns of action and reaction.

As in individuals, defensive processes in families are efforts to solve problems. These solutions can become impediments to further development when they become inflexible and nonadaptive to changing contexts.

As with individuals, in families all defensive processes are solutions to problems. For families that are in trouble, typically the problem is managing intolerable anxiety, affect, or conflict. At the family system level, complementary projective identification and defensive delineation defenses operate as shared family defenses to manage, albeit often at the price of one or more members becoming "ill," the anxiety and conflict within the family. The result for the family system is often a variably stable, relatively fragile, but persistent baseline state that is vulnerable to recurring episodes of crisis.

These defenses are "shared" in multiple ways: They are used by all members of the family system; they are used in repetitive patterns that are both familiar and particular to the family; and the family operating as an entity may apply them to others outside the boundary of the immediate family. That is, the shared family defenses can be used to address individuals, groups, and systems outside the family that are perceived as destabilizing or threatening to the family system's shaky state of equilibrium.

THE "STUCK" FAMILY SYSTEM AND THE TREATMENT ALLIANCE

In hospital, partial hospital, and residential treatment settings, as in others, the early phase of treatment requires the development of a tripartite working alliance that extends from beyond patient and staff to encompass the family, as well. This working alliance is fundamental to maintaining a holding environment to support the process of therapeutic developmental change (Shapiro, 1982). This alliance is especially needed in the treatment of individuals with significant psychological disturbance who have not achieved developmental separation from family. For example, the fact that a family is paying for the patient's treatment can be enough to stimulate powerful conflicts around dependency and autonomy that can quickly impact the task of creating a working alliance. When the family pays for the treatment, it can also generate competing claims as to who "owns" the treatment. Parents may feel that their payment entitles them to become part of the treatment team and to extend their parental authority into areas of clinical authority. Most importantly, when this competition is present, it can affect the patient's need to take up his or her authority by claiming ownership of the treatment.

The patient's developmental failure not only reflects problems in the family system; it also contributes to them. This complementary process contributes to the systemic cycle of repetitive action and reaction in the form of a family drama scripted by the unconscious dynamics of projective identification that can keep the patient and family unable to achieve developmental growth. Typically, the script for this family drama contains unconscious fantasies, assumptions, and agendas that are the products of distorted perceptions (Shapiro et al., 1977). These unconscious family agendas can also interfere with the establishment of a working alliance in the treatment system and thereby function as a form of resistance to treatment.

The family of a new Riggs patient is typically a system in crisis. The family members are organized in roles that are supported by an array of defenses that allow the family to manage itself and maintain its ability to function in the context of crisis. These defenses and roles are adaptive if they are flexible enough to allow learning and change in response to changing situations. If they are too rigid and inhibit learning, they become a form of resistance to the treatment process. Rigid family defenses typically strive to maintain the status quo of the family system and thereby actively resist the treatment's goal of bringing about therapeutic change (Zinner & Shapiro, 1972). From the clinician's perspective, the family of the treatment-resistant patient often presents as a "stuck" system unable to resolve its problems. Interestingly, this type of family system can present itself in different ways along a continuum from "rigidly constricted" to "unstable, uncontrolled fluidity" of role relations (Ackerman, 1966, p. 90). At one end of the range, rigidity can impair adaptation through learning, whereas at the other, instability and fluidity cause profound confusion or even loss of identity for the family and its members.

THE INVITATION TO JOIN THE FAMILY SYSTEM

From the point of admission the family system defenses are challenged by the introduction of the treatment team. As the treatment process proceeds, new information is introduced into the family system and new ways of understanding the family experience and context are offered. This new information is intended to affect the family system. The tendency of the family system to maintain its functional or dysfunctional status quo is challenged by the therapeutic intent of the treatment. Although the conscious manifest position of the family system may be to welcome change, the paradoxical effects of the family's unconscious fantasies and conflicts, and the family's unconscious wish to maintain the status quo, can combine to evoke resistance.

One of the ways family resistance manifests itself is through an unconscious invitation to the clinicians to take up complementary roles in the family. When clinicians are incorporated into the family's drama, they become less effective sources of new information and can be "managed" to maintain the family system's status quo by the familiar patterns of the family system of defense. The unconscious use of projective identification within and by the family creates powerful transference and countertransference dynamics that may unavoidably result in the clinician's unconscious acceptance of the invitation to "join" the family because of the way elements of the clinician's own life history are "hooked" by the family system's dynamics. This mutual unconscious re-creation of the family drama, involving family members and clinicians, is an application to family therapy of the psychoanalytic notion of enactment described in Chapter 2.

Within enactments all parties that are part of the treatment system quickly come into conflict and competition. It is common, then, for all parties in the treatment system to take up their authority in their roles (e.g., patient, father, mother, spouse, payer, individual therapist, family therapist) to engage in the conflict. Yet, because the treatment system has unconsciously taken in the distorted perceptions of the family system, the role-based "authority" being exercised is distorted. If clinicians accept the unconscious invitation to join the family and enter into a family enactment, the resulting drama will reveal conflicts and patterns of interaction that uncannily mirror the patterns of interaction and conflicts of the family system. In this way the "error" of entering an enactment may provide the clinician's best opportunity to understand and potentially interpret the family system's problems. Of course, this optimistic scenario is only possible if the clinician becomes aware of the unconscious enactment into which he or she has entered, and is able to translate the family system's behaviors into language and affect that are recognizable to the family members. The clinician's conscious translation of family behavior into language and affect becomes the therapeutic interpretation, the intervention for change offered back to the family system.

In family work with treatment-resistant patients, learn to detect, analyze, and use enactments, especially as they invite clinicians to join the family's characteristic defenses.

THE DYNAMICS OF THE FAMILY DRAMA

From the beginning of treatment the identified patient is in the focal family role. Yet other family members (parents, siblings, spouse, children, etc.) constellate themselves in an array of roles that serve both to maintain family system functioning and to provide "platforms" from which family members may act out and communicate family dynamics. In the early phases of treatment the family roles present as a variety of recognizable manifest types. Common parental examples of these manifest types include, in inevitably oversimplified language, the "anxious concerned parent," the "angry parent," the "avoidant parent," the "hysterical parent," the "loving parent," and the "heartbroken parent." The affect communicated in these manifest roles is absolutely genuine and demands the clinician's respect and care. Yet these types are not merely descriptive. Each type may also contain and communicate meanings constructed from previous family experience. These covert meanings generate the patterns of a family drama, and the family drama often follows a covert unconscious script, "the themes of which are some combination of adaptive and functional family 'work' tasks and a variety of unconscious fantasies, or covert assumptions, often conceived as a hidden agenda" (Zinner & Shapiro, 1972, p. 523).

Powerful anxieties are often present within the complicated construction of the family drama. These anxieties can be manifest in a variety of forms. In one form the parent takes up oversight authority in the "functional family work task" (Zinner & Shapiro, 1972, p. 523) of assessing the treatment staff. This assessment most often takes the form of a variety of spoken and unspoken questions: Can the clinician understand the family's experience? Will the clinician agree with the family's perceptions and theories about the problem? Does the clinician, and by extension the entire institution, present itself as a trustworthy and competent caretaker of the identified patient? Will this potential treatment be helpful or result in disappointment? The reasonableness of these questions belies how, in some families, they may also represent the unconscious fantasies and assumptions that underlie the dynamics that keep the family system stuck and the patient locked into the identity of "treatment resistant."

For example, the question of whether the staff can be trusted to safeguard and protect the patient from harm is, on the manifest level, a responsible parental concern. Moreover, the parents' role-based sense of authority for maintaining oversight of their child's safety appears to be equally rational and justified. But consider this parental position when the child is an adult who, despite symptoms and past crisis, is fundamentally able to make his or her own assessments about the competence of staff and is able to work collaboratively with staff around managing safety. The parents may be taking up their authority in a way that infantilizes the patient, undermines his or her authority, and reinforces fixed stereotyped assumptions about who in the family is "ill," who is "healthy," who is "impaired," and who is "capable." According to Shapiro (1982):

> We observe a complementary use of projective identification of dystonic aspects of their self representation by these parents, which blurs their capacity to experience themselves as separate from the particular child in areas of conflict.
> Through the use of this shared defense, parents fail to perceive accurately the reality of the child, developing defensive stereotyped delineations of him. (p. 212)

It is important that these stereotyped assumptions about the patient cannot be reconciled with direct observations of the patient's abilities and functioning. These stereotypes are the "defensive delineations" that find their origin in disavowed aspects of the parents that structure the projective identification processes of the family system.

The family system adopts the use of projective identification as a family defense in unconsciously resisting the threatening potential of the treatment to disturb the family system's status quo. By this mechanism the treatment team, and even the treatment institution, can become players in the family drama. There are many examples of this phenomenon. Consider the not uncommon parental concern that staff is motivated financially to make the patient dependent to extend the length of treatment to generate more revenue. The parent raises this question with the self-evident authority of parental financial oversight. Yet this conscious position may contain an unconscious fantasy about the danger of dependency that originates in the parent's family-of-origin experience and is being projected into the treatment context.

In the examples offered above, family members are acting in their family roles and taking up the authority they derive from those roles. The identified patient takes up authority in the treatment process in both the patient role and in his or her family role. The parents exercise their parental authority in their family roles of mother and father. The spouse, children, and extended family members, when involved, similarly exercise the authority derived from their roles. Clinicians also take up authority based on their training, expertise, and experience in their delegated roles as individual and family therapists.

As Muller describes in Chapter 6, the concept of the Third provides a means to understand and interpret the dynamics of the treatment system, including the way the interlocking system of roles in the treatment system represents aspects of the Third. The roles of child, father, mother, and clinician all rely on complex cultural contexts that are the source of their meaning. It is this larger cultural context that gives meaning to words such as *health*, *autonomy*, *success*, and *failure* in the treatment process. The cultural context also gives meaning to the "tasks" that define the function and purpose of both professional and family roles, the family system, and treatment system. This larger context of the Third acts as the frame of reference for reality-testing the ways in which particular roles are taken up. This frame of reference is key to examining and understanding the treatment process and its intrinsic elements of intervention and interpretation. When family dynamics, or clinical interventions, are guided by unexamined unconscious conflicts, fantasies, and assumptions, the function of the larger cultural context of the Third may be replaced by the self-referential and self-confirming logic of the irrational. Family therapy can function as a process through which the family system introjects the Third as a necessary condition for this family task. By extension, family therapy supports the patient's development within the context of the family system.

CLINICAL EXAMPLE AND DISCUSSION

The following example is from work with the family of a previously treatment-resistant young adult woman who had comorbid mood and personality disorders. In this example family therapy played an integral role in establishing a working alliance that allowed for the containment, awareness, reflection, and interpretation of the family defenses that both contributed to the patient's treatment-refractory illness and kept the family stuck in terms of its developmental task. The process of alliance building required that the conflict and competition among the multiple authorities involved in the treatment system be contained, understood, and interpreted in terms of a larger context made up of past experience, conscious and unconscious agendas, and shared goals.

Before offering the case, it is worth defining the several roles in which the family and individual therapists worked. The doctoral-level individual therapist provided four-times-weekly individual psychotherapy. There were also several kinds of family work conducted by the family therapist, who was a clinical social worker. These included family consultation meetings by phone with the parents, who did not live in the local area, intended to help them understand the treatment program, serve as a point of liaison to them, and gather family history as part of the initial evaluative phase of treatment at Riggs, which culminates in a case conference near the end of the first 6 weeks of treatment. These meetings did not include the patient; their format is based on a Bowenian model of working with separate parts of the family system (Bowen, 1978), and they contribute significant data that the family therapist integrates into a developing formulation of the family dynamics. In addition, there were separate meetings between the family therapist and the patient focused on the experience of family meetings and social work casework needs. The family therapist also coordinates the discharge planning process, which includes both the patient and the family.

There were two kinds of meetings in which the patient and her parents met together with staff: family meetings and family therapy. Both of these were co-facilitated by the family therapist and the patient's individual therapist, who acted together, but in somewhat differentiated roles, as a family co-therapist team. The co-therapist structure provides a means of integrating clinical thinking about individual and family dynamics and creates a potential synergy between these two modalities of treatment. The full family meetings were initially for the purpose of gathering some history and completing an assessment of family dynamics, but later shifted to family therapy based on explicit negotiation of an alliance with all parties to engage issues in the family system and consider the possibility of change.

Ms. R was a single 28-year-old woman who sought admission for "treatment-resistant" depression, chronic feelings of being "empty, worthless, helpless, and hopeless," and persistent thoughts of suicide. Multiple attempts at outpatient treatment were not successful and twice ended in crises. She had one previous suicide attempt by overdose of prescribed medications in the context of conflict with her psychiatrist. Although Ms. R was able to complete college with difficulty, and had begun a career as a teacher's aide, her vocational performance was inconsistent, and she had recently been unable to work. She complained of a constricted social life and felt "emotionally stunted" compared to peers. She experienced a persistent desire to be physically held and comforted by others, regularly asking not only her mother, but also previous therapists to hold her. She acknowledged that her multiple difficulties had kept her very attached to her family and dependent on them for support.

From the beginning Ms. R's parents presented as anxious and somewhat suspicious of the treatment process. Mr. R's focus was on the cost of treatment and its value. He was clear that family resources would allow only a limited length of stay. Although staff acknowledged this limit and identified the helpfulness of its clarity for setting achievable treatment planning goals, Mr. R remained suspicious that the limit would not be held by staff and that the treatment would become an unmanageable burden on the family. He took up his authority in the role of paternal steward of family finances and initially limited his engagement to this singular focus. This position made it difficult to proceed with the clinical assessment tasks of obtaining family history and developing a clinical formulation of the family experience. Curiously, it was this process of clinical assessment and formulation that constituted part of the value for which Mr. R was paying.

As the family assessment meetings unfolded, it emerged that Mr. R's own father had emigrated to the United States as a young adult after the Second World War to escape the postwar consolidation of Soviet hegemony in Eastern Europe. He was reported to have had difficulty acculturating, became increasingly isolated, and drank heavily. Mr. R's mother was the strong matriarch of the extended family system. Described as "controlling, tough, and critical," she was feared for her quick judgments and even quicker temper. Mr. R described his parents as emotionally closed and unable to understand the feelings of others. He felt particularly unclaimed by his father, who rarely shared activities with him, as he observed other fathers do with their sons. Mr. R's only sibling was a brother who for decades was disengaged from the family and a "heavy drinker."

Meanwhile, Mrs. R's initial postadmission focus was on whether staff was adequately attending to her daughter's needs. For a considerable time Mrs. R had taken up her maternal role as the primary provider for her daughter's emotional needs. Because of her daughter's ongoing difficulties, this role had been a considerable source of frustration, as a result of which Mrs. R experienced an ongoing state of anxiety. However, despite her anxieties, Mrs. R consistently strove to maintain an outwardly optimistic and positive attitude when providing her daughter with support. The separation imposed by the treatment appeared to heighten Mrs. R's level of anxiety dramatically. She engaged in frequent interrogation of staff, including many elaborate "what if" scenarios, to assess staff competency in meeting her daughter's needs. As with Mr. R, her singular focus interfered with the tasks of clinical assessment and formulation.

In her family of origin Mrs. R described her father as "cheery but emotionally unavailable." He'd had an alcoholic father (Mrs. R's grandfather) who "was a significant source of family shame." Mrs. R's mother had struggled with lifelong depression that left her unable to function for significant periods. During one of these periods, when Mrs. R was a very young child, her mother was hospitalized for a "nervous breakdown." Mrs. R's experience in her family of origin was described as one of "growing up in the dark"—the family avoided any direct discussion of her mother's depression and kept it secret from others. Mrs. R stated that she adapted to the family context by becoming increasingly self-reliant and by refusing to be a burden to her parents. She regarded this adaptation as a positive source of personal strength. It is notable that Mrs. R had been a teacher, but stopped working when she became pregnant with her first child, the patient.

Mr. and Mrs. R had been married for nearly 30 years, but had separated within the last 2 years. Their decision to separate was a "complete shock" to the patient, members of the extended family, and friends. No one had any idea that the couple had any difficulties in their marriage. Both parents described the relationship as "emotionally empty." For many years they had felt mutually resentful, and both anticipated divorce as a welcome relief.

The patient reported in an assessment meeting with the family therapist that her father continually confronted her with his judgment that she "behaves badly" in order to gain attention and elicit emotional responses from others. At the same time, she found her mother's supportive, encouraging, positive acceptance of her illness frequently infuriating. Both parental stances left her feeling unseen, unheard, and unsatisfied in her need. Significantly, she was aware that she did not allow herself to express these "negative" feelings in the family because "It's not how we are." She was largely unaware of how these dynamics contributed to her own depression or her self-destructiveness. The individual therapist's initial clinical formulation hypothesized that the patient became developmentally stuck, with her sense of agency compromised, by well-intentioned attempts to help her that unwittingly fostered emotional dependency and identity diffusion.

Once the family history and assessment were obtained, some elements appeared to stand out as important for initial formulations about family dynamics. The father had experienced his father as abandoning and his mother as rigid, controlling, and judgmental. He compensated for the lack of feeling emotionally "seen" and understood by his parents by developing a counterdependent stance as an adult that resulted in problems sustaining emotional connection and intimacy in his marital relationship. He became "emotionally closed," much like his own father.

The mother had responded to her "shameful," "emotionally closed" alcoholic father and chronically ill and unavailable mother by also adopting a counterdependent stance. Yet the mother went one step further in taking up the role of family caretaker. As caretaker she could feel a sense of emotional connection that re-created her bond with her mother, while, at the same time, defending herself against experiencing her own unmet needs. She could also project her disavowed needs into another. One working hypothesis was that the patient had introjected her mother's projections and was unconsciously acting out the sadness and neediness that was experienced but disavowed by her mother. Consistent with projective identification processes, the mother unconsciously identified with her daughter's depression and neediness. She experienced her daughter's behaviors as confirmation that these characteristics were in *her daughter* and not connected to her own cheery and positive stance in life. These ideas became the basis of a formulation of the family dynamics that was held in mind by the clinicians.

Meanwhile, in the separate family consultation discussions with Mr. and Mrs. R, the family therapist initially focused on carefully addressing the parents' concerns, providing education about institutional processes and standards of care, establishing initial boundaries around their adult daughter's treatment, and creating a container for managing anxiety by providing a holding environment for exploring affect. These efforts led to enough reduction in anxiety for the process of taking a family history to proceed.

Unfortunately, these initial efforts were only partially successful in creating a working alliance because they did not directly address the connections between conflicted authority positions, projective identification dynamics, and covert unconscious agendas that increasingly impacted the treatment. Despite repeated attempts at family education, both in discussions and using written material, the individual and family therapists had the repeated experience that information provided to the family was either not heard or not remembered. During the first 2 weeks each new conversation quickly became a repetition of the same pattern of questions about costs or competency, and inquiries about the patient's discussions in the psychotherapy. These questions were delivered with escalating levels of insistence and self-justified demand. The family therapist had the experience of being unheard, much like the patient's reported experience in the family. Notably, during one of these discussions the family therapist found himself so "pulled in" and reactive to the family system that he began arguing with the parents in a way that was clearly counterproductive to the therapeutic task. The family therapist began to sense that he was caught in an enactment and sought consultation to clarify why he was becoming "stuck" in work with the family.

In peer consultation the family therapist realized how the family's behaviors had stimulated a countertransference response that resonated with aspects of his own family experience. He realized his own past experience of feeling unfairly judged had made him vulnerable. The patient's father's hostile and suspicious stance had evoked an increasingly rigid, detached, and judgmental response in the family therapist, followed by an argumentative response by the family therapist, which led him to recognize that he was engaged in an enactment. The family therapist's awareness of this countertransference response and his use of peer consultation allowed a reflective examination of the unconscious dynamics within the treatment system as a whole. From this larger frame of reference the family therapist was able to see that his response both recreated the patient's father's experience of his rigid, critical, controlling mother, and allowed the father to unconsciously identify with the introjected but disavowed rigid, controlling, and judgmental parts of himself that had been projected into, and unconsciously acted out, by the family therapist.

The peer consultation helped the family therapist link his countertransference reaction with elements of the family's history and experience, while allowing a richer formulation and providing the basis for interpretation. It became clear that the parents and treating clinicians were in a fight in which each side felt authorized by their role, but in which the behavior in role was off task. The parents were exercising their parental authority to protect their own and the patient's interests. Yet the parents' positions repeatedly dismissed information about how the clinicians were also acting in the interest of the patient. The parents' avoidance of engaging in the assessment process was experienced by the treatment team as a communication that their agenda was in competition with the agenda of treatment. As a result, the family therapist had become increasingly rigid and concrete in the role of family educator. He experienced the father as demanding, critical, and intrusive. He experienced the mother as unrelenting in her investigations of staff competency, and he felt increasingly frustrated by her acting as if the treatment team were lying or withholding. The parents' repetitive demands to get answers to the same questions that had already been answered felt like neediness in a displaced form. With the help of the peer consultation, all these aspects could be seen as interconnected dynamics reflecting elements of the family experience.

The manifest conflict over competing authority roles required an interpretation that linked the conflict to the expression of unconscious fantasies embedded in the family history, but interpretation was not fully possible until the family members had signed on at least tentatively to engage in family therapy with a goal of change in the family system. The opportunity to provide this interpretation came in one particular family therapy session (80 minutes), in which the parents and patient met with the family therapist and the individual therapist, who together co-facilitated the meeting.

This family meeting began with a repetition of the same parental questions that had already been addressed several times. The co-therapists then reviewed key elements of the family history that the patient did not know and engaged family members in actively remembering and integrating their own family stories. As this work progressed, interpretations were made that linked the manifest content of past and present behavior to assumptions and fantasies embedded in the family experience. These interpretations provided a larger context, derived from the multigenerational culture of the family system, which placed current conflicts in perspective. This progressively deepening process led to two important interpretations that were offered to the parents.

The first interpretation linked Mr. R's behavior toward staff with unconscious assumptions he held as a result of his relationship with his parents. Mr. R could see that he held the assumption that staff, like his parents, would not listen to him, acknowledge his needs, might attempt to take control of the family away from him, or most disturbingly, judge him as lacking as a father. Similarly, Mrs. R was able to take in the second interpretation, which was offered to her, that she took up her maternal authority as a means of expressing her unconscious fantasy that staff, like her mother, would prove incapable of providing required maternal supplies and would leave her daughter "in the dark," needing to fend for herself as her own family of origin had left her. Her persistent interrogation of staff was an attempt to uncover the illuminating truth that would free her from being "in the dark."

The patient's participation in this interpretive process provided her with new information about her parents and family that was useful in altering her perceptions of them and of herself. The patient was able to put her father's critical and judgmental style into a multigenerational perspective that gave it meaning and context. She was able to see that she and her father both struggled with the experience of not having their needs seen or met. In a similar manner, the patient was able to see how she and her mother both depended on others to address and contain anxieties about daily life.

This new awareness placed the patient's "treatment-refractory" illness in the context of a shared family culture—a culture whose hallmark was conflict over dependency and counterdependency. The patient's behaviors could be understood as a more symptomatic expression of the same conflicts that her parents experienced. More importantly, the patient's internal conflicts could be understood as not having been created in a vacuum. Psychologically, the patient served as the container for the unconsciously disavowed and projected dependency needs of the parents, whose own functioning might have been affected had their dependency conflicts not been unconsciously split off. As they heard and internalized the interpretations, family members and the family system as a whole were able to gain perspective and see how all members were connected by previously unrecognized but shared characteristics. For the patient this experience provided a richer and more textured understanding of her parents and her connections with them. It allowed her to see them as more complex than simply as "critical" and "overly sympathetic." It allowed the parents to see their daughter as less separated from them by "illness" and to understand that the current family problems began before this family configuration ever existed.

The key to this interpretive work was the family therapist's ability to become aware of and use clinically his unwitting acceptance of the unconsciously extended invitation to join the family by accepting and internalizing the projective identifications that constituted the shared family defense. Central to the concept of the structural Third addressed by Muller in Chapter 6, the family therapist gained this awareness in the context of peer consultation, which provided a structure for examining his thinking and responses from a frame of reference larger than his own.

Similarly, the family used the family therapy frame of reference to engage in a progressively deepening process of examination and interpretation that resulted in a shift in perspective, self-understanding, and interaction with others.

The interpretive process resulted in change in the family system. The interpretations offered resonated with both parents, who were then more able to differentiate the clinicians from the stereotyped, defensive delineations they had unconsciously applied. The parents came to experience the family co-therapists as seeing and understanding them in a way that allowed them to better see themselves. The clinicians could now be differentiated from the family's unconscious fantasies and experienced as helpful to the family. This shift helped establish a working treatment alliance between the patient, the family, and the treatment team, with a level of trust, recognized shared goals, and a common sense of purpose. The parents' previous pattern of stuck defensive questioning and suspicion toward the treatment team was no longer required. Further, the parents could now experience the patient as more than "manipulative" or "ill," and could begin consciously to see aspects of themselves in her. The patient became less "stuck" in her perceptions of herself and her family. She was better able to integrate a more complex experience of her parents that differed from the flat "defensive delineations" previously held. She could now understand her parents' behaviors as part of a meaningful historical family context. Similarly, the work done with the family had a synergistic effect on the individual therapy, allowing the patient to better acknowledge split-off parts of herself and to begin to experience herself as a more complex person. She was also better able to take up her "patient authority" in negotiating with her family for support and for respect of her own boundaries.

CONCLUSION

The R family demonstrates a family system unconsciously reacting to the treatment process and to the treatment team as posing threats to its dysfunctional state of equilibrium in the early phase of treatment. It is important to remember that even nonadaptive defenses in a family, as in an individual, are attempts to solve a problem, and that old and familiar solutions are not easily given up. New information or new approaches that might alter the family experience may be experienced unconsciously as a threat to the maintenance of the solution the family has adopted over time for managing anxiety and conflict. Even as a family is asking for help for an "ill" member, it may also, paradoxically, act in ways that resist this help, and may unwittingly contribute to embedding a member in the role of "treatment-resistant" patient. Although consciously the R family hoped that treatment would bring welcome change, the unconscious fantasies and conflicts of the members constituted a resistance. These dynamics often result in difficulty, or even failure, to achieve a working alliance that supports the therapeutic process.

> When family system issues contribute to treatment resistance in a patient, change in the patient may require change in the dynamic equilibrium of the family system. A precondition for such change in the family system is negotiation of an alliance to engage in family therapy, that is, to examine and engage issues in the family system with an eye toward the possibility of change.

The family system often "invites" the treatment team to join the family by taking up roles that complement family dynamics and activate familiar shared family defenses. This invitation is offered through the mechanism of projective identification. The pull for the treatment team to join the family is an unconscious invitation to enact problematic unconscious family conflicts that may have contributed to the family being developmentally stuck, and the patient appearing treatment resistant. And when clinicians unwittingly accept the invitation, generally through the way it "hooks" their own vulnerabilities, they have entered an enactment. Such accepted invitations or enactments represent an opportunity for the treatment team to directly experience the unconscious family agenda and make it available for interpretation. Family therapy provides a structural Third for the naming, examination, integration, and resolution of the unconscious assumptions, fantasies, and agendas that may keep the family, and sometimes the clinicians, stuck—and the identified patient "treatment resistant."

REFERENCES

Ackerman, N. (1966). *Treating the troubled family*. New York: Basic Books.

Bowen, M. (1978). *Family therapy in clinical practice*. New York: Jason Aronson.

Shapiro, E.R. (1978). The psychodynamics and developmental psychology of the borderline patient: A review of the literature. *American Journal of Psychiatry, 135,* 1305–1315.

Shapiro, E.R. (1982). The holding environment and family therapy with acting out adolescents. *International Journal of Psychoanalytic Psychotherapy, 9,* 209–226.

Shapiro, E.R., & Carr, W. (1991). *Lost in familiar places: Creating new connections between the individual and society.* New Haven, CT: Yale University Press.

Zinner, J., & Shapiro, R. (1972). Projective identification as a mode of perception and behavior in families of adolescents. *International Journal of Psycho-Analysis, 53,* 523–530.

Chapter 13

A Team Approach to
Treatment Resistance

Sharon E. Krikorian, PhD, and
J. Christopher Fowler, PhD

Patients who engage in destructive and chaotic behaviors present serious treatment challenges to psychiatry. The Austen Riggs Center has made its mission helping these "treatment-resistant" patients become people who take charge of their lives. Throughout this volume our colleagues have articulated some of the special challenges of a clinical population that requires more than the customary provisions of psychiatric care to emerge from treatment resistance. In this chapter we describe an approach to teamwork that may be applicable in many clinical settings, and is not limited to the Riggs setting.

Among the techniques and interventions used in the psychosocial and biological treatment at Riggs, three broad principles anchor our work: engaging the patient's authority, prioritizing the importance of relationships in effecting change, and working to discover the underlying meaning of behavior. During stormy transference–countertransference enactments (particularly those involving life-threatening acting out), patients and staff can lose their grasp on these principles and fall into chronic crisis management instead of adhering to dynamic treatment. It is at such crucial moments that staff members and the patient often need the treatment team and the authority of the team leader to offer a "third" perspective on the enactment.

> Treatment-resistant patients benefit from the work of an integrated psychodynamic treatment team when they cannot form stable treatment alliances, are seriously self-destructive, and/or provoke intense emotions that are hard for any one treater to bear.

When teams function optimally, they balance management and interpretation, as described in Chapter 9 on renegotiating the treatment frame. Teams respond to crises by recognizing the realistic risks posed by the patient's behavior, and then by setting reasonable limits on self-destructive actions. When the crisis is somewhat contained, the team can then approach the crisis as a meaningful communication about something that is being repeated from the patient's life. By doing so, the team recognizes the crisis as an interpersonal communication embedded in the patient's distressing actions. This recognition helps staff metabolize intense emotional reactions to a patient's destructive behavior and provides a dynamic framework for approaching the problem. This reflective, nonpunitive approach helps open a psychological space for engaging the patient in the study of the repetition and its meaning. Direct engagement takes seriously the patient's authority and provides opportunities for rebuilding a damaged therapeutic alliance. Such moments may occur at points of crisis or of transition as patients deal with the anxieties and conflicts of taking on more autonomy and responsibility for their lives. When patients and staff create the necessary reflective space during moments of crisis and ruptures in the treatment alliance, patients have the opportunity to learn about their underlying conflicts and to develop new modes of dealing with powerful feelings, gradually replacing destructive acting out defenses with higher-level defenses. In this process of transforming action into language, the patient often begins to discover his or her identity and voice as a member of a community.

> The psychodynamic treatment team functions as a "third" in difficult treatments, offering a reflective space to understand what is being mobilized in the patient and in the team.

THE FUNCTION OF TREATMENT TEAMS

Psychodynamic treatment teams oversee three functions of psychosocial treatment. These include:

1. *Information sharing among treatment providers.* This is an ongoing team function, but is especially important as treatment begins and as team members work together, along with the patient, to formulate a dynamic understanding of the patient's symptoms, behaviors, and personality organization in the context of his or her family and social environment, and biological contributions. This information sharing is critical for constructing a treatment plan with well-matched interventions and therapeutic goals. As new information flows into the team, members can evaluate how the treatment plan and interventions are progressing, and can openly renegotiate a treatment plan when particular interventions fail or are contraindicated.

2. *Provide a holding function for patients.* This holding function consists of setting realistic limits on patients' self-destructive behavior and helping to rebuild alliances when impasses develop and ruptures in the therapeutic alliance occur. Renegotiating a genuine alliance, with an agreement to work toward understanding self-destructive and self-defeating symptoms, is often effective in shifting from chronic crisis management to genuine treatment in work with previously treatment-refractory patients.

3. *Provide a consultative and holding function for team members* when they become embroiled in power struggles with patients or each other as a result of intense countertransference reactions often involving transferences that are split across team members or between disciplines. This holding function encompasses containing and interpretive functions as team members grapple with countertransference elements and the emergence of parallel processes within the team that may reflect intrapsychic and family dynamics.

Psychodynamic treatment teams working with treatment-resistant patients have three principal functions:

- Sharing information among treatment providers.
- Providing a holding function for patients.
- Providing a consultative and holding function for team members in the face of splitting or intense countertransference reactions.

The first function of teams is to gather, share, consolidate, and integrate information to develop a dynamic formulation that will be a guide as ongoing treatment is monitored. This function includes meeting with the patient to negotiate a treatment plan with a set of mutually agreed upon interventions and treatment goals. The individual therapist is responsible for developing and updating the dynamic formulation, but all team members contribute to the evolving formulation by helping the therapist grasp aspects of the patient's character organization and range of functioning that may not be readily apparent during psychotherapy sessions. In this way, team members broaden their understanding of the patient in different contexts and across various relationships.

Teams provide a number of functions that can be subsumed under the rubric of holding and containing. Shapiro and Carr (1991) describe the mutative effects of providing these functions:

> . . . containment of impulses and interpretation take place through acknowledging individuality (curiosity), bearing painful affect (containment), and putting in perspective (empathic interpretation in context). The containing and interpreting that occurs within the holding environment provides individuals with the opportunity to become aware of their projections and to reinternalize them. Through so doing they achieve a more complex sense of themselves, a more empathic view of others, and a strengthened ability to join with others in different roles in a shared task. In other words they grow and develop. (p. 39)

Mental health professionals working with self-destructive patients recognize that setting limits on destructive acting out is often a crucial component of containment necessary for sustaining treatment. In an open setting like that at Riggs (as with outpatient teams), limits are not established through physical control and environmental restriction, but through recognizing the realistic limits of clinicians in agreeing to continue working with a patient. This requires a focus on the importance of the therapeutic relationship and continual attention to the state of the alliance.

When patients engage in the kind of self-destructive or life-threatening behaviors that led to their hospitalization, the team is mobilized to enforce appropriate limits and boundaries. When the patient's life is at risk, limit setting is relatively straightforward and is the only issue to be addressed until the threat is contained. The multiple meanings and communications of the behaviors may be sorted out later, after the immediate threat is contained. Often destructive acting out is risky but not imminently life-threatening. Under these conditions pursuit of meaning is the team's priority. For example, Zerbe (1988) observed that many patients seek containment of destructive urges and feel relief and gratitude when confronted about their behavior in a direct but nonpunitive manner. Carrying out such limit setting successfully is balanced by the need to bear the countertransference anxieties required to tolerate some symptoms (e.g., superficial cutting). Many patients use these symptoms as their only claim to an identity and to personal authority, and struggle to discover their meaning and put it into words instead of action.

> Optimal "holding" of patients occurs when limits are not set through physical control and environmental restriction (except when necessary in acute inpatient settings), but through recognizing and discussing directly with patients the realistic limits of clinicians in agreeing to continue working with them. This requires a focus on the importance of the therapeutic relationship and continual attention to the state of the alliance.

Kernberg (1976) suggests that a major aspect of hospital treatment is diagnosing the nature and causes of the ego's breakdown in its control function, with a goal of facilitating "reestablishment of boundary control" (p. 258). He proposes that this reestablishment is accomplished by holding patients accountable and responsible for their behavior as a way of developing internal control. Limit setting provides a psychological containing function, but also introduces the real provision of a holding environment that communicates to patients that their behaviors are meaningful. Approaching limit setting from this angle focuses particular attention on ruptures in the therapeutic alliance (Safran & Muran, 1996; Safran, Muran, & Samstag, 2001; Chapter 8, this volume).

Since Greenson's (1967) formulation of the therapeutic alliance, clinicians and researchers have found that a strong or deepening therapeutic alliance contributes to positive treatment outcome. Although variations in the definition of the alliance abound (Frieswyk et al., 1986; Horvath & Luborsky, 1993; Luborsky, Crits-Christoph, Mintz, & Auerback; 1988; and Chapter 8, this volume), most agree that therapeutic alliance pertains to the therapist–patient bond, collaboration, and shared commitment to treatment goals within individual psychotherapy. These characteristics are based on the experience of the therapist as supportive and helpful, while there is an agreement to engage in mutual work toward understanding and changing the dynamic forces that obstruct the patient's progress in order to reach a set of mutually agreed upon goals. Initially it was believed that a consistently strong alliance promotes the most change and growth for patients, but experience and research suggest that the repair of ruptures in the alliance is also a powerful factor in the change process (Safran & Muran, 1996; Safran, Muran, & Samstag, 2001). We have found this to be true in working with patients who act out self-destructively when injured by perceived rejections and slights (Plakun, 1994). The team often plays an important role in helping the patient and individual team members discover the source of injury and then find ways to reestablish a mutual engagement. Frequently this process involves inviting the patient to a team meeting in order to explore the sources of tension and disagreement.

Working with intense countertransference reactions is a crucial aspect of the holding function of teams. Building on Winnicott's (1965) concepts of "total environmental provision" (p. 43) and "holding environment," various authors (Muller & Robinson, 2001; Stamm, 1985; Wells et al., 2006; Zerbe, 1988) highlight the value of the team as a structure for gradually integrating the patient's projections and unmanageable affects. Stamm (1985) emphasizes the "work ego" of treatment teams as she stresses the responsibility of the team leader to "metabolize" and contain emotions evoked within the patients and staff in order to provide a stable and secure environment for optimal treatment. We have discovered that any team member, including the team leader, may get swept up in countertransference reactions. At those moments when the team leader is off task, others may be called upon to demonstrate leadership through providing the objective perspective that the team needs. Hence, the team as a whole functions as a container for all its members. By creating an atmosphere of mutual respect, patients and staff can develop a sufficient level of comfort to "risk self-disclosure . . . to use it for understanding one's personal reactions and thus for helping the patient" (Stamm, 1985, p. 435).

When teams function well, members can appreciate the varied experiences staff have of patients from their differentiated roles (Haslam-Hopwood, 2003; Stamm, 1985; Wells et al., 2006), the team process is maintained, powerful negative feelings are detoxified, impulsive action can be suspended, and clinicians working directly with the patient can feel grounded in their roles and work.

Countertransference anxieties can overwhelm individual team members when a patient's extreme symptomatic behavior strains the normal containing functions of the team. These anxieties can lead to conflicts within a team that immobilize it or lead to a focus on management of crises far more than on interpretation of their meaning (Kernberg, 1976; Main, 1957; Sacksteder, 1997; Chapter 9, this volume). Splitting is a common form of breakdown that occurs when personality-disordered patients stir intense and polarized countertransference reactions, in which some staff take on a role of loving protector or guardian, whereas others feel angry and tortured by the patient's attack (Gabbard, 1989; Greene, 1993; Main, 1957). Gabbard (1986) describes such patients as having "the capacity to gain a unique position in the lives of their treaters, characterized by an intense, although mutually ambivalent, attachment on the part of both treater and patient" (p. 333). Splits among staff can usually be handled by openly addressing the feelings and reactions staff members have toward the patient. However, Gabbard (1989) suggests that some splits may also represent unresolved differences among staff that are triggered by borderline patients, whose unconscious splitting and projective defenses are in the service of "emotional survival" (p. 447). At such moments, the team leader, another senior therapist, or, for that matter, any team member, can provide a crucial consultative function by helping the affected team members integrate split transferences, intense countertransference reactions, and anxieties. This type of intervention helps staff members discuss and acknowledge the projections of the patient's internal world and familial dynamics. In this way split countertransference reactions can be collected and integrated in a team meeting.

Treatment teams are also affected by external pressures from families, insurance companies, legal systems, and hospital accreditation bodies, as well as by internal organizational pressures that may make it difficult for the team to hold onto its task. Eisenberg (1997) discusses how hierarchical structures within an institution may impact staff ability to manage anxiety and function optimally on teams. A particularly difficult institutional dynamic is activated when a treatment fails. It may be quite painful to discover that a patient has been lying to members of the team, for example, about secret substance dependence, and requires transfer for chemical dependency treatment. The psychotherapist may experience the breach most pointedly, but any team member may feel betrayed and defeated. At these times it is crucial that the team leader provide an opportunity for staff members to discuss and process the negative outcome, for it can easily taint their reactions to the next new patient who resembles the departed patient. Teams, like families, can be susceptible to the transmission of trauma (see Chapter 5, this volume), particularly if there is a sense of shame or unexpressed anger silently held by team members.

TREATMENT TEAMS AT RIGGS

Treatment teams at Riggs are designed to emphasize interpretation of meaning and integration of information. To maximize these functions the individual therapist is responsible for integrating information into an evolving formulation of the patient. The team leader, a staff member credentialed to provide individual psychotherapy, carries responsibility for overseeing the process of integrating multiple staff perspectives of the patient, carries the hospital's administrative voice, and has decision-making authority. Although the individual psychotherapist is responsible for integrating a patient's care, the team leader oversees the unfolding of this responsibility across cases as it relates to the integration of interdisciplinary work.

Teams meet twice weekly for an hour, with the primary task of overseeing, coordinating, and negotiating the implementation of treatment plans for a dozen or more patients. The membership includes the team leader, an assistant team leader, psychiatrists and psychologists who are individual psychotherapists, nursing staff, social workers, substance abuse counselors, and staff from the milieu program, each of whom works with some or all of the team's patients. Mindful of the importance of integrating management and interpretation, there is no therapist–administrator split. It is a massive expenditure of staff resources, but we have found significant benefit when multiple perspectives from clinicians, including those not directly involved in day-to-day clinical work with the patient, are part of clinical discussions. Those not immediately involved with a patient are often able to offer consultation to the team leader and those directly involved with a patient, since they have the most neutral stance from which to notice and identify transference–countertransference problems and enactments (Plakun, 2001; Shapiro & Carr, 1991; Chapter 2, this volume). The patient's therapist and social worker generally hold information about what elements of the patient's family history are being re-created in team conflict, and the team leader oversees the process of translating team events and feelings in terms of these historical life dynamics.

Each patient is a member of the team because his or her authorization, input, and motivation (however shaky it may be) are necessary. With patients' authority in mind, teams meet with new patients soon after admission to negotiate treatment goals and clarify channels of communication and procedures for addressing conflicts and crises that may emerge. An important moment in this meeting is often clarification that a patient is indeed ready to "hire" the team to do the work. Based on this meeting and other clinical data, the therapist develops a dynamic formulation integrating the patient's presenting problems, relevant personal and family history, primary defenses, and likely unfolding transference–countertransference dynamics. Guided by the dynamic formulation, a treatment plan is defined and shared with the patient for review and comment. The joint development of a written, behaviorally focused treatment plan requires a negotiation between the therapist's psychodynamic stance, other team members who work with a problem-solving focus, and the patient. From this first meeting, the patient's voice and authorization for treatment are acknowledged and reflected in the treatment plan.

Treatment plans with treatment-resistant patients are best built around a dynamic formulation that integrates psychodynamic and behavioral views of the patient and his or her problems. It is important that the patient be part of the process of developing the formulation and the treatment plan, decide to "hire" the team, and participate in negotiating the treatment plan.

Patients periodically meet with their team to discuss treatment crises and requests to step down (or up) to other programs within Riggs's continuum of care. Since a step-down suggests that a patient is feeling ready to take on greater independence and responsibility, patients requesting such moves are asked to claim authority for the move by stating their goals for the next program and discussing the losses and consequences they anticipate in leaving their current program. Each point of transition provides an opportunity for a patient to face conflicts about more independent functioning, and thus offers an opportunity to identify and work through conflicts and losses. The team is in the position to mark and witness the associated struggles between developmental regression and progression (Muller & Robinson, 2001).

At various points in the treatment, crises may occur that are best responded to by having the patient meet with the team. Crisis meetings may come at the request of the patient or any team member, and serve as an opportunity for a forthright discussion between the patient and team.

Hypotheses are generated about what is communicated through the crisis and how best to proceed, given this new understanding. These discussions may include interpretation of the role the patient takes up within the larger therapeutic community, his or her role in the family, and how these fit with the team's dynamic understanding of the patient. When teams successfully engage the responsibility of treatment-refractory patients for their behaviors and invite them to participate as active agents in exploring meanings and motivations, these patients may discover curiosity about their own chronic maladaptive patterns and begin to take charge of their lives in new ways.

Whereas our setting is institutional, many health providers face similar challenges with outpatients, in which treatment becomes a matter of dealing with one crisis after another (Munich & Allen, 2003; Plakun, 1994). The approach we are describing can be modified for application to inpatient, residential, and outpatient settings. Outpatient treatments in repeated crisis may benefit from the creation of an ad hoc treatment team when none formally exists. Outpatient teams may best be thought of as soft assemblages of clinicians who agree, with the patient's knowledge and permission, to share information about the patient's functioning and their specific interventions. The most common form of such a team occurs when a psychiatrist prescribes medications, and a nonmedical psychotherapist carries out individual therapy. Sometimes this configuration includes a family therapist or substance abuse counselor. The question of who shall lead such teams is a thorny one, as the team leader role requires a level of sophistication with psychodynamic thinking and group process that is not common to any one professional discipline in the current treatment climate. Whether working in inpatient, partial hospital, residential, or outpatient settings, providers who work with each other in the ways described offer opportunities for previously treatment-refractory patients to change. The case of Sophie illustrates team functioning in work with a treatment-resistant patient.

TEAM FUNCTIONING: THE CASE OF SOPHIE

Sophie was admitted to the center following three near-lethal suicide attempts, the last of which left her in a coma for a week. With a history of failed treatments, failed medication trials, and over 20 psychiatric hospitalizations, she was treatment resistant and on a collision course with death. She presented a formidable challenge to any clinical setting, given her suicidal behavior, borderline personality disorder, chronic anorexia nervosa with bingeing and purging, and alcohol dependence. Her 72-pound emaciated frame provoked such intense anxieties that her family and previous doctors restricted her activities, force-fed her, and limited her ordinary human freedoms. These restrictions did little to curb her self-destructive behaviors, and her outpatient treatment degenerated into chronic crisis management.

Sophie came to Riggs not only on the advice of her outpatient psychiatrist, but also because she had grown tired of a career as a patient. She was interested in becoming a more willful and active agent in her life. This proclamation of desire gave the admitting officer the sense that Sophie might be ready to productively engage in treatment. Despite his sense that this was a high-risk admission, he judged that the risk was worth the potential benefit, given Sophie's ability to take some responsibility for her actions and to exercise a modicum of authority by claiming a desire for treatment. He explained this to Sophie, who accepted the offer of admission with the understanding that she would be responsible for keeping herself safe in the open setting.

Shortly after admission Sophie began gorging on the buffet-style meals. Nurses encouraged her to control her binges, fearing that subsequent purging could lead to a hemorrhage from known esophageal varices. Sophie's rapid resumption of self-destructive behaviors made many question her wish to change, sparking intense staff anxiety that she intended to kill herself. Nurses (who often feel the greatest responsibility for patients' physical well-being) were the most anxious about her condition, and considered her admission weight to be dangerously low. Doubts about her admission surfaced in the first team meeting, with several members raising the possibility of a transfer to a locked program if her symptoms could not be contained. The team leader urged staff to consider the dynamic meanings of her behavior.

Managing Anxiety Without Exploration Sparks Enactment

Anxiety about extreme symptomatic behavior often collapses the potential space for interpretation and reflection (Main, 1957). The risk of setting aside the interpretive task in favor of managing anxiety is that treaters and patient enter enactments as they blindly re-create family dynamics, setting up processes that confirm the patient's most conflicted relationship patterns (Plakun, 2001; Shapiro & Carr, 1991). The team leader's effort to contextualize the symptomatic behavior was, in part, an effort to shift the focus to the dynamic formulation and to invite curiosity into the team system. She was joined in this stance by more senior therapists, and by Sophie's therapist, the newest member of the team. This intervention momentarily opened a space for reflecting on Sophie's life history and the potential meanings of her behavior, but at this early stage of treatment with such a difficult patient, insights and interpretations did little to quell anxiety. When staff attempted to engage Sophie's curiosity about her bingeing and purging, she responded with agitation and defensive withdrawal. Faced with an openly resistant patient, many staff lost confidence in their ability to work with her in the open setting of Riggs.

An escalating impasse evolved in which Sophie's desperate need to hold onto her symptoms increased staff anxiety, resulting in further efforts to control and contain her behavior. As her admission weight of 72 pounds dropped to 68 pounds, and she began sporadic alcohol abuse, it became clear her life was in danger and her treatment in crisis.

Outrage and fear about her dangerously low weight rippled throughout Riggs. Pressure mounted from staff and fellow patients to transfer her to a locked setting. When patients and staff confronted her, Sophie's reaction was that losing a few pounds was "not a big deal," while insisting she was perfectly healthy at this new weight. Feedback from other patients, however, opened her eyes to the way her behavior evoked fear and outrage. There was an institutional push to suspend normal procedures and "manage" this situation by transferring her even before the team had a chance to meet with her.

The team leader had to contend with her own reaction to Sophie's behavior as well as the pressure from the institution to react quickly and transfer this self-destructive patient. Recommending discharge would certainly have conveyed to Sophie that her symptoms were beyond what could be tolerated in an open setting—a sentiment endorsed by most at the center. Transferring her to another setting would also ease the anxiety in the staff and patient group. On the other hand, Sophie would lose the opportunity for treatment at Riggs and staff members would lose the opportunity to grasp their role in an enactment.

It was clear to the team leader that Sophie's weight had crossed a line that put her treatment in serious jeopardy. However, it was also crucial that the team members, and in particular, the team leader, contain their anxiety (Stamm, 1985; Wells et al., 2006) to allow a discussion of the situation to take place with Sophie and among team members.

Recognizing Realistic Risks and Setting Appropriate Limits

Threats to a patient's life are always the highest priority. Recognizing and confronting these were important signals to Sophie that her actions were taken seriously. Sophie attended the team meeting, but, instead of relief at finding a responsive other in the team leader, she felt trapped, controlled, and coerced. While polite and contrite in the meeting, she responded to the "mutually agreed upon" limits of having her meals plated by the dietary staff by shifting to secretive binges outside Riggs, adopting an adversarial "catch me if you can" mentality. This is a common pattern in anorexic patients, but the genesis and specific meaning for Sophie were not clear. In a heightened state of anxiety, she could not make sense of her dramatic increase in purging, nor could she reflect upon the familiar repetition that was now playing out with the team. She was, in a sense, "lost in [a] familiar place" (Shapiro & Carr, 1991). Although limit setting and recognition of realistic risks were a necessary component of the team's functioning, they were insufficient to alter the course of Sophie's destructive trajectory. Something crucial was missing, despite staff efforts to understand the dynamic. The team leader wondered, "What are we missing?" She turned to the therapist for this information because the therapist is primarily responsible for integrating elements of the emerging perspective into a dynamic formulation. The therapist noted the parallel between the current scenario and Sophie's conflicted relationships with past therapists and her parents, but could not advance the discussion beyond that point. For the moment he was caught in the same enactment as the rest of the staff. The team leader encouraged team members to inhibit the urge to react reflexively to the power struggle and instead try to discover the meaning of Sophie's actions and how the staff might be engaged in a mutually destructive enactment. Was the team unwittingly engaging in a familiar family dynamic? The therapist heard this invitation as a clear message that this exploration was a primary concern of the therapy.

Crises Are Repetitions, Not Random Events

In her therapy sessions Sophie complained bitterly about feeling controlled and trapped by nurses, with little awareness of her role in provoking anxiety about her death. In the midst of a tirade against the nurses, Sophie called them "smothering mothers." This was the first hint of a central therapeutic story (Volkan, 2004).

With renewed curiosity the therapist returned to Sophie's life history and childhood development. Idyllic childhood memories of free-spirited adventures in the mountains gave way to adolescent memories of increasing scrutiny from her mother, who criticized Sophie's interest in boys and found it difficult to accept her emerging sexuality. Mother made critical remarks about her changing body and eating habits. Sophie's adolescent response to this criticism was to revert compliantly to a more childlike and acceptable position. When Sophie lost weight in an unconscious effort to please her mother, the pair began feuding over meals and caloric intake. Unexpressed conflict over Sophie's emerging sexuality and autonomy evolved into an open battle with her mother over food and weight.

The therapist slowly began to see how confrontations and limit setting activated latent relationship paradigms that led to Sophie's experience of being controlled. Not surprisingly, Sophie fought against limit setting with desperation and hostile vengeance that further escalated the crisis. Beneath her overt symptoms was a chaotic and malevolent inner world in which her mother was experienced as persecutory and controlling, while her sexuality and dependency needs were experienced as devouring and toxic. The therapist came to appreciate how she managed this inner life through absolute control of her body via starvation. He shared this emerging formulation with members of the team, the result of which was a temporary sense of relief and greater empathy for her struggle. But with each passing day, Sophie's self-destructive behaviors and weight loss eroded the therapist's confidence, leading him and other team members to press Sophie to stop her self-destructive behavior.

When Lost, Seek Consultation

The therapist recognized that he was lost in a transference–countertransference bind because he could not (and perhaps even should not) contain his countertransference urge to control Sophie's behavior. He turned to the team in hopes of gaining a perspective from a third party to this impasse. This request for consultation was different from earlier team discussions because the therapist was asking for help with transference dynamics, rather than asking the team to set limits on Sophie's behavior.

The therapist asked the team to help him think about the complicated dynamic that was unfolding. What position could he take that might open a space for Sophie to learn something about this chronic pattern? Members of the team eagerly took up the question of what was being enacted with Sophie. Clearly, her behavior was living out her struggle for emancipation from a controlling mother, while refusing to acknowledge dependent longings. What began to emerge was the staff's pattern of focusing entirely on Sophie's behavior while neglecting to consider the staff's chronic return to limit setting. Even the therapist, as the team member operating from a stance of "technical neutrality," retreated to limit setting when other interventions failed to produce the wished-for effect. Was the collapsing space for staff reflection a living out of the maternal transference?

The synthetic insight was offered by a senior therapist who noticed that the team, including the therapist, seemed caught up in a grandiose project to change a 20-year pattern in the first month of Sophie's treatment. Main (1957) refers to this as "arousal of omnipotence" (p. 135) in the staff. In the context of anxiety about Sophie's safety, the team began to lose its way, acting like a team in a locked hospital, rather than facing and using the limitations of an open setting. Hearing this gave the therapist a new perspective. He realized that this omnipotent position paralleled the behavior of Sophie's parents and that of psychotherapists since she first started seeing a psychiatrist at age 13. With this new formulation in mind, the team studied the chronic stalemate, working toward an interpretive stance. Team members began to consider how they had repeatedly enacted a parental paradigm in which they either saved Sophie from herself or disowned her as a destructive child. In such a grandiose scheme there was little room for Sophie's adult voice to make decisions and react to her environment. With this new perspective the team leader hoped to engage Sophie's authority for her treatment and invited her back to the team.

The Patient's Voice and Authority Emerge

During the team meeting with Sophie the team leader first communicated staff concern about the behaviors that were causing alarm and threatening the viability of her treatment. She made clear that Sophie could continue on her present course of action, but that Riggs was limited in its capacity to hold her treatment under these conditions. Sophie had a choice to make between engaging with the team to bring her symptoms under control, or continuing her out-of-control symptoms, in which case staff would help her find a facility that could respond to her current level of functioning.

Sophie felt rejected and threatened with dismissal from the hospital, but she reluctantly complied by stating that she wanted to preserve her treatment and promised to contain her behaviors. The team leader clarified that she did not want assurances of compliance, but rather wished to speak with Sophie about what she knew about feeling controlled by others. Sophie became interested in the line of questioning, reporting how she defeated each physician's effort whenever he or she offered ultimata to stop behaviors. The team leader acknowledged that she and the team had gotten caught up in trying to control her behavior and were dangerously close to offering an ultimatum at that moment.

The team leader agreed that Sophie was entirely capable of defeating treatment, but wondered if that was all she wanted to accomplish at Riggs. Sophie then recalled that she had asked the therapist to help her learn about the ways she defeated her efforts to develop a fuller life by pursuing thinness and ultimate control at any cost. She was chagrined at this turn of events, recognizing that she was actively endangering her chance to remain at Riggs, and not simply the victim of smothering mothers. Sophie's resolve thawed a bit, and she asked that the staff give her some space in the dining room. She felt that close scrutiny by nurses made her paranoid, which led her to flee from the dining room with stashes of food for bingeing and purging.

Repairing the Alliance

Creating an alliance with patients means that each patient and team negotiate a partnership that focuses on understanding the patient's reactions and repetitions in an effort to help the patient take charge of his or her life. In the team meeting, Sophie experienced the team leader as recognizing and validating her experience. She was then able to join the process by recalling treatment goals she and her therapist had identified and agreed to focus on in her treatment, which is part of repairing a damaged alliance (Safran & Muran, 1996; Safran, Muran, & Samstag, 2001; and Chapter 8 in this volume). At such moments the team serves a crucial function by restoring the capacity to reflect on anxiety-producing behaviors, opening a space for dialogue and negotiation. When Sophie recognized the part she was playing in the struggle with staff, her adversarial tone changed to one in which she could ask for something from nurses. Slowing down the process allowed an opportunity for Sophie, her therapist, and the team to understand a fragment of the enactment. After Sophie left the meeting some team members were hopeful that she might join in a partnership with staff around her treatment needs, while other staff members were more pessimistic.

In the next session the therapist reiterated the hospital's limitations, then offered to explore with Sophie the repeated experience of finding (and creating) "smothering mothers." He noted that he, too, had slipped into efforts to control her through interpretation, and had in a sense become a smothering mother. Sophie considered this possibility, but her associations turned to the way she had no one to help her deal with her mother's controlling behaviors. This comment helped him recognize that she was looking for a mediator to the enmeshed mother–daughter dyad. He wondered aloud if she had ever wished her father could be such a mediator. Sophie quickly agreed that this was true, and then went on to describe her father as a quiet and conflict-avoidant man who could not stand up to Sophie or her mother. Hearing this, the therapist caught a glimpse of a second transference paradigm being played out. He silently reflected on the way the team leader functioned as a "third" in creating a necessary opportunity for Sophie and the staff to negotiate a way of working together that recognized her autonomy and the legitimate concerns of the hospital staff. The therapist now could envision a way of working with Sophie that held the tensions between her wish for autonomy, her need for smothering mothers, and her desire for a paternal mediator to help her navigate a more responsible and mature way of relating.

In the weeks following the team meeting Sophie remained skeptical of the team's position because past experience taught her that therapists were easily moved into rescuing her from self-destruction. She "tested" this assumption by increasing her bingeing rituals in the dining room. When the staff did not rush to control her, she experienced a modicum of trust that her therapist and the nurses were sincere.

In the following months Sophie decreased her bulimic activity, joined the staff internist and dietary consultant in fashioning a nutritional plan, and slowly began gaining weight. She remained relatively stable and deepened her trust and reliance on the therapist, deciding she would settle in the area after she completed her Riggs treatment, asking him to be her outpatient therapist when the time was right.

Avoidance of the Negative Transference Leads to Splitting

Sophie maintained a stable, if somewhat uneasy adjustment to treatment until she requested to step down to the day treatment program 9 months after admission. This transition brought forth a reemergence of dependency conflicts and fears of a controlling mother. She became more symptomatic, with weight loss, a resurgence of bulimia, and alcohol abuse.

The therapist linked the surge in symptoms to her recent request to step down, interpreting this as a conflict between Sophie's struggle for greater independence and the dependency needs that she found so hard to bear. When Sophie bristled, accusing the therapist of trying to control her life, he retreated into a "neutral" stance, rationalizing the recent symptomatic behavior as a ploy to engage in a power struggle rather than enter the next phase of her life. Wishing to avoid another life-threatening power struggle, the therapist succumbed to Sophie's pressure by equivocating about her step-down. He unwittingly sided with her forceful declaration of independence and avoided the negative maternal transference in a false détente. Thus, the therapist unwittingly entered the role of ineffective father who could not help Sophie face the realities of her fears.

When Sophie's request came to the team meeting, few members were willing to voice opposition to it despite the escalation in Sophie's bingeing and purging. Although in the minority, the team leader was clear about her stance, and she rejected Sophie's request, making the case that an important dynamic was being played out with the team. She could not justify Sophie's step-down in the midst of increasing symptoms and another impasse in the treatment. Furthermore, she wondered what countertransference dynamic was causing the therapist to avoid Sophie's anger? Sophie's therapist reacted with outrage at the suggestion that he was missing something. He escalated the argument by insisting that the team leader was being unreasonably rigid, and was ignoring the fact that the therapist knew Sophie best: Refusal of Sophie's request for greater independence would only exacerbate her symptoms. Granting her request would signal to her that her autonomy was a mutual goal, and this would, in all likelihood, lead to a decrease in acting out. The team became polarized around this issue, with some staff aligning with the individual therapist and others with the team leader.

Mending Splits on the Team

The therapist knew rationally that Sophie's actions were not consistent with the usual context for a step-down, but felt strongly that an exception was warranted given the dynamics. The therapist felt uncharacteristically protective of Sophie, but also felt intense irritation that the team leader seemed to be ignoring his authority as the individual therapist by exerting such control over the decision. As is often the case, the intensity of the disagreements in the team suggested an enactment with this patient organized around splitting (Plakun, 1994). The team leader held firm to her decision to deny approval for a step-down, but was left feeling attacked and isolated.

When the argument resurfaced at the next team meeting, a senior therapist who was not involved directly in Sophie's treatment noted that the power struggle between therapist and team leader bore an uncanny resemblance to Sophie's primary dynamic. She wondered if the therapist was identifying with Sophie's struggle to be more autonomous because he, too, was in the process of developing his therapeutic voice, and, thus, was caught in a parallel process with Sophie.

When the therapist could internalize this useful consultation, he realized his experience of the team leader as vindictive was irrational and based on a split countertransference. He was again able to realign himself with the team leader, no longer felt obligated to protect his patient from the team leader's authority, and regained his role and perspective on his patient and her actions. The therapist was again able to use the team to speak about his anxiety about confronting Sophie. This shift led to his recognition of increasing concern about eventually treating Sophie as an outpatient, without the help of the team. Feeling held and contained by the team created the necessary perspective and psychic space for the therapy pair to deepen their work and confront negative and potentially destructive affects.

This insight helped the therapist find deeper empathy for Sophie's struggles, as well as to understand his own parallel process. It freed him to speak more directly and realistically to Sophie about the challenges they faced as the holding functions of hospital would attenuate as she moved toward discharge and outpatient treatment. The therapist recognized his dependency on the team, and especially the team leader, to take responsibility and authority for metabolizing and confronting the negative transference. If Sophie's treatment were to successfully transition beyond the hospital to outpatient status, he needed to incorporate the team role into his mind and technical repertoire. Even then he might need consultation when impasses developed.

No longer caught up in living out a split countertransference reaction, team members were in a better position to tolerate their inability to change Sophie's behavior. As the team and therapist were able to articulate their respective limitations and point out to Sophie the powerful ways she evoked their anxiety, she was better able to experience her own ambivalence about moving out of the protective environment of the hospital milieu. Over time her fears about taking up the responsibility of living independently were put into perspective. Gradually she was able to experience her anxiety consciously, claim it as her own, and use the help of others to think through how she could survive living on her own. The upsurge in symptoms abated to a point that the team leader felt Sophie could manage the challenge of living outside a Riggs residence, and approved the step-down.

Working Through Leads to Insight and Responsibility

Each subsequent transition through step-down programs precipitated a reemergence of Sophie's fears and new projections into smothering mothers. Now, however, during each repetition the intensity of symptoms decreased because Sophie had gained new internal strengths that better equipped her to recognize and deal with problematic issues. Through the team's repeated efforts to hold an interpretive frame around transitions, she was gradually able to revisit dependent longings, hatred of her neediness, and her fear and wish that people would control her. In this way she slowly began resolving internal conflicts while gaining new strengths. Such reviews continue until the issues are no longer problematic or are shrunken (Volkan 2004). The staff's increasing capacity to use the team as a space for healing splits and metabolizing intense countertransference reactions led to a greater respect for Sophie as a competent adult. This provided the catalyst for Sophie's capacity to take responsibility for her life, and to disentangle a long, crisis-ridden and self-destructive repetition compulsion. Subtle internal changes and insights led her to accept greater responsibility for actions and for preserving her life. As each crisis came more successfully and more quickly under conscious control, Sophie realized that she wanted to try living on her own without the support of the hospital. She set up a discharge plan with the help of her social worker. Realizing that she would miss the support of the staff, Sophie secured a home health aide to help with some skill deficits.

Reflecting on the final months of Riggs treatment, Sophie and her therapist reviewed her progress. During her time at Riggs, Sophie (1) learned to live alone in an apartment and to utilize peers to help with the transition to more independent living, (2) worked at a part-time job, (3) published short stories in magazines, (4) established relatively nondependent relationships with people outside Riggs, (5) defined the parameters of her conflicts and limitations in living a more independent life, (6) developed a more mature, interdependent relationship with her therapist so that she could benefit from treatment rather than reflexively reject all interventions as controlling, and (7) abstained from self-destructive behaviors (bingeing and purging, alcohol abuse, and weight loss) for more than 8 months.

Finding a Voice and Place in Society

When Sophie left Riggs after 18 months of treatment, her anorexia nervosa and borderline personality disorder were far from resolved. However, she was now able to live a more stable and productive life. In outpatient psychotherapy familiar impasses reemerged at moments of anxiety and change. Patient and therapist were able to work through the familiar binds and learn from the repetitions with greater regularity. On several occasions the therapist became embroiled in familiar countertransference enactments as a weak father or a smothering mother. When he could not find a productive way to work this through, he sought consultation with a senior therapist familiar with the case.

Sophie was particularly pleased with her ability to return to writing. Creating autobiographical short stories helped her put childhood experiences into perspective. Sophie read each story to her therapist. Initially this was to seek his approval for her talents as a creative writer. When she felt appreciated for her talents, though, she recognized that she was seeking his approval and affection as she had her father's. Later her focus shifted to the wish to share with others what she had learned through her difficult life. Her stories of familial enslavement were dramatizations of her inner life, and their resolution by breaking the bonds of slavery were lavishly heroic. Sophie smiled as she noted the romanticized twist she added to her stories, noting that her own life had not turned out so perfectly. About this she quipped, "You gotta give those young girls something to reach for." In this her therapist recognized Sophie's sublimation of the smothering mother in a new light. Sophie was imagining that other girls were living through similar struggles, and she wanted to give them hope for the future.

CONCLUDING REMARKS

Patients with "treatment-resistant" disorders and repeated crises pose a significant challenge. During such problematic treatments patients and staff often lose their grasp on the tasks and roles of the treatment. It is at such crucial moments that therapists, other clinical staff members, and the patient need the treatment team to offer a "third" perspective on what is unfolding. The optimally functioning team recognizes and engages the realistic risks posed by the patient's behavior, sets reasonable limits on self-destructive behavior, and approaches crises as meaningful communications that repeat aspects of the patient's life history and internal conflicts. Through this stance the team recognizes the intrapsychic validity of the patient's distressing actions while attending to their interpersonal meaning. This understanding helps staff members metabolize and contain intense countertransference reactions stirred by destructive behavior and offers a framework for approaching the problem. This kind of reflective, nonpunitive approach helps open a psychological space for engaging the patient in the study of the repetition and its meaning. Moments of such engagement take seriously the patient's authority and provide opportunities for repairing a damaged therapeutic alliance. Such moments often recur during a treatment and require repeated attention from the team. When patients and staff are able to repair an alliance within which they can utilize and learn from crises and enactments, they are then able to begin the process of finding and developing their identity and their voices as members of a community.

REFERENCES

Eisenberg, A. M. (1997). Institutional countertransference: The matrix of social structure and psychic structure. *Journal of American Academy of Psychoanalysis, 25,* 237–254.

Frieswyk, S. H., Allen, J. G., Colson, D. B., Coin, L., Gabbard, G. O., Horwitz, L., et al. (1986). Therapeutic alliance: Its place as a process and outcome variable in dynamic psychotherapy research. *Journal of Consulting and Clinical Psychology, 54*(1), 32–39.

Gabbard, G. (1986). The treatment of the "special" patient in a psychoanalytic hospital. *International Review of Psycho-Analysis, 13,* 333–347.

Gabbard, G. (1989). Splitting in hospital treatment. *American Journal of Psychiatry, 146*(1), 444–451.

Greene, L. R. (1993). Primitive defenses and the borderline patient's perceptions of the psychiatric treatment team. *Psychoanalytic Psychology, 49*(5), 432–450.

Greenson, R. R. (1967). *Technique and practice of psychoanalysis* (Vol. 1). New York: International Universities Press.

Haslam-Hopwood, G. T. G. (2003). The role of the primary clinician in the multidisciplinary team. *Bulletin of the Menninger Clinic, 67*(1), 5–17.

Horvath, A. O., & Luborsky, L. (1993). The role of the therapeutic alliance in psychotherapy. *Journal of Consulting and Clinical Psychology, 61,* 561–573.

Kernberg, O. F. (1976). *Object relations theory and clinical psychoanalysis.* New York: Jason Aronson.

Luborsky, L., Crits-Christoph, P., Mintz, J., & Auerback, A. (1988). *Who will benefit from psychotherapy?: Predicting therapeutic outcomes.* New York: Basic Books.

Main, T. F. (1957). The ailment. *British Journal of Medical Psychology, 30,* 129–145.

Muller, J. P., & Robinson, C. E. (2001). *Multiple holding functions of teams in residential and hospital treatment.* Unpublished manuscript.

Munich, R.L., & Allen, J.G. (2003). Psychiatric and sociotherapeutic perspectives on the difficult-to-treat patient. *Psychiatry: Interpersonal and Biological Processes, 66,* 346–357.

Plakun, E.M. (1994). Principles in the psychotherapy of self-destructive borderline patients. *Journal of Psychotherapy Practice and Research, 3,* 138–148.

Plakun, E.M. (2001). Making the alliance and taking the transference in work with suicidal borderline patients. *Journal of Psychotherapy Practice and Research, 10*(4), 269–276.

Sacksteder, J.L. (1997, Oct). *The interpretation of management and the management of interpretation.* Paper presented at Austen Riggs Center fall conference, Stockbridge, MA.

Safran, J.D., & Muran, J.C. (1996). The resolution of ruptures in the therapeutic alliance. *Journal of Consulting and Clinical Psychology, 64,* 447–458.

Safran, J.D., Muran, J.C., & Samstag, L.W. (2001). Repairing alliance ruptures. *Psychotherapy: Theory, Research, Practice, Training, 38,* 406–412.

Shapiro, E.R., & Carr, A.W. (1991). Lost in familiar places: Creating new connections between individual and society. New Haven, CT: Yale University Press.

Stamm, I. (1985). Countertransference in hospital treatment: Basic concepts and paradigms. *Bulletin of the Menninger Clinic, 49*(5), 432–450.

Volkan, V.D. (2004). Actualized unconscious fantasies and "therapeutic play" in adults' analyses: Further study of these concepts. In A. Laine (Ed.), *Power of understanding: Essays in honour of Veikko Tahka* (pp. 119–141). London: Karnac Books.

Wells, R., Jinnett, K., Alexander, J., Lichtenstein, R., Liu, D., & Zazzali,

J. L. (2006). Team leadership and patient outcomes in US psychiatric treatment settings. *Social Science & Medicine, 61,* 1840–1852.

Winnicott, D.W. (1965). *The maturational processes and the facilitating environment: Studies in the theory of emotional development.* New York: International Universities Press.

Zerbe, K.J. (1988). Walking on the razor's edge: The use of consultation in the treatment of a self-mutilating patient. *Bulletin of the Menninger Clinic, 52*(6), 492–503.

Chapter 14

Examined Living

A Psychodynamic Treatment System for Patients with Treatment-Resistant Disorders

Edward R. Shapiro, MD

Treatment resistant is a term for psychiatric disorders that do not respond to customary treatments. As noted in Chapter 1, the term may be applied to specific individual disorders, to comorbid disorders, to the patients themselves, or, as we prefer to think about it, to the limitations of the treatments offered. At the Austen Riggs Center, staff members work with patients who carry this label (Perry et al., 2009). Our patients tell us about the ways in which they have felt alienated by treatments for which the goal seemed to be to control their symptoms or even them. They consider their negative outcomes a consequence of an incompatibility between their needs and the treatment. Often, they have not felt that their ultimate responsibility for their own lives was engaged. They have shown us that they do better when they are negotiated with, rather than directed, and when we work with them toward an alliance, rather than insist on their compliance with the treatments we prescribe. Our learning about the process of this negotiation has illuminated the meaning of treatment resistance and has helped us to shape a treatment institution.

In previous chapters authors from Riggs have described aspects of the treatment of this group of patients: intensive individual psychotherapy, psychodynamic psychopharmacology, family and group work, the need for an outside perspective on dyadic therapy, engagement through a therapeutic community, the role of multidisciplinary treatment teams, the role of enactment, and the use of an alliance-based intervention for suicide, among others. In this last chapter, using Riggs as example, I focus on the treatment institution itself and how it can be structured to engage treatment resistance, learn from it, and provide opportunities for patients to shift their relationship to treatment in order to take charge of their lives.

THE PATIENTS

As noted, patients treated at Riggs meet criteria for an average of six Axis I and II disorders (Perry et al., 2009), including personality disorders (most often, borderline personality disorder). About two-thirds have suffered significant early abuse, trauma, neglect, or other adverse experiences in their families or in relation to other authority figures. Their personalities have been shaped by these experiences in ways that have important implications for relationships with their subsequent clinical caretakers (Shapiro, 1978). Children need their families and must maximize their caretakers' capacities to meet their needs. In many of these families, significant disconnection between parents and child derives from a combination of constitutional and environmental factors. The constitutional factors can include mismatched attachment styles or some form of affect dysregulation in the child (Siever & Davis, 1991); the environmental ones include the ways that parents can relive their own childhood traumas through their care of their children (Shapiro, Zinner, Shapiro, & Berkowitz, 1975). The combination can leave these children feeling unrecognized as separate individuals. These future patients' personalities—the way they are—communicate the residua of these experiences. Suppressing their anger, our patients have denied the environmental failure and lived out their unconscious anger and despair in their lives. They have withdrawn from engaging in a negotiation with the external world that might maximize their opportunities to develop through childhood. Instead, they unwittingly participate in consistently recreating the most painful aspects of their lives, one aspect of which may become resistance to treatment based on a fundamental distrust of those in positions of authority.

Psychoanalysts refer to this unconscious adaptation and shaping of the personality as *ego-syntonic*, a term that describes patients' acceptance of, and conscious comfort with, parts of themselves that are often self-defeating and alienating of others. Not infrequently, aspects of their personalities that they cannot fully discern may be difficult for others to bear.

We have learned that the best way to grasp our patients' struggles is to focus on the way they interact with people. All of us communicate our personalities by what we say and by how we say it. Others usually notice more easily than we can how our *process*—the way we do things—transmits the essence of ourselves, including our most difficult aspects. In order to see ourselves in the best possible light, we either avoid or justify the negative aspects of ourselves. To know ourselves fully—with all of our difficulties—we need the help of others who both understand us and hold us accountable. And we need that self-knowledge to help us understand and put into perspective the powerful impact of early adverse experiences.

For those patients who become labeled as treatment resistant, treatment as usual, with a predominant biological focus—that is, treatment that minimizes the opportunity to learn from relationships with others—has been insufficient. Uncontrolled behavior, disturbed relationships, suicidal despair, and an inability to contain intense affects disrupt their lives and their treatment. Periodic short-term hospitalizations for crisis management, focusing inevitably on an imposition of structural, behavioral, and psychopharmacological interventions, emphasize stabilization and compliance (Glick & Tandon, 2009). These interventions have been unable to sustain these patients' stability in treatment after discharge. To get beyond crises, many of these patients need a longer-term relationship with clinicians within a focused system that includes psychopharmacological treatment but goes beyond it. Such a system provides a working framework for specially trained clinicians who can tolerate these patients' difficult personalities long enough to help them see themselves more clearly, translate behavioral communications into language, learn how and why they have shaped themselves in this particular way, put their lives in historical perspective, and help them reshape how they deal with their interpersonal world. This is the task of a psychodynamic treatment institution.

The mission of the Austen Riggs Center is to "help 'treatment-resistant' patients become people taking charge of their lives." This epigrammatic statement emerged through discussions among patients, staff, and the Board of Trustees considering (both separately and together) the essence of the institution's work (Shapiro, 2001a). It provided the standard by which people in all roles could consider whether their efforts were congruent with the institution's mission. In addition, it stimulated ongoing work at elucidating two central questions: What is "treatment resistance" and what does "in charge" mean? Sorting out these issues illuminated the work of the entire institution.

TREATMENT RESISTANCE

Focusing on treatment resistance, we are learning how our profession's current paradigm of treatment (emphasizing biology and symptom management) has increasingly ignored the person, personality, and mind of the patient. Patients' ways of engaging the interpersonal world, their psychological structure, multigenerational history, and the subjective and personal meanings they have developed about their lives have become increasingly irrelevant to the field. Although biological treatments can help these patients reduce their symptoms, this form of relief—if not linked to psychological understanding—offers only limited possibility that they will feel in charge of shaping their lives. The predominant biological paradigm for conceptualizing and treating psychiatric illness has led to the use of the label "treatment resistant" for those patients who require more than biological intervention—who need another person to help them take themselves seriously in order to change the trajectory of their lives (Shapiro, 2001c).

> The medical model, with its biological focus, often fails to benefit treatment-resistant patients because it locates illness in the individual, bypassing recognition that we are treating a person who has developed within a particular human context.

For these patients, the repetitive behavioral struggle inherent in treatment resistance is not just a symptom of biological illness, nor simply the reenactment of painful experience. It can also be understood as a communication—and thus as a sign of hope—that someone will help them understand their experiences *and* hold them accountable for their actions. With perspective and accountability, these patients as adults might no longer have to contort themselves to fit a mismatched environment, but instead face the limitations in themselves and others in order to negotiate a better fit, using their adult authority.

Emerging from adverse early environments, these patients have made efforts as children to make the best of what was available. The deep dependence on caretakers evokes in the child a need to preserve the relationship; the caretaker must be experienced as "good." The child justifies the caretakers' limited responsiveness by experiencing him- or herself as "bad": If he or she were only better, his or her caretakers would be more responsive. The child's internal responses to this conclusion include a denial of the lack of fit, suppression of the resultant anger, difficulty in developing words for feelings, a turning of anger against the self through punitive unconscious self-criticism (sometimes manifest by an aggressive assault on the body through eating disorders, cutting, or other forms of self-abuse), and unwittingly angry behaviors toward others, often communicated through projective identification (Kernberg, 1976; Kris, 1990; Shapiro, 1978). In any treatment system, staff and other patients are inevitably caught up in each patient's powerful affective communications while induced through projective identification to react to and relive with the patient the essence of the patient's authority struggles (Kernberg, 1976; Plakun, 2001; Shapiro, 1982; Shapiro & Carr, 1991). Studying these enactments as communication can help the patient to unpack their historical significance and find their hidden meaning.

> Treatment-resistant patients with personality disorders have often developed within an early context of environmental trauma, neglect, or deprivation, and thus anticipate negative experiences with caretakers. This early history affects their ability to trust and to join in therapeutic work. Treatments work best when they include a way to address patients' experiences of failure by clinical caretakers.

TAKING CHARGE

In the course of their development, these patients may have discovered that the only way they can feel in charge in response to caretakers—whom they often experience as untrustworthy—is to resist them, sometimes only internally and passively, in the service of self-protection. This response can contribute to a pervasive lack of trust in authority figures, resulting in a chaotic interpersonal process that enacts unmanaged aggression.

> Treatment-resistant patients may experience treatment environments that direct, control, instruct, limit, and demand compliance as familiar noxious settings to which the only adaptive response is resistance. Treatments that work best avoid efforts to control and enforce compliance—and offer the possibility of a new kind of adaptation.

Because of this diffuse behavioral communication, these patients often disperse their transferences, repeatedly enlisting others who unwittingly join them in enactments, rather than bring their chaotic object world symbolically and experientially into a relatively contained transference relationship with an individual therapist. Since these patients may not have developed language to describe their painful experience, an outpatient therapist—located at a distance from the patient's behavioral enactments—often can neither discern what is happening nor help contain the impact of the behavior long enough to make sense of the transference. Riggs provides a larger human system wherein patients are invited to engage with patients and staff within a containing institutional framework designed for learning.

> These patients often fail in outpatient treatment because they communicate through behavior and disperse their transferences. The outpatient therapist often lacks opportunity to see how this behavior pattern evolves in the patient's outside world, and the patient lacks the language to report it. A setting where dispersed transferences can be seen and integrated can allow the patient to learn to use psychotherapy—and return to more successful outpatient work.

An environment wherein others make essential decisions limits the possibility for patients to notice their responsibility and take charge. Riggs is a voluntary, hospital-based institution offering a continuum of care, where all units are open, with no restrictions or privilege systems. There are myriad opportunities for patients to develop a range of relationships with patients and staff, but the choices are theirs. They participate in the shaping of their own treatment rather than simply complying with a staff design. When their characteristic behavior evokes irritation in others and they experience themselves as victims, others are available to help them notice their own responsibility, both social and political. The freedom of the open setting, coupled with a commitment to examining the meaning of what happens in that setting, makes their choices more visible, opening an opportunity for patients to see their own role in creating painful repetitions (Shapiro & Plakun, 2009). Unconscious images of the self in relation to a parent become enacted in their relationships through projective identification and are then carried by other patients and staff. Negative staff reactions to the patient and between staff members can be understood as aspects of countertransference evoked by the patient's communications (Shapiro & Carr, 1987). Placed in historical perspective, these relationships can be understood as unconscious attempts by patients to replicate and learn about their problematic earlier experiences.

> A setting that focuses on both empathy and accountability, emphasizes patient authority, focuses on areas of patient competence, and encourages engagement in and examination of relationships may provide the best opportunity for overcoming treatment resistance.

INTEGRATING DISPLACED AND ACTED OUT TRANSFERENCE FEELINGS

To facilitate the development, containment, integration, and interpretation of dispersed transferences, the therapist who is providing the intensive individual psychotherapy is a member of an interdisciplinary team, which functions as described in Chapter 13. While holding onto a perspective of the patient's mind, the therapist and the team leader each takes up a consultative role to the team's process. They listen to the intense relationships the patient develops with other patients and staff members, and consider them as potentially split-off aspects of the developing transference. The team leader endeavors to help team members unpack and understand how the team process is illuminated by the patient's history and struggles. The therapist explores with the patient what keeps him or her from focusing these acted out internal images into the therapeutic relationship.

- *Example 1.* Jennifer experienced her male therapist as empathic, responsive, available, and good. This was in stark contrast to her experience of her female nursing care coordinator, whom she found harsh, unforgiving, unavailable, and inconsiderate—an experience that justified Jennifer's angry treatment of her. The therapist, who did not experience the nurse so harshly, noted that Jennifer was presenting polarized transference views of her caretakers. To help her begin to recognize her use of splitting, he pointed out that, as therapist, he was in charge of her treatment and that the nursing care was, therefore, something that he was overseeing. He wondered about the patient's difficulty in holding him accountable for the nursing provision and raised the possibility that the patient was preserving him in an idealized space in her mind. Further exploration revealed that this preservation of an idealized parent was a defensive structure derived from Jennifer's childhood experience. Recognizing this was the first step in Jennifer's development of a capacity to hold both loving and angry feelings for the therapist in the transference.

• *Example 2.* The social worker on the team was the target of unrelenting hostility from Francine's parents for not providing them with enough information about their daughter's treatment. When Francine attended a team meeting, the team leader wondered with her what lay behind her decision not to let her parents know what was happening in her treatment. In subsequent discussions with the therapist and social worker, each suggested that Francine was covertly inviting the family to struggle with the staff rather than speaking with her parents directly about her need for a private space for her work. This opened a discussion within the family about the boundaries of privacy, shared feelings of exclusion and intrusion, and the need for all family members to take responsibility for negotiating any necessary privacy. Francine was able to recognize that her abdication from the conversation was a repetition of a childhood memory of not finding a way to preserve any sense of privacy from her anxious and intrusive parents. Discussion of these reawakened memories in the family meetings allowed family members to review the past, reveal previously hidden memories of intrusion and trauma—both in this family and in the parents' families of origin—and place their feelings in perspective.

• *Example 3.* The team leader found himself irritated at the social worker's "endless worries" about Sam's missed appointments with her. The therapist called the team leader's irritation to his attention, noting that the tension between the team leader and the social worker mirrored the split relationship between Sam's parents, where mother "worried" obsessively and father criticized her. The parents—and now team members—were having trouble functioning as a working pair in holding Sam accountable. The perspective offered by the discussion allowed the therapist to begin an exploration with Sam of his anger and grief about the inability of his parents to work together, and provided an opportunity to help the parents (and the team members) see the meaning and consequences of their stereotyped argument.

Another arena for displacement of transference feelings is in relationships between patients. The staff discourages exclusive relationships between patients for a number of important reasons, one of which is the risk of emptying treatment relationships of meaning. A pair of patients in an exclusive relationship challenges the therapist–patient pair's focus on the unfolding transference. Feelings that might otherwise have been brought into the treatment are readily displaced into the patient pair and enacted there without interpretation.

- *Example 4*. As a child, Laura was sexually abused by a babysitter and was beginning to bring into her therapy her rage at her parents for neither protecting her nor noticing the abuse. She developed an intense relationship with another patient whom she continually verbally abused. Neither patient spoke to their therapist about this tension-filled relationship, but nursing staff noticed it. When the team began to perceive this shared enactment of childhood abuse (with roles reversed), the therapist could help Laura notice the way she kept the therapist (as parent) from the necessary information he needed to help her. This observation allowed Laura to consider the many assumptions she had about her parents as a child, which had inhibited her ability to turn to them for help.

- *Example 5*. Ellen and Frank became involved in a sexual relationship while both were patients at Riggs. This action, signaling a threat to their ongoing treatments, opened a discussion with each therapist about the risky acting out of needs for intimacy. In response to the discussion, Ellen angrily confronted her male therapist, saying that he seemed to want a "one-sided" intimacy, where she could know nothing about his life. Her rage surprised Ellen and opened for examination her longing in the transference for an unavailable man, derived from her early relationship with her unavailable father. Repetitive acting out of transference feelings in her outside life had been one of the issues that had disrupted Ellen's outpatient treatment. Now, this behavior and the feelings behind it were available for exploration.

MANAGING THE SYSTEM

Arnold Modell (1984) describes how human beings are "open systems" linked by the communication of affects. How this communication functions and how it can best be used therapeutically becomes a central question for a clinical system. Affectively charged communications are the unmanaged center of our patients' psychological difficulties. Negotiating boundaries across which the dialogue embedded in these communications and split relationships can be heard, withstood (without retaliation or abandonment), and translated is a central aspect of an interpretive treatment.

Given this unremitting focus at Riggs, the need for containing boundaries for interpretation runs throughout the institution. Powerful affective communications are addressed at multiple boundaries in dyads, small and large groups, and as a total system. Managing the system can be understood as negotiating a series of task boundaries.

Any institution is comprised of many boundaries: between roles, tasks, disciplines, levels of authority, between the working organization and its board, and between the institution and the outer society. Each of these boundaries must be managed, both in terms of concrete structures (policies and procedures) and efforts to make sense of what transpires across them (interpretation). Such interpretation takes place in many forms and in different disciplinary languages in every institution. But in a treatment institution everything becomes relevant to the primary task of helping patients take charge of their communications, their affectively charged eruptions, and their lives.

• *Example* 6. A housekeeper erupts in anger at her supervisor. The supervisor places her on warning for insubordination. After review, it becomes clear that the eruption followed the housekeeper's spending 3 hours cleaning up vomit in public bathrooms shared by patients. Competent management of this event requires developing a range of questions. For example, is this just an irritable employee who needs to learn to manage her feelings at work? Is this an employee eruption that is symptomatic of an oppressive authority structure where the staff's work and commitment are not adequately recognized? Or, more clinically, has the patient community unwittingly "selected" a particular patient to vomit on the staff's building as an angry way to communicate their wish that the caretakers take more notice of their anger? Is the vomit a statement from patients that the staff's "food" is indigestible? Have they pushed a particular staff member to express anger on their behalf? Deciding which of these—and other—questions to explore—and in which context—becomes the task of the system.

At Riggs, the treatment system is constructed to maximize feedback to patients about the impact of their behavior on others (Shapiro & Plakun, 2009). The effort is to help them shift from behavioral communication of their experience (e.g., through cutting, eating disorder symptoms, suicidal behavior, inappropriate drug and alcohol use, sexual acting out) to putting their experience into words. Intensive individual psychotherapy is the ultimate venue for this translation, but every other aspect of the clinical system (family and group work, therapeutic community life, engagement in artistic and theater activities) supplements this effort. And, for staff members, their efforts to contain and understand—rather than simply react to or withdraw from—these powerful behavioral communications can evoke internal disarray in them as individuals, which they might enact through their other relationships within the institution. This countertransference dilemma can be disguised in institutional life (Shapiro & Carr, 1987), manifesting itself in interpersonal and professional tensions that affect the staff's work.

> Studying the process of the patient's behavioral communication and focusing on the interactive process between clinicians and previously treatment-resistant patients opens the possibility of developing language for patients' previously symptomatic behavioral communication—creating the opportunity for patients to gain a new perspective on what they are doing and why—and to manage themselves differently.

ORGANIZATION AND INSTITUTION

Wesley Carr makes an important distinction between "organization" and "institution" (Shapiro & Carr, 1991). *Organization* consists of the day-to-day workings of the system, the policies and procedures and structures of the organization's work. *Institution* includes the larger context, carrying out work on behalf of the larger society, and people outside the institution have ideas and images about it. Thus all institutions are "institutions in the mind."

The mission of Riggs is a clinical mission. The primary clinical dilemma for our patients is how to help them uncover the meanings behind their symptoms—the trauma and pain and rage they have experienced in their lives—while still helping them to take responsibility for their choices. They are products of their environments, delegates of their families, yet they are also individual adults with full responsibility for choosing their lives. Victimization and authority can actually go together if the past is put in perspective. For example, Laura (example 4) was abused as a child. Seeing her own repetition of that abuse with another patient, with herself in the role of abuser, allowed her to recognize the way she had identified with her abuser as a child. This recognition provided an opportunity for Laura to take adult authority for her previously denied rage.

Chapters 5 and 11 describe the ways in which our patients are bearers of painful truths—for their families and for the larger society. They represent and engage us in enactments of stories that are difficult to bear: the rage of past generations of suffering, the inability to look directly at the ways we damage our children, the sexual exploitation of the innocent in the service of past hurts. Our patients are messengers of painful truths that society cannot bear to see and learn from: Our institutional task is to help translate these truths into a language that can be grasped both by the patient and the social surround. Making this effort is our institutional mission.

Both "organization" and "institution" have to be managed—but differently. The *organization* has daily work tasks, some quite concrete: the ordering of supplies, paying bills, managing services, and providing benefits. These must be accomplished as efficiently and effectively as possible. To manage the *institution* requires attempting to articulate a task, a mission, that effectively maintains the institution's survival, meets a recognizable need of the larger society, and allows the institution to be recognizable from outside. An institution's mission is not asserted, it is discovered (Shapiro, 2001b). Once this mission is grasped—and, given the ongoing changes in society, it must continually be reshaped—managing the institution requires an ongoing effort at both articulating and assessing the images evoked in the minds of others by the institution's work.

Both *organization* and *institution* are affected by the way the staff hold and relate to the mission. Organizational tasks can be experienced as deadening or lively. Engagement in a shared institutional mission that transcends individuals contains the staff so that they can learn about, bear, and put into perspective their stressful engagements with patients. The clarity of the mission responds to the needs of the staff for a framework and a shared set of values so that they can collectively take care of the patients.

But how are nonclinical staff members brought into the larger institutional mission? Riggs provides one interesting example readily usable in other treatment settings in terms of its management of money, as I have described in Chapter 9, where business and clinical staff join to help patients and families both manage their resources and think about the feelings involved in using them.

RIGGS AS INSTITUTION

All institutions, especially one focused on work with treatment-resistant patients, need a clearly articulated mission that:

- Links the institution to the outer society by addressing a social need.
- Allows the institution to be recognizable from the outside.
- Offers a task and a set of recognizable social values that transcend individuals.
- Integrates the staff's professional commitments.
- Provides support for staff's and patients' engagement in difficult work.
- Offers a framework for the institution's development.

Discerning the ways our patients' personalities have been shaped by their human contexts (familial, social, and intergenerational), and acknowledging that they are nonetheless responsible for their own decisions, are central aspects of the institution's work. Patients are not doomed to repeat the past once they develop perspective and the recognition that they are in charge of their own present behavior.

The same is true for the work of the institution. Riggs has a history—now close to 100 years long—of developing ways of working with these patients (Shapiro & Fromm, 2000; Shapiro & Plakun, 2009). It has been shaped by its psychoanalytic past. But it is not constrained to repeat it. As society and the field of psychiatry have developed, Riggs has become unique in terms of its intensive and longer-term connection to these patients. Recognizing the psychoanalytic past allows us to see more clearly the ways psychodynamic understanding has developed beyond the dyad, into families, groups, and systems. Though intensive psychoanalytic psychotherapy remains central to our work, we have applied our understanding to the social systems around our patients and around the institution. To overcome our own blind spots, we have brought in outside consultants to help us to clarify our work, reorganize our authority structures, and develop our outside communications. These have included board members with special areas of expertise as well as formal external consultation. As with our patients, we recognize that to fully see ourselves, we need the help of others.

As a consequence, we have increasingly recognized that we have an obligation to learn from our unique exposure to patients on behalf of the field and the larger society. To help shape this institutional mission, we have developed the Erikson Institute for Education and Research as a vehicle for the articulation of our learning. We have studied our work, brought in outsiders from other fields to help teach us, and brought our learning outside. Taking in the feedback has allowed us to shape ourselves more accurately and recognize the broader applications of our unique mission. For example, learning from our therapeutic community has taken us outside the institution to consult to schools, the criminal justice system, the armed forces, health care agencies, and even the political system (Fromm, 2007; Shapiro, 2001c, 2003). Focusing on suicide has taken us into studying the impact of suicide on clinicians and trainees (Plakun & Tillman, 2005; Tillman, 2003, 2006). Focusing on personality development and treatment resistance as an opportunity to translate a behavioral communication into words has opened learning about families, social systems, and the inevitable reactions to attempting to match needs with limited resources.

SUMMARY

Treatment resistance in psychiatry is a much broader notion than the nonresponsiveness of a set of symptoms or particular disorders to ordinary, primarily biological and behavioral, treatment. It opens an examination of the nature of treatment itself: What are we treating? The notion of treating an illness, inherent in the medical model, bypasses the recognition that we are also treating a person who has developed within a particular human context. Once we begin to recognize that individuals and their contexts can create and preserve a set of symptoms in the service of attempting to manage unbearable experience, we inevitably have to broaden our notions of treatment. Paying attention to the treatment context we are creating, the ways it might reawaken painful past experiences for the patient, and the need to engage the patient as a competent ally with the treatment process can change our perspective.

I have indicated some of the characteristics of a treatment context that clinicians might usefully bring to working with patients who have "treatment-resistant" psychiatric disorders. Considering the tension between compliance and alliance and linking empathy and accountability are central components. Studying the process of the patient's communication and focusing on the interactive process between clinicians and patients opens the possibility of developing a new language for the patient's previously symptomatic communication. Holding the treatment task as primary and considering behavior as meaningful communication can allow for containment and interpretation. Recognizing that a patient's self-destructive action may involve an effort to protect a needed therapist from the patient's anger might allow for perspective on the patient's past. All of these, with the support of the range of contemporary psychiatric and psychopharmacological treatments, can help these patients to be increasingly in charge of their minds—and their lives.

REFERENCES

Fromm, M.G. (2007). The escalating use of medications by college students: What are they telling us, what are we telling them? *Journal of College Student Psychotherapy, 21*(3/4), 27N–44.

Glick, I., & Tandon, R. (2009). The acute crisis stabilization unit for adults. In S.S. Sharfstein, F.B. Dickerson, & J.M. Oldham (Eds.), *Textbook of hospital psychiatry* (pp. 23–35). Washington: American Psychiatric Association.

Kernberg, O. (1976). *Object relations theory and clinical psychoanalysis.* New York: Jason Aronson.

Kris, A.O. (1990). Helping patients by analyzing self-criticism. *Journal of the American Psychoanalytic Association, 38,* 605–636.

Modell, A. (1984). *Psychoanalysis in a new context.* New York: International Universities Press.

Perry, J.C., Fowler, J.C., Bailey, A., Clemence, A.J., Plakun, E.M., Zheutlin, B., et al. (2009). Improvement and recovery from suicidal and self-destructive phenomena in treatment-refractory disorders. *Journal of Nervous and* Delete

Plakun, E.M. (2001). Making the alliance and taking the transference in work with suicidal borderline patients. *Journal of Psychotherapy Practice and Research, 10,* 269–276.

Plakun, E.M., & Tillman, J.T. (2005). Responding to the impact of suicide on clinicians. *Directions in Psychiatry, 25,* 301–309.

Shapiro, E.R. (1978). The psychodynamics and developmental psychology of the borderline patient: A review of the literature. *American Journal of Psychiatry, 135,* 1305–1315.

Shapiro, E.R. (1982). The holding environment and family therapy with acting out adolescents. *International Journal of Psychoanalytic Psychotherapy, 9,* 209–226.

Shapiro, E.R. (2001a). Institutional learning as chief executive. In L. Gould, L. Stapley, & M. Stein (Eds.), *The systems psychodynamics of organizations: Integrating the group relations approach, psychoanalytic and open systems theory* (pp. 175–195). New York: Karnac Press.

Shapiro, E.R. (2001b). The changing role of the CEO. *Organizational and Social Dynamics, 1*(1), 130–142.

Shapiro, E.R. (2001c). The effect of social changes on the doctor–patient relationship. *Organizational and Social Dynamics, 2*, 1–11.

Shapiro, E.R. (2003). The maturation of American identity: A study of the elections of 1996 and 2000 and the war against terrorism. *Organizational and Social Dynamics, 3*(1), 121–133.

Shapiro, E.R., & Carr, A.W. (1987). Disguised countertransference in institutions. *Psychiatry, 50*, 72–82.

Shapiro, E.R., & Carr, A.W. (1991). *Lost in familiar places: Creating new connections between the individual and society.* New Haven, CT: Yale University Press.

Shapiro, E.R., & Fromm, M.G. (2000). Erik Erikson's clinical theory. In B.J. Sadock & H.I. Kaplan (Eds.). *Comprehensive textbook of psychiatry* (pp. 2200–2206). New York: Williams & Wilkins.

Shapiro, E.R., & Plakun, E.M. (2009). Residential psychiatric treatment: An intensive psychodynamic approach for patients with treatment-resistant disorders. In S.S. Sharfstein, F.B. Dickerson, & J.M. Oldham (Eds.), *Textbook of hospital psychiatry* (pp. 285–297). Washington, DC: American Psychiatric Association.

Shapiro, E.R., Zinner, J., Shapiro, R.L., & Berkowitz, D.A. (1975). The influence of family experience on borderline personality development. *International Review of Psychoanalysis, 2*, 399–411.

Siever, L.J., & Davis, K.L. (1991). A psychobiological perspective on the personality disorders. *American Journal of Psychiatry, 148*, 1647–1658.

Tillman, J.G. (2003). The suicide of patients and the quiet voice of the therapist. *Journal of the American Academy of Psychoanalysis and Dynamic Psychiatry, 31*(3), 425–427.

Tillman, J.G. (2006). When a patient commits suicide: An empirical study of psychoanalytic clinicians. *International Journal of Psychoanalysis, 87*, 159–177.

LIST OF CONTRIBUTORS

Barri Belnap, MD, is a staff psychiatrist at the Austen Riggs Center and oversees the provision of psychopharmacology services at Riggs as Chair of the Drug Usage Medical Procedures Committee. She is an organizational consultant practicing in the United States and overseas. (Chapter 3)

Marilyn Charles, PhD, ABPP, is a staff psychologist at the Austen Riggs Center, and a practicing psychoanalyst. Affiliated with several psychoanalytic institutes, she is a member of the editorial boards of several psychoanalytic journals, Adjunct Professor at Michigan State University, the author of 3 books and numerous publications, Co-Chair of the Association for the Psychoanalysis of Culture and Society, and Co-Chair of the Early Career Committee of Division 39 of the American Psychological Association. (Chapter 7)

Donna Elmendorf, PhD, is a staff psychologist and Director of the Therapeutic Community Program at Riggs. She is an organizational consultant and has written and presented in a number of clinical areas. (Chapter 11)

J. Christopher Fowler, PhD, is a staff psychologist and treatment team leader at Riggs and the Director of Research at the Erik H. Erikson Institute of the Austen Riggs Center. He is also Director of the Suicide Research Initiative at the Austen Riggs Center, an Assistant Clinical Professor at Yale University, and a faculty member of the Anna Freud Center–Yale University Research Training Program. Dr. Fowler has published and presented widely. (Chapters 1, 13)

M. Gerard Fromm, PhD, ABPP, is the Evelyn Stefansson Nef Director of the Erikson Institute for Education and Research at the Austen Riggs Center. He is a staff psychologist at Riggs, and is on the faculties of the Massachusetts Institute for Psychoanalysis, the Berkshire Psychoanalytic Institute, Harvard Medical School, and the Yale Child Study Center. Dr. Fromm co-edited *The Facilitating Environment: Clinical Applications of Winnicott's Theory* and has presented and published widely. (Chapter 5)

M. Sagman Kayatekin, MD, was a staff psychiatrist and treatment team leader at the Austen Riggs Center until 2010. He is currently Medical Director of the Professionals In Crisis Unit, Menninger Clinic, an Associate Professor of Psychiatry at the Baylor College of Medicine, and a practicing psychoanalyst. (Chapter 2)

Otto F. Kernberg, MD, is Director of the Personality Disorders Institute at the New York Presbyterian Hospital, and Payne Whitney Westchester Professor of Psychiatry at Weill Medical College of Cornell University. He also serves as a Training and Supervising Analyst at Columbia University Center for Psychoanalytic Training and Research. Dr. Kernberg has published and presented widely in the United States and overseas. (Foreword)

Sharon E. Krikorian, PhD, is a staff psychologist, treatment team leader, and consultant in the Therapeutic Community Program at the Austen Riggs Center. She has written and presented in a number of clinical areas. (Chapter 13)

David Mintz, MD, is staff psychiatrist and Director of Psychiatric Education at the Austen Riggs Center. He is a Psychoanalytic Fellow of the American Academy of Psychoanalysis and Dynamic Psychiatry, where he also serves on the Education Committee, and is on the Medical Student Education Committee of the American Psychoanalytic Association. Dr.

Mintz has presented widely and published in multiple journals. (Chapter 3)

John P. Muller, PhD, ABPP, is Director of Training at the Austen Riggs Center, and a staff psychologist and psychoanalyst. He was twice the recipient of the Deutsch Prize from the Boston Psychoanalytic Institute and in 2008 received the Distinguished Educator Award from the International Federation for Psychoanalytic Education. He has published and presented widely on Lacan, semiotics, and psychoanalysis. (Chapter 6)

Margaret Parish, PhD, is a staff psychologist, treatment team leader and consultant in the Therapeutic Community Program at the Austen Riggs Center. She is also an organizational consultant and has presented in a number of clinical areas. (Chapter 11)

Eric M. Plakun, MD, is staff psychiatrist and Director of Admissions and Professional Relations at the Austen Riggs Center, a Psychoanalytic Fellow of the American Academy of Psychoanalysis and Dynamic Psychiatry, Distinguished Life Fellow of the American Psychiatric Association, Fellow of the American College of Psychiatrists, Honorary Fellow of the American College of Psychoanalysts, past Chair of the American Psychiatric Association Committee on Psychotherapy by Psychiatrists, member of the American Psychiatric Association Assembly Executive Committee, and recipient of the Massachusetts Psychiatric Society's award as Outstanding Clinical Psychiatrist. A Harvard Medical School clinical faculty member for over 20 years, Dr. Plakun edited *New Perspectives on Narcissism* and has published and presented widely. (Introduction, Chapters 1, 2, 4, 8)

Ave Schwartz, LICSW, is Director of Social Work at the Austen Riggs Center and a former member of the faculty of the Smith College School for Social Work. (Chapter 12)

Edward R. Shapiro, MD, is Medical Director/CEO of the Austen Riggs Center, Clinical Professor of Psychiatry at Yale Medical School, and a Training and Supervising Analyst at the Berkshire Psychoanalytic Institute. Awarded the *Philip Isenberg Teaching Award* from McLean Hospital, the *Felix and Helene Deutsch Scientific Prize* from the Boston Psychoanalytic Institute, the *Research Prize* from the Society for Family Therapy

Research and the *Distinguished Psychiatrist for the Advancement of the Profession Award* from the Massachusetts Psychiatric Society, Dr. Shapiro is a Distinguished Life Fellow of the American Psychiatric Association and a Fellow of the American College of Psychoanalysts and the A.K. Rice Institute. He is the author (with A.W. Carr) of *Lost in Familiar Places* and editor of *The Inner World in the Outer World*, and has published and presented widely. (Chapters 1, 9, 14)

Jane G. Tillman, PhD, ABPP, is a staff psychologist and psychoanalyst and a treatment team leader at the Austen Riggs Center. Dr. Tillman has been Chair of the Ethics Committee and President of the Section for Women, Gender, and Psychoanalysis of Division 39 of the American Psychological Association. She is a Trustee of the Accreditation Council for Psychoanalytic Education, principal investigator of a study exploring states of mind preceding near-lethal suicide attempts, and has published and presented widely. (Chapter 10)

CREDITS

All articles are reprinted with permission.

Introduction: Plakun, E.M. (2009). A View From Riggs: Treatment resistance and patient authority—Series Epilogue. *Journal of the American Academy of Psychoanalysis, 37*(4), 699–700.

Chapter 2: Kayatekin, M.S. & Plakun, E.M. (2009). A View From Riggs: Treatment resistance and patient authority—X. From acting out to enactment in treatment resistant disorders. *Journal of the American Academy of Psychoanalysis, 37*(2), 365–381.

Chapter 3: Mintz, D. & Belnap, B.A. (2006). A View from Riggs: Treatment resistance and patient authority—III. What is psychodynamic psychopharmacology? Journal of the American Academy of Psychoanalysis, *34*(4), 581–602.

Chapter 4: Plakun, E.M. (2006). A View From Riggs: Treatment resistance and patient authority—I. A psychodynamic perspective. *Journal of the American Academy of Psychoanalysis, 34*(2) 349–366.

Chapter 5: Fromm, M.G. (2006). A View From Riggs: Treatment resistance and patient authority—II. Transmission of trauma. *Journal of the American Academy of Psychoanalysis, 34*(3) 445–459.

Chapter 6: Muller, J.P. (2007). A View From Riggs: Treatment resistance and patient authority—IV. Why the pair needs the third. *Journal of the American Academy of Psychoanalysis, 35*(2), 221–241.

Chapter 7: Charles, M. (2008). A View From Riggs: Treatment resistance and patient authority—VIII. System pressures, ethics and autonomy. *Journal of the American Academy of Psychoanalysis, 36*(3), 547–560.

Chapter 8: Plakun, E.M. (2009). A View From Riggs: Treatment resistance and patient authority—XI. ABIS: An alliance based intervention for suicide. *Journal of the American Academy of Psychoanalysis, 37*(3), 539–560.

Chapter 9: Plakun, E.M. "Chapter 1, "The Boundaries are Shifting: Renegotiating the Therapeutic Frame." In Shapiro, Edward R. (1997). *The inner world in the outer world: Psychoanalytic perspectives*. New Haven: Yale University Press.

Chapter 10: Tillman, J.G. (2009). A View From Riggs: Treatment resistance and patient authority—IX. Integrative psychodynamic treatment of psychotic disorders. *Journal of the American Academy of Psychoanalysis, 36*(4), 739–762.

Chapter 11: Elmendorf, D.M. & Parish, M. (2007). A View From Riggs: Treatment resistance and patient authority—V. Silencing the messenger. The social dynamics of treatment resistance. *Journal of the American Academy of Psychoanalysis, 35*(3), 375–392.

Chapter 12: Schwartz, A. (2007). A View From Riggs: Treatment resistance and patient authority—VI. Working with family resistance to treatment. *Journal of the American Academy of Psychoanalysis, 35*(4), 607–625.

Chapter 13: Krikorian, S.E. & Fowler, J.C. (2008). A View From Riggs: Treatment resistance and patient authority—VII. A team approach to treatment resistance. *Journal of the American Academy of Psychoanalysis, 36*(2), 353–373.

Chapter 14: Shapiro, E.R. (2009). A View From Riggs: Treatment resistance and patient authority—XII. Examined Living: A psychodynamic treatment system. *Journal of the American Academy of Psychoanalysis, 37*(4), 683–698.

INDEX